W9-DGC-249

IN LOVE WITH NIGHT

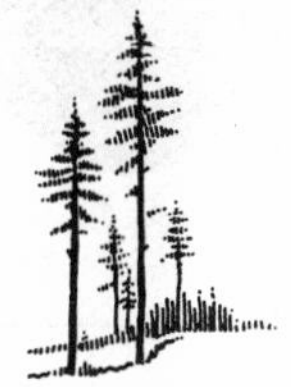

This Large Print Book carries the Seal of Approval of N.A.V.H.

IN LOVE WITH NIGHT

The American Romance with Robert Kennedy

Ronald Steel

Thorndike Press • Thorndike, Maine

Published in 2000 by arrangement with Simon & Schuster, Inc.

Thorndike Press Large Print Americana Series.

The tree indicium is a trademark of Thorndike Press.

The text of this Large Print edition is unabridged.
Other aspects of the book may vary from the original edition.

Set in 16 pt. Plantin by Warren S. Doersam.

Printed in the United States on permanent paper.

Library of Congress Cataloging-in-Publication Data

Steel, Ronald.
In love with night : the American romance with Robert Kennedy / Ronald Steel.
p. cm.
Includes bibliographical references (p. 408)
ISBN 0-7862-2555-6 (lg. print : hc : alk. paper)
1. Kennedy, Robert F., 1925–1968. 2. Kennedy, Robert F., 1925–1968 — Public opinion. 3. Legislators — United States — Biography. 4. United States. Congress. Senate — Biography. 5. Public opinion — United States — History — 20th century. 6. Kennedy, John F. (John Fitzgerald), 1917–1963 — Assassination. 7. Kennedy, John F. (John Fitzgerald), 1917–1963 — Influence. I. Title.
E840.8.K4 S74 2000b
973.922′092—dc21
[B] 00-028641

To the memory of my
mother and father

Contents

When he shall die,
Take him and cut him out in little stars,
And he will make the face of heaven
  so fine
That all the world will be in love with
  night,
And pay no worship to the garish sun.

SHAKESPEARE, *Romeo and Juliet*

Preface

Although this book deals with aspects of Robert Kennedy's life, it is not a biography. Rather, it is a study of character and circumstance, and beyond that of political mythology. In this sense it is in the style of Plutarch's *Lives*: an effort to view a historical figure against the backdrop of his times, and to deduce the impact that each made upon the other. After so much has been written about the life of this man, it seemed to me important to understand why, after all these years, he retains a place in our political rhetoric and even in our imagination. This meditation is meant as an effort to comprehend this strange and enduring phenomenon.

1

An American Dream

At some point, without ever quite intending it, American liberals, and even many conservatives, fell in love with Robert Kennedy. Like most improbable love affairs it surprised them at first. But they learned to accept, and then embrace, it enthusiastically. In the process the younger Kennedy has become, more than his brother John, more than Franklin D. Roosevelt, *the* liberal icon.

To this day, decades after his death in 1968, politicians scramble for a piece of him. Bill Clinton, in his first presidential campaign, declared himself to be a "New Democrat" in the Kennedy tradition, and on the eve of his inauguration made the pilgrimage to Arlington Cemetery to kneel at Robert Kennedy's grave. In 1998 he reassured like-minded party centrists that "a lot of what he said and did prefigured what we have tried to do in our time." To this claim leftist Democrats insisted that *they* were Kennedy's true heirs. In Robert

Kennedy's house are many mansions.

Over the years Kennedy has become the inspiration for a powerful legend. Millions believe that he embodied a new kind of liberalism: compassionate yet strong, supportive but not indulgent. And they are convinced that if he had made it to the White House, which both he and they considered his rightful inheritance, he would have transformed America. He remains the standard by which millions measure, and find wanting, today's politicians. "The yearning for Robert Kennedy — or somebody like him," a reporter wrote wistfully twenty-four years after his death, "is an open wound in some parts of America."[1]

But why is there such yearning, and why should it focus on him? The nation is not experiencing any great crisis, and has not since the Watergate episode in the mid-1970s, and arguably not since the Vietnam War. Furthermore, Robert Kennedy is a curious figure for the role of messiah. He was attorney general for only a thousand days and a U.S. senator for not much longer. He is not remembered for any single great achievement during that time. When admirers look back upon his career they speak more of what he would have accomplished than of what he actually did.

He was a receptacle into which a dissatisfied people have put their frustrated emotions and longings.

Yet this has in no way diminished his impact. "He inspired us to believe . . . that there was an opportunity to change this nation and the way we relate to each other," said Tom Bradley when he was mayor of Los Angeles. He was the ". . . last major white politician black people seriously heeded," opined *Time* magazine on the thirtieth anniversary of his death. "He seemed to be a friend of life's victims." For the critic Jonathan Yardley there was ". . . no single individual whose death has left a more lasting and mysterious sense of unexplored promise." And to Michael Harrington, whose book *The Other America* is said to have awakened John Kennedy to the shame of poverty in affluent America, "he was a man who actually could have changed the course of American history."

Such a man and such an impact deserve to be taken seriously, not only as history but also as a living reality. How we see such figures governs the way we think about politics and what we demand from those who govern us. Great yearnings and deferred dreams make their impact. They convey a special kind of truth and shape our conception of what the future can be. Because he ignited so many hopes, Robert Kennedy, like his brother John, has become, in one writer's words, "part of the dream life of America."[2]

But the dreams that Americans had about these two brothers were very different. JFK represented an imagined golden age, a fairy tale Camelot of dashing lords and lovely damsels. His death, like Oliver Stone's fantasy movie about him, brought about, in this schema, the darkness of paradise lost. Robert Kennedy, by contrast, has been viewed as a redeemer, one who came after the Fall, and so was scarred by the sins of knowledge and complicity but somehow able to transcend them — and in so doing to take a lost people with him. In this sense he held out the promise of paradise regained.

What makes RFK so contemporary, as well as so difficult to capture, is that he embodied contradiction. He was an ardent prosecutor who abused the law, a champion of black pride who allowed the FBI to torment Martin Luther King, a tardy critic of the Vietnam War who organized U.S.-sponsored assassination operations in the Third World, a fearless rebel who would not take on an unpopular president until another man cleared the way.

Despite these contradictions, perhaps in part because of them, he is remembered today by millions of Americans with an affection and an unfulfillable longing unlike those accorded any other politician. He has clearly touched something deep in the American psyche. His brief career as a politician during the years between JFK's death and his own evokes a time when it was possible to believe that a single person, by the force of his character, could change the world.

That he died before this could be accomplished, or even seriously attempted, has only added to his stature. He has become a legendary figure into whose promise we can read our unfulfilled hopes and ambitions. We have mythologized him. His life has become part of ours. As the *New York Times* stated editorially on an anniversary of his death, his story is "a version of the old legend of a knight who purifies himself through great suffering to prepare for a holy quest." Whether that quest was the presidency, the Kennedy Restoration, the transformation of American society, or a personal redemption is shrouded in ambiguity.

Much of Kennedy's allure lies in the

future conditional: in what he *would* have been, what he *would* have done. Millions are convinced that had he lived and become president, he would have quickly ended the Vietnam War, brought black and white Americans together, alleviated poverty and discrimination, and achieved a more just and humane society. He is the symbol of the politics we presumably could have had. In the words of his Senate speechwriter, Adam Walinsky, he was "the last major leader who allowed us to at least imagine we could realize the ideals of American politics."[3] It is not surprising that politicians pay him such homage, because they want to be identified — if only by association — with those ideals.

His advocates have always had a problem in relating the aggressive, vengeful, "ruthless" (to use the descriptive adjective he was never able to shake) Kennedy to the image of the gentle, caring, sensitive man who ostensibly emerged following John Kennedy's death. They give several reasons to explain the parallel existence of these two Robert Kennedys.

One, the most common, is that he was "transformed" by his brother's assassination, that the shock of that event caused him to reevaluate his life and become a different person. The great drama of Kennedy's life, Marshall Frady has written, was "his striking translation during his anguish over his brother's murder from a somewhat fierce and simplistic and decidedly dubious figure into, it seems indisputable now, a spiritually deepened moral adventurer. . . ."

A second reason, linked to the first, is that he experienced "change" and "growth" as a result of experience. By 1968 the former street fighter ". . . 'Bobby' no longer existed," Garry Wills has written. "It was a deeply changed man who was running for office now. Depth had come to him, and with it indecision." According to his aide Richard Goodwin, Kennedy's encounter with personal tragedy forced him "to explore new worlds of thought and poetry, pleasures and the manifold varieties of human intimacy . . . almost as if he were deliberately equipping himself for a larger role, laboring to become worthy of succession to his romanticized vision of the fallen leader."

Others, trying to connect the vindictive, ruthless "old Bobby" with the caring, sensitive "new Bobby" whom they discerned in his later years, declare that he was a work in progress, that he was perpetually in flux, and that his development can be marked by "episodes," like Picasso's periods. Thus, in the words of civil rights aide Harris Wofford, by 1967 this "fundamentally different man . . . seemed to move by epiphanies." Or as biographer Jack Newfield has written: "He defined and created himself in action, and learned almost everything from experience. . . . He was always in a state of becoming."

Such explanations, if true, are not comforting. Normally people are not reassured by the spectacle of elected leaders who "move by epiphanies" or are in a constant "state of becoming." What is interesting in a friend would be unsettling in a politician. But whereas writing about most politicians means examining their policies, with Robert Kennedy it means speculating on his motives.

To some he was sincere, compassionate, and idealistic, particularly in the last years of his life. To others he was calculating, rude, and unprincipled. To many he was both. He remained a mystery, even to his devoted followers, a man hidden by layers of anger and empathy, ambition and self-doubt, impetuosity and caution, opportunism and idealism. John Kenneth Galbraith has described this much-observed man as perhaps "the least known figure of our time."[4]

There is something mysterious and also novelistic about him: the rich man's son who became a saint to the poor and the neglected; the law enforcer who claimed that he yearned to be a revolutionary; the fanatic for righteousness who embraced forces of evil; the little brother who believed his destiny was to succeed the man he had sought to serve; the ruthless warrior enshrined in memory as the prince of peace.

Robert Kennedy cannot be seen or understood apart from his older brother. They form a historical diptych. Nearly as large in death as they were in life, these two Kennedys, so near and yet so distant from each other, dominate a decade that left its mark on everything that followed: on war, patriotism, and America's place in the world; on race, poverty, and notions of justice; on sexual mores and social values. Between them they split the decade, with the politically conventional John rounding out the last years of the Eisenhower era and with Robert as a talismanic figure of the willfully irrational sixties.

The brothers are united in death, encased under the marble slabs and the eternal flame meant to symbolize their reign and evoke the awe accorded martyrs and fallen heroes. They lie together in Arlington Cemetery, where the nation's heroes are buried, on a hill with a splendid panoramic view of the White House, the Capitol, and the stately federal city across the broad river. They seem to claim the site as their due, though no other president, let alone a president's brother, is awarded such a place of honor in such an imperial setting.

John and Robert Kennedy are not only united in death, but defined by death. Their deaths immortalized them. They died, as it were, on the public watch, serving as officials elected by us. Indeed, both were killed on political journeys garnering votes for their respective battles for the White House as they were seeking our political mandate.

We mark the anniversaries of their deaths — not, as with Washington and Lincoln — of their births. We speculate more on what they might have done than on what they accomplished. Their lives were a welter of successes, compromises, and failures. But through death they have become everything we want to read into them.

In John Kennedy the American people recalled a world not as it had been — with Cold War scares and battles over racial integration — but one bathed in optimism and promise: a musical comedy Camelot. Robert rose from the tumult and violence of the sixties, but in his message of reconciliation many found hope that the clash of warring factions would be gently resolved. To an America that felt twice cheated by reality, John Kennedy represented the world that should have been and Robert the one that might come to be. Together they embodied the imagined past and the imagined future.

As with the Arthurian tale it evokes, the Kennedy legend has two parts: that of the good King John, his beautiful queen, and his faithful Knights of the Oval Office — and that of his tormented follower and surrogate son, Lancelot, whose quest for the Holy Grail to redeem the kingdom ends in failure and death.

The more interesting part of the legend resides in Robert rather than in John. This dogmatic and angry, yet empathetic man emerged from his brother, first as his indispensable helper, then as his imprisoned mourner, and finally as his determined inheritor and memorializer. Over the decades John Kennedy has become the imperial JFK and entered history, a statue that we honor. We smile when we think of him, charming manipulator that he was, and we feel good about ourselves for having chosen him as our leader.

But when we think of the scolding figure we call Bobby we do not smile. He was constantly reminding us of our failures and exhorting us to do, and to be, better. He makes us reflect on all things that, just maybe, might have been.

What actually would have been, had he lived to assume the office he sought, may be a different matter. The legend tells us that the vicious campaign manager and merciless congressional investigator became a moral explorer who discovered the shame of poverty and prejudice, that the military strategist grew anguished by the war he had helped implement and became the champion of the underdog and the despised — the candidate who could have transformed America, just as he is said to have transformed himself.

This is the Robert Kennedy of legend, and the man who millions believe held the key to the nation's political salvation. Politicians have promised for decades that they embody his ideals and can lead us back to the path from which we have strayed. But it may be that this new Kennedy was in part our own creation, that we fashioned him from our needs, and that what we came to mourn was little more than our "dream life."

The myth of Robert Kennedy has become so fused with the man that it is virtually impossible to separate them. The myth is composed of three braided strands. The first is the myth of Camelot, the belief in a golden kingdom that once existed and could be re-created by him if only we believed hard enough and turned away from false tempters. The second is the liberal myth, the assumption that Robert Kennedy embodied the motivating values of American liberalism and would have pursued them with passionate conviction if he had been elected president. The third strand is the rainbow myth, that he alone among all American politicians would have been able to unite the contentious factions within society — alienated blacks and angry white ethnics, radical leftists and timorous suburbanites, blue-collar patriots and beard-wearing dropouts — into one harmonious, progressive coalition. All three of these myths resist close scrutiny.

Overriding them all is what could be

called the Bobby Myth. It is the belief that with his passing, in the words of one sixties activist turned scholar, "a promise of redemption not only passed out of American politics, it passed out of ourselves." Yet the notion that such a transforming experience as redemption can be found in the daily compromises of politics, let alone in politicians, is a disturbing one. Politics in a democratic society is about interest groups and deals, not about salvation. But this is the kind of speech to which some people are moved when talking about Robert Kennedy.

Historian William O'Neill described him as an "extraordinary human being who, though hated by some, was more deeply loved by his countrymen than any man of his time."[5] This may well be true. Yet in politics, as in life, love is not always enough. And love, as we know, is often blind. That is why we need to look at Robert Kennedy not as an idol or a mythical figure but as a man who, like everyone else, was not always clear in purpose and pure in thought. If we view Kennedy this way we have a better chance of understanding him and what it is that we sought, and continue to seek, in him.

2

The Man Nobody Knew

When we think of John Kennedy the words that come to mind are cool, ironic, charming, witty, elusive. We see a man always slipping out of the reach of causes or people who would tie him down, a man who lived for himself, and in his deepest heart, by himself. When we think of Robert Kennedy the words we use are intense, angry, vindictive, idealistic, sensitive, and, yes, ruthless; a man of contradictions. We also think of him in relation to a clan; as a Kennedy.

For most of his life Robert was the obedient son and faithful brother. Formed in the mold cast by his father, Joseph, he chose a path within the family of emulation and service. For him, as for the father he struggled endlessly to please, the family was the highest priority. Whatever served its interests was good, what did not was by definition bad.

This led Robert to view everything outside the family as hostile and potentially threatening. Rather than pleasing others he took a perverse pride in alienating them. He defied people to like him, and indicated that he did not much care one way or the other. Many did not think it worth the effort. Even those who came to admire him commented on how dislikable he was at the beginning. It was hard to imagine this impatient, angry man would ever dare seek the approval of voters, let alone that he would inspire a personality cult more intense than that of his brother.

Persuaded from childhood that he could never be the equal of his stylish older siblings, or of his glamorous parents, Robert set himself the task of being worthy of them. A loyal and ferocious guardian of the Kennedy clan's interests, he was also its nurturer and protector. Whereas many boys become ambivalent rivals of their older brothers, he remained an admiring servant his entire life. He subordinated his personal goals to Jack's ambitions. Any person who thwarted them deserved no quarter and was treated as an enemy. Subduing enemies provided a deep moral and personal satisfaction.

Although bound together by the family and its constant striving for status and power, the two Kennedy brothers were very different temperamentally. It was politics that sealed their bond. "All this business about Jack and Bobby being blood brothers has been exaggerated," their sister Eunice said. ". . . They didn't really become close until 1952, and it was politics that brought them together."

When Bobby got out of the navy in 1946 it was expected that he would work in Jack's campaign for Congress. Similarly, six years later, when Jack ran for the Senate, Bobby would quit his job in the Justice Department to run his brother's campaign. Again in 1959 he left his post on a Senate committee when Jack made his bid for the presidency. To have done anything less would have been unthinkable. It would also have been incomprehensible. Not only did he behave as though there were no higher loyalty than to the Kennedy clan, he believed it.

The family was his haven. Within it he felt safe; outside it he was in a jungle. Unlike Jack, he had few friends. The only people he trusted or felt really close to were those related by blood or marriage. Instead of being stifled by the family's incessant demands, he felt, like a priest in a monastery, embraced and protected. Psychologists tell us that shyness reflects fears of rejection and feelings of inadequacy, and that these express themselves in a resentful defensiveness. Only among Kennedys did he feel fully accepted.

Arthur Schlesinger Jr., who has described himself as "a great admirer and devoted friend of Robert Kennedy," and has written an admirable biography of him, considered him during his years as an investigator and campaign manager to be "a very cross, unhappy, angry man." Theodore Sorensen, John Kennedy's counselor and later one of Robert's political advisers, initially found him "militant, aggressive, intolerant, opinionated, somewhat shallow in his convictions." General Lucius Clay, when asked by President Kennedy to assume command during the 1961 crisis in Berlin, accepted only on the condition that he would never under any circumstances have to deal with Bobby. "I understand," the president said with a laugh.

While many people are difficult, particularly when placed in positions of authority, Bobby was gratuitously offensive. He seemed almost to take pleasure in having people dislike him. "I don't give a damn if the state and county organizations survive after November," he shouted at an earnest group of New York Democratic reform leaders in the 1960 election, "and I don't give a damn if you survive. I want to elect John F. Kennedy president."

This was not a pose or a pep talk. Electing his brother was all that mattered, regardless of how it was done or how many egos were trampled. Sometimes it was effective, sometimes not. But it usually left a residue of bad feeling that followed him wherever he went. Admirers believed that his bullying and arrogance flowed from a deep commitment to the social and political causes that animated him. Others saw it as a mark of coldness and aggression. The Italian journalist Oriana Fallaci wrote after a frustrating interview in 1965 that she had "never known a so-called shy person so capable of intimidating non-shy people. . . . As the minutes passed he became more withdrawn, more secretive, more melancholy, never shifting position, never changing the tone of his voice, which is shrill and monotonous like a horn."[1]

Hers was a common reaction. More often than not, people came away from an initial meeting with him hoping that it was their last. Whether they felt that his rude behavior emerged from barely restrained aggressiveness or from insecurities so profound that they led him to reject others before they had a chance to reject him, the reality is that he was widely disliked.

There was also an element of rowdyism in him. He was the kind of man who, had he been born poor instead of rich, might well have been a brawler and a drinker, getting into fights to work off his aggressions. As it was, he worked them off verbally in his battles with enemies, whether they were political foes or bad guys who had abused the public trust, like communists and corrupt labor leaders.

These aggressions were not merely verbal. During one of the games of touch football — the official Kennedy family sport — that he was perpetually organizing, he got into a shouting match with some college students who were batting balls in another corner of a Georgetown park. Tempers flared, somebody pushed, and in a moment he was in a bloody fistfight with one of the students. His brother Ted had to pull him away before their friendly little game turned into a brawl.

His aggressions roiled just beneath the surface and would erupt whenever he was displeased. This was widely remarked by many who had to deal with his violent and easily aroused temper. "If one of you guys writes one more time about his looking like a choirboy, I'll kill you," a State Department official barked at a reporter. "A choirboy is soft, cherubic. Take a look at that bony little face, those hard opaque eyes, and then listen to him bawl somebody out. Some choirboy!"

He was a street fighter and in many ways a fanatic. Imbued with a religious faith based on dogma, he needed only to convince himself that a cause was morally right in order for him to justify virtually any means to pursue it. He believed, for example, that Joe McCarthy was right in his accusations that communists ran loose in the government and thus had no qualms about serving him regardless of his methods. It was the virtue of the cause, as he perceived it, that gave him justification. He was, in his own view, a fighter for righteousness.

During his campaign for the presidency and particularly after his death, his emotional stubbornness and unshakable moral certainty were seen as virtues. He was no longer described as a fanatic avenger, or a dogmatist, but a person of deep principles. In the words of Hans Morgenthau, an unsentimental analyst of power politics, "that same emotional and moral reaction, which proved to be a dubious asset for

Robert Kennedy as a politician, became the source of his final triumph as a charismatic leader."[2]

If this is true, it is in part because the times demanded it. The 1960s were not years of lukewarm emotions and guarded commitments. Kennedy himself learned that when, from fear of defeat, he refused to challenge Lyndon Johnson directly until he was pushed — and was criticized for his caution. The era not only created leaders who raised high expectations; it also rewarded — or destroyed — them for this. Kennedy sought and encouraged deep emotions from his public, as it did from him.

Part of his appeal, particularly in the late sixties, was that he seemed to be an unhappy man. It was with the troubles, not the triumphs, that millions identified. The opposite was true of his brother. One could admire John Kennedy, find him engaging and attractive, even be in thrall to him, as many were. One could even, in a flight of fantasy, wish to be him — if only for an hour. No one, on the other hand, would want to be Robert Kennedy. He was too driven, too conflicted, too visibly distressed.

As Arthur Schlesinger expressed the

dichotomy, JFK "was at bottom a happy man, Robert a sad man. John Kennedy seemed invulnerable, Robert desperately vulnerable. One felt liked by John Kennedy, needed by Robert Kennedy." That sense of need, and even of desperation, was an important part of his appeal. Life around him was not more gracious, but more unsettled and intense. If JFK was a man to enjoy or admire, Bobby was one to follow — or to fear.

And many did fear him, beginning in the early 1950s when he worked for Senator Joe McCarthy, and extending through his crusade against labor union crooks, and later as attorney general and presidential candidate. For every person who loved Bobby Kennedy and yearned to follow him wherever he led, there was one who with equal passion distrusted or even despised him. Few major figures in American political life have aroused such intense and conflicting emotions.

Gore Vidal, who disliked him for reasons perhaps as much personal as political, in the mid-1960s described him as a "dangerous, ruthless man . . . a Torquemada-like personality with none of his brother's gift for seeing things other than black and white." For Vidal his strengths were also his weaknesses: "his obvious characteristics are energy, vindictiveness, and a simple-mindedness about human motives which may yet bring him down."[3]

In the early years of his public life Bobby displayed the dogmatism of a fanatic or a religious convert. Whatever cause he followed or opinion he professed was morally right. It had to be or he could not justify his belief. He often gave the impression that his own triumph and that of the cause of virtue were the same thing. Unsurprisingly he was frequently viewed as self-righteous and intolerant.

He was not a man whom one could approach easily, or who was able to make strangers feel comfortable. Suspicious of outsiders, he accepted them hesitantly and only after a long period of trial. Periodically, he would give vent to a furious temper that he did little to control until late in his life. Many, on encountering his cold manner and disdainful gaze, came away with the impression that he was irredeemably rude and arrogant. Wherever he went he left a trail of disillusioned admirers or even enemies. Unlike his brother, he had a knack for self-destructive behavior and for making life even more difficult than necessary. Like many emotionally insecure people, he dared others to dislike him and made it easy for them to do so.

Robert Kennedy's biographers relate stories of those who were treated rudely, or even contemptuously, by him on their first encounter, but who then somehow broke through the wall of his reserve and became admirers. One of his Justice Department aides, John Seigenthaler, recalls an initial meeting where Kennedy received him for a job interview with "a veil over the eyes, tense lips, flared nostrils, his overcoat on with the collar turned up." He immediately accused his baffled guest of being late and stalked out of the room. But Seigenthaler persisted and eventually felt that Kennedy had become a close friend.

In his revealing study of the Kennedys and Martin Luther King, Harris Wofford recalled that his first meeting with Bobby in 1957 "did nothing to make me want his brother to become president . . . already Bobby's reputation was that of an arrogant, narrow, rude young man." Yet Wofford also wrote that by the late sixties "I wanted him to be president more than anyone I had ever supported." Journalists, too, were often won over — at least by the mellower Kennedy who ran for president in 1968.

Many who covered that campaign ended up deeply sympathetic to him. Richard Harwood of the *Washington Post* had long considered Kennedy to be an arrogant, narrow-minded rich boy. Yet after only a few months of covering the 1968 campaign this reporter asked the paper to relieve him because he had grown too close to the candidate.[4]

So long as John Kennedy was president and Bobby played the role of bodyguard and enforcer his social ineptitude was not particularly important to him. He didn't care that people disliked him. This showed that he was doing his job, as he defined it. It was only when he struck out on his own, after Jack's death, that he had to construct a new public persona.

John Kenneth Galbraith's observation that Robert Kennedy was a man nobody knew rested on the fact that he made such contradictory impressions on people. He was either idealistic or cynical, shy or aggressive, sensitive or callous, trusting or suspicious, affectionate or cold, vulnerable or guarded, unaffected or imperious. The impact he made depended directly on the relationship that he had with them and on the degree of trust they placed in him. Because of his own intensity, however one read his motivations, he triggered extreme reactions. If he was one of the most loved, he was also one of the most hated, Americans of his time.

When we think about John Kennedy, and we get beyond the style, and the celebrated "special grace," we speak of what he did and what he would have done. We may be disappointed by or admiring of JFK, but we are not mystified by him. But with Bobby it is quite different. We ask who he was and why he was that way. If we put JFK on a pedestal, we lay RFK out on a couch. One brother is there to admire and mythologize, the other to analyze and deconstruct. Jack is an icon, Bobby an enigma.

One journalist phrased it well by writing that with Bobby "the man keeps getting in the way of the politician . . . everyone was always wondering what made Robert Kennedy tick, as if he were a time-bomb." He did seem perpetually primed to go off, as though the forces that animated him were too volatile to contain. Understandably he alarmed many even as he inspired others. Of no other politician has there been such disagreement or confusion about who he was.

Harris Wofford later wrote that "there

was something in his basic character, temperament, and religious convictions that led naturally toward tragedy." The thing about tragedy is that it seems natural only after it happens. Kennedy's fate could also have been failure or irrelevance. Indeed that might have happened had he further pursued the path of caution and not run for president in 1968. Then rather than yearning to know what he might have done, we would hardly think of him at all. He would be just another ambitious, but failed, politician: an heir who was only apparent.

Nearly every death is a tragedy to someone, or even to many. What is poignant about Robert Kennedy's, and what raises it to a higher political dimension, is that it occurred as he was somewhere in midpoint on his strange political journey. He seemed to have at least partially transcended the vindictive and dogmatic person he had been, but had not yet become whatever it was he was heading toward. He was different things to different people because they read themselves and their needs into him. People found him a compassionate tribune of the underclass, or a revolutionary warrior for justice, or a tough law enforcer who would quell disorder, or an honorary love-child of the Woodstock generation, or simply one who would restore what they charitably remembered as the golden age of the mythical Camelot. As Henry Fairlie has written, when many people speak of Robert Kennedy "one will usually find that they are talking about the impact of the man on themselves. It is hard to think of another politician into whose life so many people read themselves with such indulgence."[5]

It is unlikely that he knew where he was going as he doggedly pursued the mission to fulfill what he believed to be his brother's legacy. Yet even had he won the presidency that would not have been the end of his quest. His campaign was not only for the presidency, but for a kind of meaning that could not be found in the necessary compromises of politics. He wanted more out of political life than it could give. He was in search of a cause, even when he was not certain what it was. As a youth this had pulled him toward the church, which offered an explanation for every puzzle. But politics is not a religion; it is only a method. It can keep idle fingers busy, but never fill a vacant heart. That vacancy was what made his life such a troubled one.

During the late 1960s, from their own scattered reading of Jean-Paul Sartre and Albert Camus, some of his leftist admirers claimed that he was at heart an existentialist, to use the fashionable word of the time. Yet this is an overagitated reading. There is little evidence that he defined himself in action, or that, as they claimed, he felt alienated from society. If he expressed to them some secret kinship with revolutionaries like Che Guevara, it is because that is what they wanted to hear. He was, it is true, fascinated with guerrilla movements, but mainly because he himself, ever since childhood, had always been to some degree an outsider.

During his last years he kept pushing beyond the limits of politics. He had embarked on an ascetic pilgrimage, and, like most pilgrims, he was looking for himself. At the end of the trail for this lonely wanderer lay not a rainbow nor the Grail. Rather he seemed to be waiting for words from some whispered inner voice, some shaft of illumination that would answer the terrible questions: Who am I? Why am I here? Where am I going?

Ultimately he found what he was looking for in the legacy that he would make his own. He would go beyond JFK's truncated, stylish thousand days to become the paladin of the underclass, the defender of the weak and the despised. He would be the transforming spirit. In this he would find some redemptive meaning for his life and for the legend he would try to create. It is for this, and not for his "legacy," his intensity, or his ambition that we remember him.

3

Family Values

Every idyllic childhood is an unhappy one in its own way, and Robert Kennedy's was no exception. From the picture books and hagiographic literature it would seem that the Kennedy children led a joyous existence. It was certainly a privileged one. The houses in suburban Boston and later New York, the beachfront mansion in Florida, and the summer compound on Cape Cod, where life has been described as an unending round of touch football games and boat races, reinforce the image of a happy and loving family.

The parents doted on their children and trained them for success — or at least they did when they had the time. Joseph Kennedy was often away, attending to his various business, political, and romantic deals, and his neglected wife, Rose, made a life of her own based on compulsive shopping, travel, and prayer. She took great pride in being on the list of the best-dressed women in America. When at home this fashionable, pious lady left her children largely to the care of servants. During the seven years after they bought the Hyannis Port house in 1929, it is estimated that Rose made seventeen trips to Europe. John Kennedy, who resented both his mother's prolonged absences and his father's cavalier treatment of her, once told a woman friend, "My mother is a nothing." According to his friend Chuck Spalding, from his family John learned that there was "only one way to treat a wife — and that was the way his father had treated his mother."[1]

Joseph Kennedy was inspired by a goal, fueled by resentment and ambition, first to become so rich that the Boston Brahmins would be forced to respect Irish newcomers like himself, and second, through his wealth and instruction, to have his sons rise to such heights that the Boston snobs would be humbled. This campaign for admiration and power consumed his life.

It is said that he took great pride in the training and accomplishments of his children. This is true, but insufficient. In fact he lived through his children — that is, his sons — seeing in them the means by which his own ambitions could be achieved. They became the trained, idealized versions of himself. If he could not be president of the United States (one of his more fanciful ambitions), then one of his sons would be.

The obvious candidate for this role was, of course, his eldest son, whom he named, of course, after himself. When that son fell in battle, the mantle passed, without hesitation and without protest, to the next male in line. Thus was John Kennedy groomed for president, and following his death, did Robert and Edward become candidates. So imbued were the sons with their father's ambitions that none even questioned the role assigned to them.

Joe Jr., the namesake, a handsome and dutiful young man, died too young to have shown any considered opinions of his own. His letters to his father during a European sojourn in the late 1930s echoed the sentiments of anti-Semitism and the appeasement of Nazi Germany that sullied his father's tenure as ambassador to Britain.

It may even have been his eagerness to please his father that contributed to his death as an airman in World War II at the age of twenty-nine. Young Kennedy, according to Arthur Krock, the *New York Times* columnist who provided literary services for the family,* volunteered for a highly dangerous mission over Germany because he "was seeking to prove by its very danger that the Kennedys were not yellow. That's what killed that boy. . . . And his father realized it."

Before Joe Jr.'s death, Jack had shown little interest in politics. Insofar as this charming playboy ever thought of a career, he assumed that he would do some writing and maybe become a journalist. Though irreverent and skeptical, he nonetheless did not seriously consider defying his father. On his discharge from the navy he ran for Congress. "It was like being drafted," he later explained. "My father wanted his eldest son in politics. 'Wanted' isn't the right word. He demanded it. You know my father."

The same imperative applied to the other sons. Bobby thought he might be a lawyer. It was his father who ordered him to run Jack's political campaigns and ultimately, despite his qualms, become attorney

* *Among Krock's services was editing and finding a publisher for Jack's undergraduate thesis,* Why England Slept, *and later lobbying the Pulitzer committee to award the youthful senator its biography prize for the largely ghostwritten* Profiles in Courage.

general in his brother's administration. Even the unfortunate Ted, an affable man who evolved from a playboy to a diligent senator, entered the family profession because it was expected of him, and for the same reason made his run — hapless and halfhearted as it was — for the presidency. As Bobby later said of Ted's 1962 bid for Jack's Senate seat: "The person who was primarily interested in having him run was my father . . . just as I would never have been Attorney General if it hadn't been for him, I don't think my younger brother would have been Senator nor my older brother President."[2]

One might be tempted to argue, like Krock, that Joe was responsible for the tragedies that befell his sons as they sought political glory. But this would be going too far. He did impose his will upon his boys, just as he had on the financiers, lawyers, and movie moguls with whom he bargained and connived. But his sons were not just boys. They became young, and then mature, men. He even provided them with private incomes so that they might have a sense of independence. They could at any point along the way have said no. They could have rebelled.

None did — or at least none of the males. Only the high-spirited Kathleen, three years younger than Jack and five years older than Bobby, defied her parents' plans. The most immediately appealing of the Kennedys, Kick, as she was called, shocked her parents by marrying an immensely rich and titled British Protestant, and after his death conducted a well-publicized affair with another, already married, one. When she died in 1948 in a plane crash with her lover, her indignant mother refused to attend her funeral.

Defiance had been followed by tragedy. But so had obedience, in the case of Joe Jr., and ultimately Jack and Bobby. And so too had innocence. Rosemary, the mentally retarded eldest daughter, was subjected by Joe, without her mother's knowledge, to a prefrontal lobotomy in hopes of improving her condition. When the operation failed and worsened her condition, he placed her in an institution and she never lived with the family again. It was no small thing to disappoint, let alone defy, such a powerful father, such a religious and rigid mother, and the internalized pressures of being part of a team. For that is what the Kennedys were, an eleven-member collective as big as a football squad and as determined to win.

Bobby, ten years younger than Joe Jr.

and eight years younger than Jack, lay deep in the shadows of his brothers, but far outside their daily concerns. For children such an age gap is enormous; he was virtually of another generation. Small, shy, and insecure, he would cower in fright as his two brothers fought for dominance. Sometimes at night, from the next room, he would hear Joe banging Jack's head against the wall in frustration over his younger brother's clever taunts.

Bobby, the little brother, emulated them both and pushed himself to secure their recognition and approval. His whole childhood was an effort to win approval from the people he cared about most: his parents and his brothers. He carried over much of this behavior into his adult life, reinforcing the reputation for toughness that he believed was a measure of worth. "I always found him a touching figure under the bad manners," Gore Vidal observed in a charitable moment. "He was obsessed by his relative inferiority to his older brothers. As a result, he had to be twice as tough as everyone else, have twice as many children. What a tense life it must have been — and, finally, sad."[3]

His fear of appearing weak warred with the gentle side of his nature: the side he learned to repress in order to win respect. He showed this in his affection toward his mother. He was apparently the only male who relied on her emotionally and who shared her strong Catholicism. He strictly observed Mass on Sunday and wrote her constantly from his various schools, closing his letters with "oodles of love" and myriad Xs for kisses. She called him her "little pet."

Bobby was Rose's child. Their letters exude concern and affection. She encouraged him to observe the rules of his faith, and he was eager to do so. While studying at St. Paul's, an Episcopal school in New Hampshire, he complained to her that the Protestant Bible was being used too frequently. He asked to go elsewhere, and Rose arranged for his transfer to the Portsmouth Priory, a strict Benedictine school.

He faithfully attended Mass the rest of his life, and spent his career hunting and punishing malefactors — in this way remaining true to the deepest elements of his character. Had he been born in a poor family he might have become a priest — or a cop. Jack, by contrast, was a Catholic when it suited his political purposes. As Jacqueline, an irreverent skeptic, said to

Arthur Krock during Jack's 1960 presidential campaign: "I think it is unfair for Jack to be opposed because he is a Catholic. . . . Now if it were Bobby: he never misses Mass and prays all the time."

Bobby's ardor, religious at least in inspiration, was a critical part of who he was. His crusades against evil, his tendency to see everything as black or white, his later expressed compassion for the neglected, and his insistence on viewing politics in personal rather than abstract terms all stemmed from his religious feelings. He was naturally intolerant. For him there could be no two sides to truth, to virtue, or to justice. In a family of operators and in a nation of pragmatists, he was a believer and a crusader.

As a scrawny, sensitive child captivated by his religious instruction and clinging to his mother, Bobby did not fit easily into Joe's conception of a Kennedy warrior. Later Rose claimed that for a time she feared he would not be tough enough, that he would become, in her words, a sissy. But this was not the path to acceptance in the Kennedy family; it was a virtual guarantee of exclusion. The best that a little boy concerned with Jesus and small animals could hope for was to be treated as a misfit, affectionately but condescendingly, like the sad Rosemary.

Even as a child Bobby was determined that this not happen. Displaying the grim tenacity for which he was later renowned, he forced himself to be stronger, and to succeed on the harsh terms set by his older siblings. In a family where competition was the language of communication, he would speak as loudly as he could. At the age of four he jumped from a boat at sea in an effort to show — until fished out by his brother Joe — that he could swim ashore.

There was something desperate about the ordeals he set for himself. "Nothing came easy to him, but he never stopped trying," one Kennedy biographer quotes Jack's Choate roommate and longtime sidekick LeMoyne "Lem" Billings as saying. "He *willed* himself into the water to learn to swim, and he willed himself onto the football field." He would win his parents' love by doing what was expected of him. Since they valued punctuality he would never be late. Once, when the family was sitting down to dinner and Joe's nightly seminar on world events, he ran so fast to get to the table that he crashed through a plate-glass door.

Yet what he most wanted long eluded

him. He was trying to meld what he was with what he felt he should be. “While he secured his mother’s love by being so good, so gentle, and so religious,” in Billings’s words, “it made him even more invisible to his father.” What Joe admired was strength, toughness, force, and determination, and this is what he sought to instill in his children. He treated them as though they were in training for an athletic meet. For him sports was a Darwinian metaphor for life, a contest in which the strongest and most determined took the spoils.

Although Joe Kennedy often neglected his children, they were the most important thing in his life, even more than his business deals, sexual liaisons, or political ambitions. And certainly more important than his wife. “Children evoked in all the Kennedy sons the strongest emotions they would ever know,” in Billings’s view. “This was true for Bobby and Teddy as well as for Jack. They were all oriented toward their kids far more than toward their wives.”[4]

After dinner Joe would invite each child to come talk to him individually, and when out of town he would write them and they would write him. Mixing criticism and encouragement with an emphasis on success, he would above all stress the importance of winning. For him success was always measured in material terms. In the more than two hundred letters he wrote, biographer Doris Kearns Goodwin has noted, not once did he suggest any moral principles for his children to observe.

All children want to be loved by their parents and will endure the worst abuse or neglect to gain it. Bobby was no exception. But his nature was in conflict with the values his family respected. He struggled with this problem his whole life. The soft, or emotional, side of his character, the side that expressed itself in his religious devotion and his closeness to his mother, separated him from the boisterous, competitive spirit of his father and older brothers.

Instead of withdrawing or rebelling, he responded to the powerful competitive pressures of the family by striving to do what the strongest member of the family expected of him. He learned to compete ferociously. "When you come from that far down you have to struggle to survive," he later said of his childhood. In the words of Chuck Spalding: "Bobby felt he was weak. He felt he had to toughen himself up and get rid of that vulnerability everyone had remarked on since he was a boy. This was the way for him to get someplace in the family. The drive was incessant, just fierce. He simply remade himself. He got so he could just go through a wall."[5]

Unlike ironic Jack or rebellious Kathleen, Bobby adapted to the family's values. Over his shy and sensitive nature he grafted Joe's aggressiveness. He grew a tough outer skin to protect himself and to behave as the person his father wanted him to be. "Bobby's a tough one," Joe proudly told a reporter in 1957. "He'll keep the Kennedys together, you can bet." Joe even awarded him his highest praise. "Bobby's like me," he once said, "he's a hater."

To be a Kennedy child was to be in perpetual training, coping with unceasing competition and achievement. The desire to please incessantly demanding parents took a toll on all the children. Kathleen handled the pressure by rebellion, Jack by emotional detachment, and Bobby, consumed by anxieties over self-worth, by punishing transgressors.

The sensitive and loving little boy became an awkward and self-conscious adolescent. "He used to walk with his head way down, buried in his neck, like a bird in a storm," one of his classmates at Milton

Academy recalled. At dances "he mostly stood on one foot with the other toe resting on top, his hands way down in his pockets." Displaying a sullen defensiveness, virtually daring anyone to like him, he had few friends.

Following Bobby's visit to his parents' winter estate in Palm Beach over a Christmas holiday, Rose wrote a friend that though her sixteen-year-old son "plays a very good golf game . . . he is very unsociable. . . . He absolutely refused to go to the Bath and Tennis [Club] and when he has gone out he doesn't seem to like any of the boys here." Nor, she might have added, did this awkward adolescent give them any reason to like him.

"What I remember most vividly about growing up was going to a lot of different schools, always having to make new friends, and that I was very awkward," Bobby later said of this unhappy period. "I dropped things and fell down all the time. I had to go to the hospital a few times for stitches in my head and leg. I was pretty quiet most of the time. And I didn't mind being alone."[6]

Adolescence is a hard time for most people, and he was hardly unique in being often unhappy. But in his case awkwardness was compounded by insecurity and isolation. For him to say that he "didn't mind being alone" was to admit failure in the game of popularity that adolescents prize so highly. This had to have been painful for him. And it left a protective armor that he carried around the rest of his life: the armor of seeming indifference to, and even hostility toward, strangers until they demonstrated acceptance.

Sports offer a means of connection on a nonverbal level, and football more so than almost any other game. It became for Bobby the means for acceptance and validation. He remained devoted to it his entire life. The playing field was his social club, his campfire confessional, his analyst's couch. Through sports he broke out of his isolation at Milton Academy by becoming a friend of the school athletic hero, Dave Hackett, and later at Harvard by finding a group of classmates with whom he did not feel inadequate and uncomfortable.

Invariably the smallest person on the team, Bobby could show his worth by fighting harder, by playing even with broken bones, by never giving up. In a sense his whole life was a test — a test to overcome his greatest fear: that he was inadequate. Years later, during the traumatic period after Jack's death, he underlined in his notebook the precept of Emerson: "Do what you are afraid to do." This was the credo he tried to live by. It led him to take foolhardy risks with his life by scaling unclimbed mountains, riding rapids, and stalking wild animals. And it ultimately led him, after many doubts and misgivings, to try to become the vessel of his brother's purpose.

He constantly tried to do more, to overcome his weakness and his fears, to work harder and be tougher than anyone else. Emulating his parents, he even had two more children than they: eleven to Joe and Rose's nine. He never fully outgrew his gnawing fear of failure or his adolescent obsession with worthiness.

The first time he met Jimmy Hoffa he challenged the labor leader to a push-up contest. As a Senate staff lawyer investigating union racketeering, he told mobster Joey Gallo: "You think you are tough, but you're not, and I would like to show you up in a fight." In some ways he never graduated from the playground.

John Kennedy once said of his childhood that "we soon learned that competition in the family was a kind of dry run for the world outside." No one took this more to heart than Bobby. The incessant contests and races that dominated the childhood of the Kennedys were viewed as a training ground for later battles. All the children, including the girls, played football. It was obligatory: the official Kennedy family sport, passed on from one generation to the next. For Bobby particularly it was not so much a game as a gladiatorial combat. In no other endeavor did he so apply his father's teaching that winning is everything. He played as though his very being depended on winning. He was sometimes accused of being a dirty player.

For someone uncomfortable with words and insecure with strangers, sports was a way of belonging. When he returned to Harvard in 1946, after a short and uneventful stint in the navy at the end of the war, he signed up to play football. Even though he was smaller and younger than the other players, most of whom were veterans, he was determined to make the team. He made up in grit for what he lacked in weight and skill, and at the end of the season was rewarded with a varsity letter by a sympathetic coach: the first Kennedy to win one.

But it wasn't the letter that he played for.

It was to measure himself against others, to prove he was not weak, and to be accepted as an equal. Football for him was a test of manhood. "Except for war," he once said, "there is nothing in American life — nothing — which trains a boy better for life than football."[7]

As a college student, football was not merely an athletic pastime; it was his social life. Although rich and well-connected through his family, he could never fit in with the society swells at Harvard as his brothers had. He shunned the one social club that offered him an invitation, and avoided the parties and dances where women from the nearby schools were invited to meet eligible Harvard men.

Instead he hung out with the football players, many of them not only older war veterans, but also from working-class backgrounds. He did not advertise that he was the ambassador's son, although they found out soon enough. Nonetheless they grew used to him, and came to admire his grit and lack of pretension. Kenny O'Donnell, a townie who befriended Bobby on the team and later became a key member of the Kennedy political entourage, was one of the several football players who served as ushers at Bobby's wedding.

These men were his friends not only because they were his teammates, but because they too, for a different reason, were outsiders at Harvard. They were not sophisticated or rich; they were never asked to join an exclusive club, nor invited to debutante balls. Bobby chose to be with them, to make his social life among townies and vets. Like most outsiders, he felt comfortable only among those who were not his social or intellectual peers. This is why he gravitated so naturally toward children, whose judgment he did not fear, and to the downtrodden, whom he thought he could help. With them he did not need his suit of armor.

Some of the qualities by which he was later defined — his brusqueness with strangers and subordinates, his rudeness and anger, his arrogance and ruthlessness — stemmed from his insecurities. He was one person to the outside world and another to his intimates. Neither really knew him. For most of his life he did not really know himself.

Because of these internal conflicts people have disagreed about who was the "real" Bobby Kennedy. The "good Bobby," to use Jules Feiffer's clever dichotomy, seemed always at war with the "bad

Bobby," the gentle healer with the calculating politician. But there was only one Bobby. The "bad Bobby" was grafted onto the "good Bobby" in childhood. This was the price of acceptance in the family and the coat of protection against the world.

4

True Believer

It was wise of Bobby at this point not to follow Jack's lead and seek a career in politics. He had neither the temperament nor the patience. Nor did he have any serious goals. He had drifted through Harvard without making a noticeable impression on either his professors or his classmates. These early postwar years were a time of intellectual ferment on campuses as the wartime alliance of America and Russia mutated into the Cold War. But these debates largely passed him by, as he spent his afternoons on the football field while accumulating mostly Cs and Ds that landed him on probation. When he got his degree in March 1948, his departure was little noticed. One of his classmates, later a prominent doctor, described him as a "kind of nasty, brutal, humorless little fellow." The judgment was fairly widespread.

He had little sense of what to do with his life. It would have been easy for him to go into one of his father's business operations, or to find a niche somewhere in the state or federal government bureaucracy. He might even have tried a career in journalism — a field in which he had shown some interest by filing reports for a Boston paper on a six-month trip to Europe and the Middle East that he made just after completing his course work. Instead he decided to go to law school.

Although even Joe's blustering and blandishments could not get him into Harvard Law School with his abysmal "gentleman's" grades, he did manage to gain admission to the respected University of Virginia. To the surprise of his family he did quite well, graduating in the upper half of his class and becoming the first Kennedy to earn a graduate degree. As head of the speakers' bureau he brought a number of well-known people to campus, including such cronies of his father as Justice William O. Douglas, columnist Arthur Krock, Senator Joseph McCarthy, and Joseph Kennedy himself.

Although McCarthy had not yet achieved his later notoriety, it was Kennedy's invitation to Ralph Bunche, a black American, that provoked serious controversy. Bunche was chief deputy to the secretary general and the highest-ranking administrative official at the United Nations. When accepting the invitation, Bunche refused to speak before a racially segregated audience, as Virginia law then required. Kennedy joined others in a challenge that induced the university's president to circumvent the ban.

This did not mean that Kennedy was an early crusader for civil rights. Not for a dozen more years, and then under very different circumstances, would he be motivated to question the laws of racial exclusion on a broader level. But this incident did indicate his unwillingness to go along with what he perceived as an injustice when he was directly involved.

He was not a man who operated by abstractions. He learned not by reading or thinking but by observing. Civil rights, like poverty, was mostly an abstract issue until he could see its effects firsthand. This is one of the reasons, as attorney general and later as senator, he traveled so much. It was how he learned. Stories abound of his visits to urban ghettos and Appalachian and Deep South villages where he saw the apathy and misery of the "other America." He operated best from his emotions rather than from his intellect, from his feelings rather than from theories.

His emotions were engaged in situations where he could see and touch. Where he saw children suffering from malnutrition or people crowded in hovels he would declare that this was "not acceptable" and demand that something be done. This was the caring, feeling Kennedy of the late 1960s — the "good Bobby." But where he had to operate from intellectual abstractions such as the "national interest" his instinct was to divide the world into good guys and bad ones.

The capture, unmasking, and punishment of bad ones gave him a special pleasure beyond that of simply doing his job. He saw himself, and wanted to be seen by others, as a crusader for righteousness. As with other righteous people, like Woodrow Wilson, he often felt misunderstood. To be good he had to be tough. Being a tough guy was part of his identity, a way in which he dealt with himself and the world. This toughness later became, for many people, part of his appeal, and in 1968 won him the support of some who admired George Wallace.

At the end of his junior year in law school Bobby became, at age twenty-four, the first of the surviving Kennedy children to marry. The athletic and prank-playing bride, Ethel Skakel, also hailed from a large and wealthy family and was, if possible, even more pious in her Catholicism than Rose. Thirteen months later the first of their eleven children was born.

When Bobby graduated in June 1951 he had no clear idea what to do with his law degree. His father found him a job investigating tax evaders and suspected communist agents for the Justice Department. But he quit that after only a few months for more important family business. Jack's 1952 campaign for the Senate was faltering badly. Someone was needed to pull together a disheveled organization and keep Joe Kennedy from trying to control everything. Bobby came. Twenty-six years old, arrogant, self-righteous, and determined, he knocked heads together and ran roughshod over the old pols.

It was a family division of labor. Bobby sweated and screamed his way through the campaign, doing the dirty work, while Jack gave statesmanlike speeches and charmed the ladies with his boyish appeal. Jack always took the high road, leaving the messiness to others. "The entire handshaking, small-talking side of politics was repugnant to him," organizer Lawrence

O'Brien recalled. It was also good strategy. Running against the patrician Henry Cabot Lodge, who came from a distinguished family of politicians, he had to avoid being labeled just another pretty-boy opportunist with a rich father.

Bobby's job was to keep him on the high road. Once during the campaign he shouted at a local candidate who he felt was riding Jack's coattails: "I don't want my brother to get mixed up with politicians!" The politician objected, and Bobby knocked him to the ground. Jack had to be kept above such crass maneuvers. "Don't give in to them," he told Bobby of the local pols' efforts to muscle in on his organization, "but don't get me involved." Jack used the same tactics eight years later in his campaign for the presidency, with Bobby consigned to the role of enforcer. It was this role of campaign manager that gave birth to the image of the "ruthless" Bobby.

That Jack was above and beyond such behavior was not only a tactical maneuver but a reflection of his temperament. In contrast to Bobby's intense emotionalism, Jack was ironic and detached. Even as a child he had established an emotional distance. In this way he protected himself from his mother's disciplined coldness and his father's insatiable demands. He avoided showing need and had trouble displaying affection. As a child his mother said she never saw Jack swept away by anger or uncontrollable tears. Even his best friends confessed that they did not really know him.

He dealt with the world through irony and wit. Because he was a clever and engaging fellow, this made him a desirable companion while providing the protection he sought. Later, when Jack entered political life, these qualities were extolled as evidence of his sophistication. The Kennedy "cool" was greatly admired in the outposts of the New Frontier. Thus was a defense mechanism turned into an attribute of superiority.

Although Jack was an intelligent man with a nimble mind that cut through cant, he did not have the passions or deep personal convictions Bobby was later to acquire. "Like his father, he was intent on the pursuit of power, and left it to the intellectuals to rationalize his deeds," biographer Richard Whalen has written of JFK. "He was in politics, not to advance an ideology, but to derive personal satisfaction. His politics was as self-centered as his father's fortune-building."[1] There was no shortage of intellectuals eager to do the rationalizing.

Bobby's devotion to Jack, and to the family's wider ambitions, was equally driven. Where it differed from Jack's was that gratification lay not in the exaltation of the self but in its submergence to the family. That is why Joe eventually came to value Bobby, although he had never taken him seriously as a child. When he boasted that Bobby would keep the family together what he meant was that Bobby would, unlike Jack, put the family above himself — that is, he would put Joe's ambitions above his own.

Although Jack's technique was to ingratiate himself with people by his charm and wit, and Bobby's was to distance them with his hostility and moodiness, both shunned open displays of emotion as a sign of weakness. The preferred mode of discourse was kidding. This permitted familiarity without the danger of vulnerability or sentiment. It can also be, as Freud has taught us, a sublimated form of hostility.

Jack, who was much more at ease with people, and with himself, than Bobby, turned this into an art form. His sidekick Lem Billings, with whom he was as close as he ever got to anyone, was the object of endless gibes about his weight, looks, intelligence, and appeal to women. Through cords of humor and good-natured ridicule he bound Billings to him, as he later did others. Significantly, as Garry Wills has observed, the humor was directed against them rather than against himself.

Jack's other distancing technique was that of distorting people's names. He gave many of his friends personal, sometimes disparaging, nicknames. Billings, for example, was Lemoan or Pneumoan. Instinctively Jack recognized that renaming people was a way of asserting control over them. He did this even to his brother, who hated being called Bobby, but could never shake the childhood diminutive Jack insisted on using. Bobby retaliated by doing the same to others once he had the chance. Theodore Sorensen, known as Ted, had this taught to him when he received a note from Bobby after JFK's assassination. "Teddy, old pal," it began, and ended with the signature "Bob."[2]

The 1952 Senate campaign was a critical event for both Kennedy brothers. It catapulted Jack to the national political stage and won Bobby the respect of his family. He had shown that he could be counted on, and that he had to be taken seriously. Toughness and tenacity had paid off. Jack might not have been able to make it without him. Although he had no interest in running for office himself, he began to see politics as the arena in which he could make an impact and at the same time do some good.

Everything came together for him with Joe McCarthy. Later, after McCarthy had fallen into disfavor and disgrace, Bobby's admirers argued that his involvement with McCarthy was merely a brief aberration of his youth, the exuberance of an unsophisticated young man. This was meant to assuage uneasy liberals. But in fact the relationship with McCarthy was so significant that on the senator's death in 1957 — four years after Bobby stopped working for him — he said that he had lost an important part of his life.

In early 1953, when Bobby went to work for him, the communist-hunting senator from Wisconsin was at the peak of his influence, the most controversial political figure in America. His florid accusations of communist agents destroying the United States from within struck a chord of response among Americans confused by a conflux of disturbing developments: the

Iron Curtain across Eastern Europe, atomic spies, a Soviet nuclear bomb, a communist victory in China, and the Korean War.

McCarthy had a ready answer for these problems, and millions listened. Joe Kennedy was one of them. He had grown increasingly cranky and conspiratorial after his falling-out with Roosevelt, who had refused to offer him an important government post because of his isolationist pronouncements as ambassador to Britain. Kennedy liked McCarthy's slash-and-burn attacks on liberal Democrats. He also liked the rowdy amiability of the hard-drinking junior senator from Wisconsin, and had invited him to Hyannis Port for several weekends of family fun and games. McCarthy had even dated Eunice and Jean, though Joe probably would have drawn the line at having him for a son-in-law.

Bobby, then, knew McCarthy not only as a communist hunter, whose rough tactics he admired, but also as a family friend and a lively, ribald fellow Irishman. From his vantage point working for McCarthy was a job made in heaven: he could be at the center of the action and perform a patriotic service. His father took care of the details. Having funneled money into McCarthy's campaigns, as he had with other politicians whom he considered potentially useful, Joe asked the senator to name Bobby as the chief legal counsel on his Senate investigative committee.

McCarthy, however, had already decided on an even more brash, aggressive, and intelligent young lawyer from New York. Roy Cohn, then but twenty-five (two years younger than Bobby), was already known as a communist hunter for his work on the prosecution team in the trial of atomic spies Ethel and Julius Rosenberg. His legal skills and elastic scruples made him highly desirable to McCarthy. Bobby got hired, but had to settle for a job as an assistant counsel. The two young lawyers, fighting over the same turf, took an instant dislike to each other.

Jack was not happy that his brother was working for McCarthy. This had nothing to do with the senator's methods or goals. Jack showed no great concern for McCarthy's unfounded accusations and civil rights abuses. He just did not want a member of his family to be involved with such a controversial figure, particularly at a time when he sought the support of liberals for his own political ambitions. His reasons for keeping a discreet distance from McCarthy were, as speechwriter and aide Theodore Sorensen later admitted, "political, not ideological."

Bobby's reasons for serving McCarthy were just the opposite. Being an investigator suited his temperament and reflected his convictions. Although Cohn had relegated him to the minor task of investigating trade between American allies and China, Kennedy turned it into a politically useful issue for McCarthy. With Americans fighting Chinese troops in Korea, he gained media attention for the investigation, and when it was finished filed a report condemning "this shocking policy of fighting the enemy on the one hand and trading with him on the other." This embarrassed the Eisenhower administration, which pointed out that the trade did not involve strategic goods, and saw the whole inquiry as a McCarthy publicity ploy.

Bobby was zealous in carrying out his investigation, but he had little influence over McCarthy, who took most of his cues from Cohn. When McCarthy appointed Cohn to head the entire investigative staff Kennedy was locked out of any position of influence. Cohn was running the show and had no use for him. In frustration he resigned after only six months, and spent the rest of 1953 in a dull job his father had found for him working for a commission to reform government.

Liberals never let Robert Kennedy live down his association with McCarthy. Nor did he ever apologize for it. In his mind he had no reason to do so. He liked McCarthy, shared many of his beliefs, and saw him not as a malign force or an unprincipled opportunist, but as a patriot. Later, when that became an unpopular position to take, he excused McCarthy as being a well-meaning but gullible victim of the manipulative Cohn. "At that time, I thought there was a serious internal security threat to the United States," he told an interviewer a decade later in a different political climate, and ". . . that Joe McCarthy seemed to be the only one who was doing anything about it." Then after a few moments' reflection he added — whether from conviction or prudence — "I was wrong."

His relationship with McCarthy was probably the most difficult part of his career for his later admirers to handle. It seemed to go even deeper than politics. Something about the senator's character touched him. He was sincerely fond of McCarthy, seeing him as a "very complicated character," as he later said, who felt no personal rancor toward those he vilified, and who was sincerely puzzled that they resented him for destroying their reputations. "He would get a guilty feeling and get hurt after he had blasted somebody," Kennedy maintained. "He wanted so desperately to be liked. . . . He didn't anticipate the results of what he was doing. He was very thoughtful of his friends, and yet he could be so cruel to others."[3]

Many people with a less charitable view of McCarthy would find this comment an example of self-delusion or duplicity. Probably it was a bit of both. But it also showed Bobby's eagerness to defang an issue that continued to haunt him for the rest of his political career. Efforts by his admirers to attribute this episode to softheartedness actually diminish Kennedy by making him seem naive.

Robert Kennedy not only liked McCarthy, but respected him and applauded his activities as well. In 1951 he asked McCarthy to be the godfather of his first child, Kathleen. This was more than sympathy for an underdog, for at the time McCarthy was riding high. Even after

McCarthy, in a fit of manic excess, accused President Dwight Eisenhower and the U.S. Army of knowingly harboring and promoting communists, Kennedy — then working for the Democrats on the committee — put most of the blame on Roy Cohn's "misconduct."

Jack Kennedy, rather than criticizing the man his brother had worked for and his father supported, simply ducked the whole issue. Recuperating in the hospital from back surgery at the time of McCarthy's censure by the Senate in 1954, Jack failed to vote at all, although he could easily have paired with another senator without getting out of bed. He was the only Democrat who did not vote or pair on the crucial issue. Instead he helped chief writer Theodore Sorensen draft his book *Profiles in Courage*. There he extolled the bravery of legislators who had taken grave political risks in defense of their moral principles. The book, with Arthur Krock's lobbying, was ultimately awarded the coveted prize in biography by the Pulitzer board of editors, even though the advisory panel of jurors had not even listed it among its eight recommendations.

As for Jack's politics, it was not so much that he supported McCarthy; he just did not feel strongly about him. Furthermore, as he later explained in a moment of candor, "I had all these family pressures." Bobby, for his part, remained faithful to McCarthy until the very end. In January 1955, a few weeks after the Senate voted to censure McCarthy after public opinion turned against him, Bobby made another gesture of support. The occasion was a banquet given by the Junior Chamber of Commerce in which he was among those honored as one of the ten outstanding young men of 1954. The speaker was Edward R. Murrow, the well-known broadcaster who had helped turn the tide against McCarthy with a stinging television documentary. As Murrow rose to speak, Kennedy pointedly rose from his seat and stalked out of the room.

McCarthy, deprived of media attention and an admiring audience, descended deeper into drunkenness and died in May 1957. Bobby was deeply shaken by his death. He cried when he heard the news, and that day wrote in his journal: "Very upsetting for me. . . . I dismissed the office for the day. It was all very difficult for me as I feel that I have lost an important part of my life — even though it is in the past."

To emphasize this loss of an "important

part" of his life he attended the services held for McCarthy in the rotunda of the U.S. Senate, and then, in a more significant tribute, flew to Wisconsin to be at his burial. At the funeral he stayed in the car most of the day. When recognized by reporter John Bayley, he said, "I don't want to tell you how to write your story, but if you choose not to mention I was here, I'd appreciate it."[4]

The McCarthy episode was not simply an insignificant and overblown incident in Kennedy's life, as his admirers insist, but a central and telling event. In some real way he identified with McCarthy: not simply McCarthy the Red hunter who recognized evil and sought to extirpate it, but also McCarthy the victim who was ultimately punished for his beliefs. Kennedy saw himself in both roles, identifying himself with McCarthy triumphant and McCarthy scorned; McCarthy the prophet and McCarthy the martyr.

He found McCarthy's death so "very upsetting" because for him the errant senator was a kindred spirit — one engaged, as he was himself, in the struggle against evil. Like himself, he believed, McCarthy faced a hostile world that would not understand him. Like him McCarthy suffered for his dedication to a noble cause. Like him McCarthy had become, in his disgrace, an underdog.

For someone who had struggled his whole life to gain validation in a family of ferociously competitive achievers, nothing captured Kennedy's sympathy more than the underdog. The more McCarthy was attacked, the more did Kennedy identify with him. In his eyes McCarthy was a fighter for virtue, just as he was himself. In his defeat Kennedy saw not an ironic justice but a cruel martyrdom.

5

An Enemy Within

The legend tells us that Robert Kennedy was a moralist. For him, as his wife once said, it was "always the white hats and the black hats, the good guys versus the bad guys." Gray was an unknown hue. As he grew older the objects of his scorn broadened: from international communism to corrupt labor officials, organized crime, die-hard segregationists, and finally even Lyndon Johnson. His moral certainty focused his energies and made him a formidable opponent. Like most moralists he could be self-righteous and relentless. This inspired the behavior which was often, and with some justice, described as ruthless.

Nowhere was this behavior so aggressively evident as in his work as a Senate staff investigator. Although he had quit McCarthy's subcommittee in frustration at being subordinate to Roy Cohn, he was back six months later working for the Democrats as minority counsel. And when the November 1954 elections produced a Democratic majority, John McClellan became subcommittee chairman and named him chief counsel.

Kennedy assured the press that under the new leadership the committee was "not a whit less interested in rooting communists out of government than it was when Senator McCarthy ran the show." This was true. He was involved in more investigations of communists than he had been when McCarthy was chairman. But after McCarthy's demise, and the country's weariness with subversive clerks and dentists in the bureaucracy, there was little more mileage left in leading anti-communist posses.

Seeking out new malefactors, Kennedy found a rich lode in the Teamsters union, where high officials with links to organized crime had siphoned off workers' dues for their own benefit. The thought of honest working men being cheated by their own greedy leaders provided Kennedy with a moral cause. In a series of widely publicized hearings that brought him national attention, he forced the Teamsters chief, Dave Beck, to take the Fifth Amendment sixty-five times to avoid self-incrimination. Ultimately Beck was evicted from office and sent to prison for larceny and tax evasion.

Kennedy was making a name for himself as a relentless prosecutor, but it was not the kind of name that pleased his father. Not only did Joseph Kennedy have useful ties to Teamster officials (and, it was widely believed, to crime syndicates as well), but he feared that Bobby's prosecutorial zeal would antagonize organized labor and thus hurt Jack's presidential ambitions.

But Bobby's moral principles had been engaged. He considered Beck to be corrupt and his successor, the more intelligent and crafty James Hoffa, akin to absolute evil. Hoffa, a self-made man who had quit school at fourteen, had fought with cops and management goons, battled other unions for the right to organize drivers, and used thugs and gangsters to pursue his ends. Short, pugnacious, muscular, and disciplined, he took pride in hard work and loyalty.

Also like Kennedy, he was always eager to prove his toughness. In every way they were adversaries made for each other. Kennedy, Hoffa complained, "was a man who always made a big thing out of how strong and tough he was, how he had been a football player or something at Harvard." Kennedy, for his part, later wrote of Hoffa: "When a grown man sat for an evening and talked continuously about his toughness, I could only conclude he was a bully hiding behind a facade."

Hoffa was in some ways the kind of man Kennedy could have admired. Through sheer grit and determination he had risen from poverty, fought for the working man, and led a personal life of puritan abstinence. But along the way he had conspired with criminal forces. This triggered Kennedy's moralistic energies. For him the punishment of Hoffa was not a task but a crusade.

"Bob, who had an underlying distaste for the kind of people his father used to buy, recognized the devil in Hoffa . . . something absolutely insatiable and wildly vindictive," the columnist Murray Kempton wrote. ". . . He recognized in Hoffa a general fanaticism for evil that could be thought of as the opposite side of his own fanaticism for good . . . and, therefore, involved direct combat."

Kennedy had some inkling of this himself. After talking to one of Hoffa's associates he jotted on a notepad that the man "said that I was too e[n]meshed with

Hoffa — that it was like Nixon on Alger Hiss." Just as Nixon was inspired to peaks of cunning and emotion by his passion to convict Hiss, so Kennedy found in Hoffa the object of his most intense desire. "My first love is Jimmy Hoffa," he confessed to an interviewer. The fight against Hoffa not only inspired him, but catapulted him onto the national stage — just as Hiss had done for Nixon. Each inquisitor was locked in embrace with his nemesis.

To fortify his case against Hoffa, Kennedy subpoenaed a rogue's gallery of Mafia chiefs to testify, including Joey Gallo, a labor-management racketeer and murder suspect; Tony Provenzano, a Teamster official who took the Fifth Amendment forty-four times; and Sam Giancana, the chief hit man for the gang that took over from Al Capone in Chicago. Kennedy, who a few years later would learn of the mobster's compromising link to JFK, taunted and tried to humiliate Giancana by making insulting remarks while questioning him, such as "I thought only little girls giggled, Mr. Giancana."[1]

Although the hearings were dramatic, Kennedy failed to convict Hoffa on bribery charges, and the Teamsters defiantly reelected him. But one side effect of the hearings — with their revelations of rigged union elections, intimidation of dissidents, misuse of funds, and collusion with gangsters — was to spur sweeping anti-union legislation that punished the good unions along with the Teamsters.

The effort to nail Hoffa consumed all of Kennedy's energies. It became a holy cause. The hearings went on for months, and more than 1,500 witnesses testified. Yet it all came to naught when the jury failed to convict. Hoffa was right when he predicted that when it was over he would still be head of the Teamsters and Kennedy would be "running off to elect his brother president."

Which is precisely what happened. In August 1959, Bobby resigned from the McClellan subcommittee to help Jack win the 1960 nomination. In one sense he had failed, for Hoffa continued maddeningly to elude him. But the experience had also been gratifying and even exhilarating. Not only had it made him a public figure, but it had shown that he could do something on his own as well. He had become more than just his father's son and his brother's brother. At this point he was better known in the country than was Jack.

Bobby had made an impact with his own

abilities. He had won the respect of those he cared about and the scorn of those he hated. "For the first time in his life he was happy," Lem Billings recalled. "He'd been a very frustrated young man, awfully mad most of the time, having to hold everything in and work on Jack's career instead of his own. I think he found himself during the Hoffa investigation."

He also made a good many adversaries. Civil libertarians were disturbed by his relentless cross-examination of witnesses and by his efforts to discredit those who invoked their right to remain silent. "No one since the late Joseph McCarthy has done more than Mr. Kennedy to foster the impression that the plea of self-incrimination is tantamount to a confession of guilt," wrote Yale law professor Alexander Bickel. From the hearings Bickel concluded that Kennedy was "a man driven by a conviction of righteousness, a fanaticism of virtue, a certitude about guilt that vaulted over gaps in the evidence."[2]

For liberals the problem with Kennedy's conduct of the case was that he first decided that Hoffa was guilty and then searched for charges on which he could be convicted. Normally prosecutors determine that there has been a crime and then set about to find out who committed it. One of the reasons that Kennedy professed such scorn for liberals was his belief that they desire the end but get squeamish about the means; they need tough cops to do the dirty work. To his mind being liberal meant being weak, and there was nothing he held in greater contempt.

From Kennedy's family background and religious training it is not surprising that he would see conflict as a clash of absolutes. The notion that certain constraints had to be observed, or that he might even be wrong, went against his value system. For him extremism in the defense of justice was no vice and moderation no virtue.

This was particularly true where it concerned those he believed were demonstrably evil, like communists and Jimmy Hoffa. In Kennedy's mind the Teamster leader had assumed monstrous proportions. Hoffa had become his white whale. Only in one other case were Kennedy's passions to be so aroused: in the hunt to destroy Fidel Castro. With both these men he lost all sense of proportion, inflating the sins of the hunted until they matched the fanaticism of the hunter.

Robert Kennedy's departure from the McClellan subcommittee to run Jack's

1960 campaign did not slake his determination to nail Hoffa. No sooner did Robert Kennedy become attorney general than he set up a special bureau in the Justice Department popularly known as the "get Hoffa squad." Under the direction of Kennedy's handpicked aide, Walter Sheridan, sixteen lawyers and twice as many FBI agents were deployed for the hunt.

The effort to nail Hoffa went on for years. Finally, after the expenditure of a remarkable amount of time, money, and energy on this single case of labor union abuse, a jury in 1964 sent Hoffa to jail. Kennedy had finally gotten the kill he wanted. Yet instead of being elated, he was depressed. By that time he was living in a different world than when the hunt began, years earlier. Jack was dead and the New Frontier had been replaced by Lyndon Johnson's plans for a Great Society.

When the verdict was announced, he showed no emotion. It was as though an important force had passed from his life. He and Hoffa had been locked into their personal vendetta for so long that it was like the end of a love affair. When his staff at the Justice Department gave a party to celebrate Hoffa's conviction, Bobby put a damper on the festivities. "There's nothing to celebrate," he said.

But of course there was a great deal to celebrate — if the conviction of Hoffa was what he really sought. Yet capturing the prey meant that the chase was over, and it was the chase that had excited him. As his white whale Hoffa was his nemesis and thus one of the most important things in his life. Kennedy was not the kind of hunter who found happiness in mounting stuffed animal heads on his wall. For him the thrill came in the pursuit. He sought out conflict because that is where he felt most alive.

On leaving the Rackets Committee in 1959 he enlisted journalist John Seigenthaler to ghostwrite a book about what his publishers called his "dramatic struggle with the ruthless enemies of clean unions and labor management." Published in 1960, it was an engaging tale that contributed to his growing reputation as a fearless inquisitor. The title he chose was a catchy one, but revealed more about himself than he may have intended. He called it *The Enemy Within*.

6

Running Interference

When Jack Kennedy opened his bid for the 1960 presidential nomination, he had naturally taken for granted that Bobby would quit his job on the committee, suspend his chase after grafters and gangsters, and sign up for service for as long as he was needed. The notion that he could have other priorities had not even been considered by Jack, by the family, or even by him.

He became the cop, devising strategy and enforcing discipline. The job required someone totally dedicated to Jack's ambition and ideally indifferent to his own. This campaign reinforced the reputation for ruthlessness he had earned as a Senate inquisitor and manager of Jack's earlier campaigns. "He has all the patience of a vulture without any of the dripping sentimentality," said one of the reporters assigned to cover JFK's race. Bobby took it as a compliment. "It doesn't matter if they like me or not," he explained. "Jack can be nice to them. . . . Somebody has to be able to say no."

Jack agreed. With his facility for enlisting people to serve him, he "recognized that the campaign required a son of a bitch," in Arthur Schlesinger's words, "and that it could not be the candidate." Rather than resent Jack's demands, Bobby felt grateful and needed. Service was the method he had found for gaining validation within the family. He was Jack's protector and enforcer. "Whenever you see Bobby Kennedy in public with his brother," a reporter said to Murray Kempton at the 1960 Democratic convention, "he looks as though he showed up for a rumble."[1]

JFK's strategy for 1960 (which Bobby was to adopt eight years later in his own bid for the presidency) was to demonstrate his vote-getting abilities by winning big in a few key primaries and then cutting deals with party bosses who controlled large blocs of delegates. This strategy had been challenged in West Virginia by the ebulliently liberal Senator Hubert Humphrey. The Kennedys badly needed to carry this heavily Protestant state to break the taboo against a Catholic in the White House.

Bobby, as campaign director, brought in Franklin D. Roosevelt Jr., son of the liberal icon whose name was revered in the state. In the last days of the campaign Roosevelt implied to voters that Humphrey, who had had a medical deferment during World War II, was a draft dodger. The contrast with the young hero of *PT-109* fame was pointed and obvious. The infuriated Humphrey rightly blamed the slur on Bobby, complaining that as campaign manager he showed "an element of ruthlessness and toughness that I had trouble either accepting or forgetting."[2] It was also an example of the behavior that even the supposedly reformed "good Bobby" was to show eight years later in his own contest for the nomination with Eugene McCarthy. Jack carried the state and demonstrated finally that the Catholic issue was a dead one.

By the time Jack got to the convention he had the nomination sewed up. Lyndon Johnson, despite strong backing in the South and from party leaders, had failed to mount a serious challenge. Liberals, horrified equally by the prospect of Kennedy or Johnson, made an emotional plea for Adlai Stevenson, the man who had led them twice to defeat. Gene McCarthy's eloquent nominating speech for Stevenson roused the liberals to one last hurrah. But Kennedy money, liberally dispensed by Joe, and the Kennedy political steamroller corralled the votes.

Jack had dangled the vice presidential slot before half a dozen hopefuls in order to gain their support for his own nomination. But when the time came to choose, the normally cool and decisive candidate made a hash of it. Partly from need for a running mate who could improve his chances in the southern states, partly as a good will gesture, he offered the post to Lyndon Johnson. He figured that the powerful Senate majority leader might be too proud to accept it, but would be grateful for the invitation. To his surprise, but not necessarily disappointment, Johnson accepted.

Party liberals, along with organized labor and civil rights groups, were outraged. To their minds Johnson was too southern, too conservative, and too linked to big-money oil and gas interests. They pressured JFK to retract the offer and anoint a certified liberal.

Kennedy, known for his cool and unsentimental political calculations, had put himself in the line of fire between two bitterly opposed factions. He realized, as his father kept pointing out to him, that Johnson could be helpful in winning crucial electoral votes in the South, and he did not want to alienate such a politically powerful senator. But he also feared a revolt by northern liberals who never felt that his heart was with them.

Not wanting to compromise himself any further, he called on Bobby to run interference. With JFK's approval Bobby made three visits to Johnson's hotel suite as the convention delegates waited for official word of Jack's choice for vice president. Each time he tried to talk Johnson off the ticket. At one point he suggested to the proud Texan that he would be happier in the post of Democratic party chairman. "Shee-it!" replied Sam Rayburn, Johnson's mentor and Speaker of the House.

Finally realizing that Johnson would not withdraw, and fearful of splitting the party further, Jack bowed to the inevitable and made the choice of Johnson official. Trying to avoid responsibility for a comedy of errors, he put the blame on his brother. "Bobby's been out of touch," he told *Washington Post* publisher Philip Graham of the failed effort to talk Johnson off the ticket, "and doesn't know what's happening."

For Bobby, as for Jack, it was, as usual, good cop/bad cop. Commenting a few years later on Graham's report that he was "out of touch," Bobby laughed at the notion that he was operating behind Jack's back. "Obviously, with the close relationship between my brother and me," he explained, "I wasn't going down to see if he would withdraw just as a lark on my own: 'My brother's asleep, so I'll go see if I can get rid of his Vice President!' " To Graham's widow, Katharine, Bobby said that her husband "didn't know us; we — my brother and I — never would have been apart."[3]

In this he was surely right, for they operated as a team. And they were to do so increasingly during the three years of Kennedy's presidency, when Bobby remained not only his henchman, but his confidant and adviser as well. Bobby was for all practical purposes the deputy president, consigning the proud Lyndon Johnson to a role of largely ceremonial irrelevance.

The feud between Bobby and Johnson, which was to grow to monumental levels of contempt and vituperation in the years that followed, began during those confused days in July 1960 in Los Angeles over the struggle for the vice presidency. Johnson felt abused by the experience and never forgave Bobby for how he had been treated then and during the thousand days of Jack's presidency.

As it turned out, John Kennedy probably could not have won without Johnson, who brought in the electoral votes of Texas and several southern states. Kennedy's margin of victory was only 120,000 votes of a total 68 million cast — the narrowest in history. The Catholic issue had hurt him in the South but helped him in the Northeast and industrial Midwest.

Kennedy also could not have won without the black vote, which came to him more by accident than by coherent plan. In late October, as the campaign was going into its final days, Martin Luther King was jailed for trying to integrate a department store snack bar in Atlanta. Civil rights adviser Harris Wofford, who knew King, urged the candidate to phone the minister's wife to offer his sympathy. Jack thought it a good idea and spoke for a few minutes with Coretta King. When Bobby heard what had happened he exploded. "Do you know that three southern governors told us that if Jack supported Jimmy Hoffa, Nikita Khrushchev or Martin Luther King they would throw their votes to Nixon?" he shouted at Wofford. "Do you know that this election may be razor close and you have probably lost it for us?"[4]

But on reflection Bobby decided to make the best of what he considered a political gaffe and put in his own call the next day to the Georgia judge who had sentenced King. The civil rights leader was soon released on $2,000 bond. From a legal point of view the calls of both Kennedys were meaningless; from a political one they were astute. King's father, an influential Southern Baptist minister, swallowed his suspicion of Catholics and urged his followers to vote for John Kennedy.

Though hardly a champion of civil rights, Kennedy won two-thirds of the black vote nationwide. In Illinois, which he took by only 9,000 votes, he won 250,000 votes in black wards. He probably also could not have carried New Jersey, Michigan, South Carolina, or Delaware without a large black majority. Eisenhower blamed Nixon's loss on the phone calls.

One reason the vote was so close was that for many people there seemed hardly a hair's breadth of difference between the candidates. Arthur Schlesinger, a former Stevensonian who had swung over to Jack, felt obliged to write a campaign pamphlet tellingly entitled "Kennedy or Nixon —

Does It Make Any Difference?" Many were not sure that it did. But Kennedy's stylish geniality and vague promises to "get the country moving again" won over marginal voters ready for a new face. The election was hardly a mandate for change. But then the victor had no serious reformist agenda.

This was confirmed by the choices he made for key posts in his administration. The candidate who had promised to get rid of the old faces with outdated ideas immediately reappointed two warhorses long scorned by liberals: Allen Dulles at the CIA and J. Edgar Hoover at the FBI. To head the Treasury he named a Wall Street banker and Eisenhower's undersecretary of state, Douglas Dillon; to run the Pentagon a Republican corporate executive, Robert McNamara; and to forge a more dynamic diplomacy at the State Department, a foundation administrator of deeply orthodox views, Dean Rusk. Kennedy had considered choosing J. William Fulbright, the thoughtful chairman of the Senate Foreign Relations Committee, as secretary of state. But Bobby talked him out of it on the grounds that some African nations might complain that Fulbright, as a southerner, had a weak civil rights record. Later, when Bobby started using Rusk as a scapegoat for administration failures in Cuba and Vietnam, he said that he regretted having vetoed Fulbright.

By mid-December, Bobby's own future remained undecided. Initially he was unsure whether he should hold a job in his brother's administration and toyed with the idea of running for governor of Massachusetts. He even mused that he might like to be president of a college — taking for granted that this was simply another family plum to be handed out. But there was little doubt that he would go into the new government in some role. "I had to do something on my own, have my own area of responsibility," he told an interviewer in 1965. By this he meant that he should not simply be his brother's cleanup man.

But the decision had already been made for him by his father. Joe was insistent that he be named attorney general. This was an audacious demand, given that Bobby had no obvious qualifications for the job. He had never practiced law, argued a case before a jury, or been a district attorney. All he had ever done was graduate from law school, chase bad guys as a congressional investigator, and run his brother's political campaigns.

Yet Bobby had one supreme qualification that put him high above other candidates. He was dedicated to Jack and to the family in a way that no outsider could ever be. This was critical because Joe realized, better than the president-elect himself, that Jack needed protection. Not protection so much from his political opponents as from his own Justice Department, particularly from the head of the FBI, J. Edgar Hoover.

Hoover, who had run the FBI since before Bobby was born, was too politically entrenched in office to dismiss. Jack, with his thin electoral margin, had realized that it was dangerous even to try. Hoover was not an enemy if properly deferred to. But as head of the nation's domestic spy and law enforcement agency he had a thick dossier of incriminating evidence on virtually every politician. And the Kennedys had reason to assume that he knew things about them that could have seriously compromised, or even destroyed, Jack's presidency if they ever became public.

Somebody, Joe realized, had to keep Hoover in check, somebody who put Jack's political survival above all other considerations. The FBI was administratively a branch of the Justice Department. This put the director at least theoretically under the control of the attorney general. If Hoover could not be evicted from his post, he could at least be contained. That was Bobby's task.

For a few days Bobby offered a perfunctory resistance, but the pressure was more than he could handle. At a breakfast meeting at Jack's house in Georgetown the older brother lay down the law. He told Bobby, according to an aide who was there, that he needed at his side someone he could trust totally, someone "who's going to tell me the unvarnished truth, no matter what." Then he pulled out family loyalty as the clincher. If he could ask people like McNamara and Rusk to give up their careers, "men I don't even know . . . certainly I can expect my own brother to give me the same sort of contribution."[5]

Of course up to this point Bobby had done nothing but contribute to his brother's welfare. At some point it might have been thought that he had done enough. Yet when Jack had called for a show of loyalty, Bobby could do only what was expected of him. It was what he had always done. And he could not help being dazzled by the audacity of such a brazen display of nepotism. It showed, as he said admiringly, that Jack had "the guts of a burglar."

The Kennedy family knew no higher praise. This behavior is what their father had taught them to admire, and how Joe had grown rich. Audacity had been the key to Joe's success as a predatory entrepreneur. For the older Kennedy, as for his sons, audacity and courage always had a sexual component. And sex was inextricably associated with power and domination. That was the major component of Joe's and then Jack's relationships with women, and it spilled over into politics. Caution in their lexicon was unmanly; audacity was virile. The language of the New Frontier was couched in the vocabulary of sexual politics. "Let's grab our balls and go," Jack said to Bobby as they went to tell the waiting reporters that the president-elect was naming his own brother as the nation's protector of the laws.

This was the end of Bobby's halfhearted attempt to carve out some kind of independent life for himself. He never really meant it, and he never had a chance in any case. "I did it," he later said, "not so much to become attorney general as to be around during that time."

7

His Brother's Keeper

His appointment was treated as something between a joke and an outrage. *The Nation* called it "the greatest example of nepotism this land has ever seen" and *Newsweek* termed it a "travesty of justice." The critical Professor Bickel of Yale Law School declared in *The New Republic* that on his record "Robert Kennedy is not fit for the office." Compared to these the *New York Times* showed relative restraint in judging that "his experience is surely insufficient to warrant his present appointment."

There was much to support the charges. The idea that the thirty-five-year-old presidential brother and campaign manager would impartially uphold the law without regard to political considerations strained the credulity of many. If Bobby now had thousands of deputies, he still had only one client: John Kennedy. And there was nothing he would not do to protect him. "He would have taken a bolt of lightning for Jack," his deputy John Seigenthaler later said. "He really didn't care if he was regarded as a great Attorney General. All he cared about was his brother's presidency."[1]

Yet he took his wider responsibilities seriously, recruiting a qualified staff of senior lawyers from top law firms and universities and attracting some of the idealistic young people who had flocked to Washington to enlist in what a Kennedy phrase-maker called the New Frontier. Despite his youth and inexperience he was, in terms of his energy and dedication, eventually considered even by skeptical critics to have been an exceptionally able attorney general.

Initially he focused on what he knew best: chasing bad men. Expanding the scope of the Justice Department's operations, he gained new investigative legislation from Congress to resume his war on the racketeers he had first targeted as a Senate investigator. He also was driven by the demands of the times to focus increasingly on the struggle of black Americans for full equality and justice. At first suspicious and even hostile to many civil rights leaders, he responded increasingly — if sometimes reluctantly — to their demands.

Eventually, and particularly after he left office, this seemingly harsh and cold law enforcer became a hero to millions of blacks who believed that he had made their cause his own.

He was not an easy man to work for. Driving his staff as hard as he did himself, he made little effort to charm or seduce. Like many rich men he paid low wages, found it easier to borrow money from his employees than to carry change, and expected his aides to double as domestics and chauffeurs when needed by his large brood. However, he also inspired deep loyalties among many who worked for him. He was as determined to be a good attorney general as he was to face down his fears and be a winner at whatever he tried.

And he could be relentless, or what many called ruthless, in dealing with those he considered to be evil or enemies. The sense of humor he showed among friends would turn into sarcasm or anger when he was crossed. Witnesses he had examined as a Senate investigator sometimes emerged shaken from the ordeal. One union official broke into tears under his relentless questioning. "His face, when it lacks that boyish, photogenic grin, is not a pleasant sight," wrote one man who worked for him. "It has a certain bony harshness, and those ice-blue eyes are not the smiling ones that Irishmen sing songs about."

He was his brother's bulldog, and his methods made him deeply disliked by those he challenged. Big businessmen almost uniformly distrusted him for his aggressive behavior in rolling back a price rise in 1962 by the steel companies that JFK opposed. His action troubled not only them, but civil libertarians as well. "I had the grand jury," Bobby later told an interviewer of his move against company executives. "We looked over all of them as individuals. We were going to go for broke: their expense accounts and where they'd been and what they were doing. I picked up all their records and I told the FBI to interview them all — march into their offices the next day. We weren't going to go slowly. I said to have them done all over the country. . . . All of them were subpoenaed for their personal records. . . . Under the circumstances we couldn't afford to lose."[2]

Such tactics disturbed even those who supported the objectives he sought, and they intensified persistent doubts — evidenced in his harassment of suspect union officials and his obsession with nailing

Jimmy Hoffa at virtually any cost — about his commitment to civil liberties. Like many crusaders in pursuit of righteousness, he showed a disturbing tendency to justify whatever behavior he found useful.

Yet in one critical area he showed surprising caution and even timidity. Liberals assumed that he would use his vaunted toughness to rein in the freewheeling, indeed virtually independent, director of the FBI. The much-feared J. Edgar Hoover had for decades run the bureau as his private fiefdom within the Justice Department. But the Kennedys were deferential toward Hoover. "It was important, as far as we were concerned, that he remain happy and that he remain in his position," Bobby later explained. ". . . It was much better [for] . . . what we wanted to do . . . that we had him on our side."

What he meant was that they needed Hoover on their side because he had the potential to do considerable harm both to JFK's goals and his reputation. With his powerful links to Congress and his extensive dossiers on the private lives of politicians, Hoover was too deeply entrenched and too well connected to dismiss. The best that could be hoped for was to neutralize him. At this task the Kennedys proved to be no more successful than their predecessors had been.

Bobby was strikingly passive toward Hoover, allowing the FBI to continue its controversial practice of wiretapping and bugging people under investigation — most notably in its harassment of Martin Luther King — and failing to enlist FBI agents to protect civil rights demonstrators in the South. As Victor Navasky writes in his study of Kennedy's performance as attorney general: "During President Kennedy's life Robert never *attempted* to control either the Director or the FBI . . . he tempered his efforts to influence the FBI so as not to embarrass his brother."[3]

Even though Bobby tried not to cross Hoover, their personal styles made them clash almost constantly. The FBI director was a deeply conservative man who insisted that his agents keep their hair short, be clean-shaven, and never take off their suit jackets in the office. He was deeply shocked to serve under an attorney general who came to the office with a huge dog, worked in shirtsleeves, put his feet on the desk, and threw darts at a target on his wood-paneled walls.

But style was only the visible part of their disagreements. Hoover and the FBI had become famous for chasing crooks and communists, with an emphasis in recent years on the latter. With spies and communist dupes in short supply, Kennedy tried to steer a reluctant Hoover back toward criminals. He won authority from Congress for new powers to deal with organized crime, and stretched the rules of the Internal Revenue Service to nail racketeers on tax-evasion charges.

By 1963 the number of indicted mobsters leaped fivefold from what it had been when Kennedy took office, and doubled again the following year. He continued the pursuit of corrupt union officials and their Mafia enforcers that he had begun in the Senate. He ordered the IRS to impose tax liens on mobsters Santos Trafficante and Carlos Marcello, whom he had first targeted while on the Rackets Committee. After his deportation, Marcello (later a suspect in the JFK assassination investigation) was picked up on an FBI wiretap telling another mafioso: "Don't worry about that little Bobby son-ofabitch. He's going to get taken care of." Then he added, in a seeming reference to the president: "The dog will keep biting you if you only cut off its tail. But if you cut off the dog's head it will die."[4]

The other mobster Robert Kennedy was particularly eager to catch was Sam Giancana. During the Rackets Committee hearings he had ridiculed and provoked the Chicago Mafia chief who directed thousands of agents and controlled some $2 billion in gambling revenues. Yet he failed to win an indictment against him. Although he had revealed Giancana's links to key mob figures in Las Vegas and Florida, there were two other connections that Kennedy did not investigate. One was to the CIA. The other was to his brother, the president.

Giancana was one of the gangland figures cultivated by Frank Sinatra. The singer had also been brought into the Kennedy entourage through Peter Lawford, a sometime actor, Kennedy brother-in-law through his marriage to Patricia, and unofficial procurer of starlets for JFK. The president was as fascinated by show business as Sinatra was by politics. Through the ever-obliging Lawford the singer met the president and was enlisted to orchestrate his inaugural ball. Sinatra, who had many girls, in early 1960 did his new friend, the president, a special favor by introducing him to a favorite: Judith Campbell, later known as Judith Exner. A striking brunette who was, Sinatra had assured JFK, even better looking than Elizabeth Taylor, Campbell deeply impressed the president.

In her 1977 book, *My Story*, she recounts the idiosyncrasies of their love-making and their assignations in various cities around the country, including JFK's invitation to travel with him on *Air Force One*. Kennedy, she relates, was obsessed with the sex life of the stars and insisted on knowing who the sexual partners of Sinatra and other show business people were. She kept him informed frequently. White House logs show more than seventy phone calls from Campbell to the president.

Campbell relates that while conducting her affair with Kennedy she also became involved with Giancana. The Mafia don boasted that he was responsible for the crucial nine thousand votes in Chicago that allowed Kennedy to win Illinois in the 1960 election. In 1988, Campbell claimed that at Kennedy's request she arranged secret meetings during the 1960 campaign during which Kennedy asked for Giancana's help — and that in 1961 she carried envelopes back and forth between the two. Giancana's interest in her, she later came to suspect, rested primarily on her affair with John Kennedy.

While the president's affair with a Mafia party girl was a secret to the nation, it was not to J. Edgar Hoover. The FBI director had a long dossier on Kennedy that went back more than twenty years to JFK's wartime affair in Washington with a Danish woman, Inga Arvad, who had been photographed with Hitler and was under surveillance by the FBI as a possible Nazi spy. Only Joe's intercession with the secretary of the navy saved Jack from losing his commission, though he was kicked out of intelligence work. The story was hushed up and the navy quietly transferred Kennedy to duty in the Pacific. It was expunged from the navy's records, but not from J. Edgar Hoover's files on prominent people.

Although Hoover found Jack's promiscuity distasteful and potentially dangerous, what led him to confront the president directly over the issue was Campbell's connection to Giancana. For the president to share a mistress with a Mafia capo meant opening himself to possibilities of blackmail by organized crime. If this connection had become known Kennedy would have been so morally compromised that he would likely have had to resign in disgrace.

Jack's obsessive promiscuity had gone beyond the point of boyish exuberance to that of political self-destruction. Even a normally compliant and adoring White House press corps would not have accorded him that much slack.

The danger was even worse than it had first seemed. An FBI sting operation in Las Vegas had revealed through wiretap evidence that Giancana was linked to the CIA. The agency, as part of its secret effort to topple Fidel Castro, had engaged the mobster to use his gangland connections to assassinate the Cuban leader. Thus it was that the president of the United States was not only sleeping with a Mafia moll, but sharing her with a mob capo engaged by his own intelligence services to murder a foreign leader.

Kennedy handled Hoover's revelation with his customary cool. After the director left his office he made one short, final phone call to Campbell and then did not see her again. On Bobby's advice, he also severed relations with Frank Sinatra, angering the singer by canceling a scheduled visit to his home in Palm Springs and compounding the insult by staying instead with Republican Bing Crosby, Sinatra's chief rival.

Hoover's bombshell did not noticeably affect the president's behavior otherwise. He continued to have sexual relations with various available women, both inside and outside the White House, and in 1963 was involved with a part-time prostitute born in East Germany who was suspected of being a communist agent. In that case Bobby intervened fast, deporting Ellen Rometsch on an air force transport plane even before the FBI completed its investigation and threatening with an antitrust suit a newspaper chain that was considering printing the story. The brother whom JFK in 1963 had described to Ben Bradlee as "a puritan, absolutely incorruptible," also knew how to bend the rules, as in the use of the FBI and the Internal Revenue Service, when duty demanded.[5]

On the issue of JFK's flamboyant promiscuity, Michael Beschloss, in his analysis of Kennedy's diplomacy, *The Crisis Years*, writes that JFK's "lawyers, his father, and his brother Robert evidently used financial payoffs, legal action, and other kinds of threats to silence women who had been involved with Kennedy and, for breach of promise or other reasons, threatened to go public." The Rometsch case provides another example of JFK's reckless willingness to put his presidency in jeopardy to any group or even foreign government that wanted to use or destroy him — and of Bobby's equal willingness to cover up for the brother whose fate was so entwined with his own.

Jack's affairs stemmed less from a quest for pleasure than from a craving for excitement and, like his father, for defying society's rules with impunity. He particularly liked James Bond movies. He "seemed to enjoy the cool and the sex and the brutality," his friend Ben Bradlee, then Washington bureau chief of *Newsweek*, has written.[6] Like his father he had a succession of women. They were so interchangeable — secretaries, starlets, prostitutes, students — that often he did not bother learning their names.

For a president under constant surveillance his behavior was reckless. But that is what made it exciting to him. Rather than hiding his trysts he conducted them even in the White House, under the eyes of the Secret Service. White House staffers covered for a licentious boss who gave some of them, in Richard Reeves's words, "an excited feeling that they had been accepted into a private Kennedy circle." Sex, according to people close to him, had no connection to feeling. It was power and compensation. His old chum Lem Billings, who knew him as well as anyone did, believed that John Kennedy "knew he was using women to prove his masculinity, and sometimes it depressed him."

Like Lord Byron, whose life fascinated him, and whose lame leg paralleled JFK's own weak and disease-wracked body, he was determined to make an impression on people by flamboyant sexual behavior. "With his sense of worth, well-being and masculinity undermined by his own body and by a mother who could not hide her hostility toward him, Kennedy had drawn upon his talents for self-projection to put forward an image that made him notorious to authorities but admired by many of his peers," historian John Hellmann has observed.[7]

Although Bobby was not ostentatiously promiscuous like Jack, and lacked his flair for self-dramatization, he too tried to overcome the disadvantage — in a culture and a family that emphasized power and aggressiveness — of his shyness and small stature. His compensation took the form not so much of sex but of a compulsive physical competitiveness. He became tough and wiry, and would drive himself, and those willing to accompany him, to exhaustion in feats of daring and endurance. The sport of touch football, where players were sometimes injured by the ferocity of the game as he played it, was dwarfed by the feats of mountain climbing, rapids running, wild animal hunts, and fifty-mile hikes that engaged him so compulsively. Like Jack, but in a different way, he was always trying to prove something. Whereas Jack tried to exert dominance through charm and seduction, Bobby did it through hostility and aggressiveness. But the behavior had the same source in feelings of insecurity and fears of weakness. And "to be obsessed with winning," Nancy Gager Clinch has written, "is to be obsessed with failure."[8]

Bobby, unlike Jack, did not view sex as a semi-public performance so much as an occasional break from his demanding family life and increasingly numerous children. Reports link him to involvements with a number of women, some of them prominent in the social and entertainment world. Given the prevailing ethos in the Kennedy family, where sexual prowess and promiscuity were viewed as a badge of masculinity, it strains credulity to imagine that he was immune to such virtually obligatory demonstrations of virility. Among the starlets, socialites, and political groupies to whom he was linked, it is also widely believed that in the difficult months after JFK's death he and Jacqueline were drawn very tightly together. The notion that this Kennedy was the one male in the family who was a "puritan" is hard to sustain.

Of the various women in the orbit of the Kennedy brothers, the one whose star power matched their own was Marilyn Monroe. Jack was introduced to the diva by the helpful Peter Lawford and continued to see her for the next two years. Frequently she would call him on his White House line. At the president's forty-fifth birthday celebration at Madison Square Garden she appeared, dressed in what Adlai Stevenson described as "skin and beads," to sing a breathlessly suggestive rendition of "Happy Birthday." Jacqueline Kennedy chose not to attend the performance.

But Marilyn was too needy a woman for a busy man. As Jack's interest waned, she turned to Bobby for comfort and reassurance. How much more is a matter of speculation. He has been accused of being with her on the day she died from a barbiturate overdose in Los Angeles in August 1962, and even of having contracted for her murder to prevent her from carrying through her threat to tell the media about her affair with the president. Such accusations are less interesting for what they tell us about Bobby's sex life than for the suspicions they reveal about a family so intent on gaining and holding power. Whatever his degree of involvement with her — whether simply as Jack's protector or also as Jack's surrogate — Bobby's ultimate concern was to prevent any political harm from befalling his brother.

By now Marilyn Monroe and the Kennedys have entered the realm of legend: the neurotic woman who was every man's sex fantasy; the smooth leader of the Free World who lived on borrowed time and made his own rules; and the faithful little brother who wanted only to serve, but who himself later learned how to make his celebrity serve his politics.

The Kennedys cultivated celebrity — and celebrities. It was one of the ways they drew to them the flocks of helpers and admirers who gratified their needs and served their ambitions. For those in their orbit, proximity to the light — to be invited to the fabled dinners (or better yet the private film showings) at the White House or to elaborate and often raucous soirees that Ethel Kennedy would organize with tireless abandon at Hickory Hill, their suburban home in Virginia — was a sign of acceptance into a privileged inner circle. The glamour rested not only on presidential power but on family money, and the particular "style" that John and Jacqueline cultivated so successfully, and from which Bobby also benefited.

It was a style that depended on more than power, more than wealth, more than style and grace. It also depended on success. Power that fails to subdue once unleashed is power that is compromised. This the Kennedys learned with regret and in anger.

8

Troubleshooter

Robert Kennedy was not his brother's friend in the sense of being a crony. JFK had others who filled that role: the amiable Lem Billings, whom he could chide; ribald buddies like his navy chum Red Fay or journalist Ben Bradlee, with whom he could trade dirty jokes and stories about women. Bobby was more: he was a protector, an alter ego, and, to a degree unknown to the public at the time, the deputy president.

When he made his bid in 1968 for the White House, he cited his foreign policy experience as a qualification for the job. This might have been considered a curious claim for one whose job as attorney general was to punish domestic lawbreakers. But he was not amiss in making it. He played a major role in virtually every aspect of foreign policy in his brother's presidency, and was the key American negotiator — indeed the only significant American negotiator — during the dangerous confrontation with the Soviet Union over Cuba. He was deeply involved in the planning of the early stages of the Vietnam War. In addition, he took actions under his brother's authority, and at times in his absence, on a number of major foreign policy issues. For all practical purposes he played a more important role than did the secretary of state, and was more responsible for the ensuing consequences.

It is often said that John Kennedy wanted to be his own secretary of state, which is why he appointed a compliant administrator like Dean Rusk to the post. But it is generally not known how reliant he became on Bobby both for advice and for making decisions. This began as early as May 1961 when Rafael Trujillo, dictator of the Dominican Republic, was assassinated. With JFK in Europe, Robert simply took over the U.S. response. ". . . Nobody seemed to be doing anything" to prevent communists from trying to gain power, he told an interviewer several years later. ". . . I guess I had the major responsibility of trying to work out some plans. . . . We moved the fleet in closer." When asked about suspicions that United States officials had engineered the assassination of a chief of state, Bobby replied: "They wouldn't have done it without telling *me*" (italics added).

It was Bobby who pushed hardest for the use of counterinsurgency forces against communist-led rebels in the Third World. The Alliance for Progress, designed to squelch radical forces in Latin America through U.S.-sponsored economic development programs, was one of his favorite projects. It was Bobby whom JFK instinctively called on when the Bay of Pigs invasion collapsed, and he who handled the ransom of prisoners taken by the Cubans. From that time on he became his brother's deputy for foreign policy. As he said in 1964: "I then became involved in every major and all the international questions."[1]

But it was the Cuban missile crisis of October 1962 that brought them together as a foreign policy team. It demonstrated to Jack that in the end there was only one person on whom he could fully count; one person on whose judgment and discretion he could rely, and who would put his interests above all others. While this event helped forge a tighter bond between the brothers, it also strengthened the forces that were to provoke a personal tragedy.

Cuba has been a national obsession ever

since 1959, when Fidel Castro and a ragtag band of revolutionaries seized control of the government from a U.S.-backed dictatorship, and then, whether by prior design or perceived necessity, turned it into a communist dictatorship. Nothing like this had ever happened before in what was deemed to be America's sphere of influence, and from the start U.S. officials worked to overthrow Castro.

On assuming office in January 1961, John Kennedy inherited a secret plan to use U.S.-based Cuban exiles to invade the island and depose the regime. The operation had been orchestrated by the CIA, which had trained the exiles at bases in Florida and Central America, and provided weapons and transport. Kennedy, assured that Castro had little popular support and could be easily toppled, approved the plan. But in order to avoid embarrassing charges of American aggression against an island that had long been a virtual American colony, the president insisted that U.S. forces not be used in the attack. For public purposes he sought what the CIA called "plausible deniability."

That doomed the plan. Without air support from American fighter planes the ill-equipped invaders were routed on the beach at the Bay of Pigs, with many killed and the rest captured. It was that rare thing: a perfect disaster. Kennedy inveighed against the CIA and the Joint Chiefs of Staff for encouraging him in this ill-fated venture. His aides labored to persuade an admiring press corps that the failure was not Kennedy's fault, but that of the "experts" who had presumably misled him. In fact he had not been "misled," but was undone by his own arrogance and bad judgment.

Kennedy denied that he knew about plans to invade Cuba before his inauguration as president. But this defies belief. His friend Senator George Smathers confirmed that Kennedy knew about the plans before his election. Presidential speechwriter Richard Goodwin said in 1981 that Kennedy "may very well have known" in October 1960 (when he attacked opponent Richard Nixon in a TV debate for failure to get rid of Castro) of the CIA's plans, and in his 1988 memoir, *Remembering America*, writes that the CIA's briefings of Kennedy during the campaign "revealed that we were training a force of Cuban exiles for a possible invasion of the Cuban mainland."[2]

For public purposes JFK officially accepted responsibility, but shortly got rid of the two officials most responsible for the operation: CIA director Allen Dulles and his deputy, Richard Bissell. A former Yale economics professor touted for his brilliance and mordant wit, Bissell had been a Kennedy favorite and, until this fiasco, was being readied to take over Dulles's job when the veteran spook retired. He became the fall guy, though he always insisted that the operation could have succeeded had Kennedy not blocked a U.S. air strike.

The only other way the landing might have succeeded, failing direct U.S. air support, was if the Cuban leadership were to be wiped out. This alternative was based on more than wishful thinking. In September 1960, during the last months of the Eisenhower administration, the CIA had contracted the Mafia to use its operatives in Cuba to assassinate Castro. The operation continued when Kennedy assumed office, and was a major reason both Kennedy and the CIA leadership were so confident that the exiles' landing could succeed. It might have, had Cuban intelligence services not foiled the plan, and had the CIA not been totally wrong in believing that the mass of Cubans did not support Castro.

The failure of the invasion did not mean that the administration had given up its plan to get rid of Castro's regime by one means or another. In the fall of 1961, John Kennedy startled a *New York Times* reporter by asking: "What would you think if I ordered Castro to be assassinated?" When the reporter replied that he thought it would be a bad idea, the president hastened to reassure him that he did as well.[3] But why would he ask such a question of anyone, let alone of a journalist, if he were not considering it, and wanted to test how it would be treated in the media — and to put himself on record as being against it?

How much the Kennedy brothers knew about the CIA's assassination scheme is a matter of dispute. Their admirers insist that it was an entirely rogue operation, and that had they known they would have vetoed it. But in 1975, long after the death of both John and Robert Kennedy, the Senate Select Committee on Assassinations revealed, after a scrupulous and thorough inquiry, that beginning in 1960 agencies of the U.S. government organized at least eight plots to kill Fidel Castro. Most of these took place when Kennedy was president.*

The major reason Bissell was so optimistic that the Bay of Pigs landing would succeed was that, as he told an interviewer in 1984, "assassination was intended to reinforce the plan. There was the thought that Castro would be dead before the landing." This was no secret to Havana and Moscow. The Soviets were convinced, according to historians who later gained access to the Kremlin archives, that "the Kennedy administration had expected Castro to die before he could rally support for destroying the invasion." This was also the view of Kennedy's friend George Smathers, who stated in 1964 that the president had told him a few weeks after the Bay of Pigs fiasco that he had been "given to believe" by the CIA that when the invaders landed Castro would be dead.[4]

Although Robert Kennedy had not been directly involved in the planning of the Bay of Pigs operation, he took its collapse as a personal defeat. For him this defeat was not

* *The CIA conspired during this period to assassinate the leaders of the Congo, Iraq, and the Dominican Republic, and, in 1970, Chile.*

a signal to reevaluate assumptions, but to redouble efforts and get even. Arguing impassionedly to the Cabinet that the Kennedy team could not take this failure lying down, he insisted that it must "either act or be judged paper tigers in Moscow." He was so distraught and eager for action that Walt Rostow, McGeorge Bundy's hawkish deputy at the National Security Council, reassured him that there would be other opportunities to prove the administration's mettle. One place he had in mind was Southeast Asia.

Authorized by JFK to oversee the CIA's plans to eliminate Castro, the attorney general insisted on the importance of winning the war with Cuba, even though the administration had lost the battle. "Our long-range policy objectives in Cuba are tied to survival far more than what is happening in Laos or the Congo or any other place in the world," he wrote in a memo to his brother. The Castro situation could not be allowed to fester: "The time has come for a showdown, for in a year or two years the situation will be vastly worse." With some prescience he argued that "if we don't want Russia to set up missile bases in Cuba, we had better decide now what we are willing to do to stop it."[5]

The Bay of Pigs changed the relationship

between Bobby and Jack. After this experience Jack realized that he needed someone by his side whom he could trust totally, who would ride herd over the feuding bureaucratic rivals, who would not shrink before any task of any nature, and who would never neglect the wider political interests of the Kennedy administration and the Kennedy family. From this time on Bobby became, in effect, the deputy president: the person who sat in for Jack during Cabinet meetings, hounded the bureaucracy, treated even the highest officials as though they were family servants, and made a stunning range of foreign policy decisions.

Bobby's first task was to organize a united front to dispel accusations that Jack had acted imprudently in Cuba by ignoring the cautionary advice of more experienced Democrats such as Senator J. W. Fulbright and statesman Chester Bowles. Bowles's pre-invasion misgivings on the landings had been leaked to the press, to the Kennedys' considerable embarrassment. Encountering the undersecretary of state in the hallway, Bobby jammed a bony finger into his soft stomach: "You should learn to keep your mouth shut and remember that you were *for* the Bay of Pigs."

A week after the failed adventure on the beach, Jack assembled the National Security Council for a planning session. Bowles argued that Castro's position was so secure that only a costly American invasion could dislodge him. "That's the most meaningless, worthless thing I've ever heard," Bobby spit out angrily at the senior statesman. "You people are so anxious to protect your own asses that you're afraid to do anything. All you want to do is dump the whole thing on the president." Continuing in this vein he contemptuously concluded: "We'd be better off if you just quit and left foreign policy to someone else."[6]

Jack sat coolly watching this attack, saying nothing. Nor did anyone else dare to speak. Bobby was clearly playing the role that Jack had assigned him.* It would not be long before Bowles, who spoke unpleasant truths and had concerns beyond the reputation of the Kennedys, would be

* *Richard Goodwin later wrote of this outburst: "I became suddenly aware — am now certain — that Bobby's harsh polemic reflected the president's own concealed emotions, privately communicated in some earlier, intimate conversation. I knew, even then, there was an inner hardness, often volatile anger beneath the outwardly amiable, thoughtful, carefully controlled demeanor of John Kennedy."*[7]

pushed out of office.

A few weeks after the Bay of Pigs, Bobby established his own secret line of communication with the Kremlin through a young Soviet military intelligence officer, Georgi Bolshakov, who operated under cover at the Soviet embassy. From this point on the two men met about twice a month as private, nonofficial emissaries to negotiate on behalf of Kennedy and Khrushchev. Through this link conducted by Bobby, JFK served as his own secretary of state. Bobby's initiative and freedom of action made him, in effect, a conegotiator with the president.

The fiasco at the Bay of Pigs persuaded JFK to give unprecedented decision-making powers to Bobby, and it inspired in both brothers an obsessive determination to punish Castro for their embarrassing defeat. With an American invasion ruled out because of the effect such aggression would have on U.S. relations with Latin American states, the Kennedys turned to the CIA. In doing so they followed a pattern of earlier presidents who found the agency's capacity for clandestine operations suited to deeds they were constrained from performing in the open.

Bobby became JFK's link to the CIA's

anti-Castro operations and its incessant goad. As Richard Helms, who took over covert operations from the disgraced Bissell, and later became head of the CIA, told historian Michael Beschloss: "The whip was on the Agency all the time from the president through Bobby: 'Get on with this thing!' He wanted Castro out of there." Bobby had summoned Helms to his office at the Justice Department in January 1962 and told him that the elimination of Castro was "the top priority in the U.S. government. All else is secondary. No time, money, effort, or manpower is to be spared."[8]

As Robert Kennedy learned more about covert operations and the CIA's virtually unlimited resources for conducting secret wars, he was drawn excitedly into the shadowy world of counterinsurgency. This was the Kennedys' answer to communist-inspired "wars of national liberation" in the Third World against Western-supported regimes. Commando teams known as Special Forces — or more popularly Green Berets — were set up and instructed in methods learned from Mao Tse-tung, Ho Chi Minh, and Fidel Castro. Bobby was entranced by the notion of brawny fighting men who would live in the jungle and enlist peasants in the struggle against communism. He kept a talisman green beret on the chair behind his desk even after he went to the Senate.

Bobby fell in love with the notion of counterinsurgency, and the Green Berets were his kind of fighters. For him they were the incarnation of a scrawny boy's childhood fantasies: the jungle ingenuity of Tarzan matched with the toughness of the Foreign Legion. He brought them to the Kennedy family compound at Hyannis Port, where they swung from trees, scaled walls, and emitted such fierce noises that brother-in-law Sargent Shriver forbade his children to be around them. At Hickory Hill, he assembled his troops for seminars on how to swim among Third World peasants like Mao's fish in the sea.

To erase the shame of the Bay of Pigs fiasco, Robert Kennedy put together a small team, known cryptically as the Special Group (Augmented), or SGA, to do clandestinely what the administration was blocked from doing openly. General Maxwell Taylor, whom Bobby had picked as JFK's personal military adviser, ran the group under his supervision. Nothing was off-limits. As Robert McNamara later explained: "We were hysterical about

Castro at the time of the Bay of Pigs and thereafter."[9] No one was more hysterical than Bobby, and no branch of the government more useful to him than the CIA, with its immense covert action capabilities.

In Robert Kennedy's eyes Fidel Castro had assumed gigantic dimensions. The fact that he had humiliated the Kennedys by surviving their attempts to destroy him was only part of the reason. Castro was a continuing, provocative affront for what he was. The qualities he marshaled — bravery, cunning, defiance, and inspirational leadership — were ones that Bobby admired. A figure of towering dimensions, Castro had created and led a popular revolution, and from his impoverished island successfully resisted the most powerful nation on earth. Infuriatingly, he had survived U.S. blockades, invasions, and assassination plots.

While Bobby was in an office writing legal briefs or haranguing witnesses, the Cuban leader had inspired millions around the world with his rhetoric and bravado. His very existence was a reproach, and he had to be destroyed. Castro was another of Bobby's white whales, just as Jimmy Hoffa had been. He could not rest until he had brought down this infuriating presence.

Nothing was ruled out: sabotage, invasion, even assassination. Under Jack's presidential order to "use our available assets to overthrow Castro," Bobby set up an action program under the code name Operation Mongoose. Its existence was an official secret, its activities clandestine, and its mission to overthrow — by one means or another — the government of Cuba. "My idea is to stir things up on the island with espionage, sabotage, general disorder, in an operation run essentially by the Cubans themselves," Bobby explained at a White House meeting in November 1961.[10] In short, what he proposed was a U.S.-financed and -directed terrorist operation.*

To run it he appointed the infamous Edward Lansdale. A former advertising man and air force officer with a reputation

* *Later, when courting the left in preparation for his presidential bid, he took a different approach. Asked to prosecute American students who had visited Cuba in defiance of a State Department travel ban he refused, saying, "What's wrong with that? If I were 22 years old that is certainly the place I would want to visit." A few years later he became an honorary revolutionary. To a leftist admirer who tried to flatter him by saying he belonged in the hills with Fidel Castro and Che Guevara instead of behind a desk, he replied ingratiatingly, "I know it."*[11]

for cutting through bureaucratic inertia and indoctrinating the peasants, he had won fame in the Philippines in the early 1950s for organizing the defeat of communist-led rebels. He was the thinly disguised hero of the best-selling novel *The Ugly American* and the anti-hero of Graham Greene's *The Quiet American*, a corrosive portrait of a naively idealistic man who destroys a society in order to save it. Lansdale was Bobby's kind of man. He combined anti-communist fervor with a skill for knocking heads together and spilling blood in a noble cause.

Lansdale personified Bobby's fantasies of leading a counterrevolution. "We are in a combat situation with Cuba," Bobby informed a group from the Pentagon and the CIA in January 1962. At the same time he told John McCone, the former Republican businessman who had become the new director of the CIA, that Cuba was "the top priority in the U.S. government — all else is secondary — no time, money, effort or manpower is to be spared."[12]

McCone argued for direct U.S. military force against Cuba before the Soviets turned the island into an impregnable base. The Kennedys, fearful of the political fallout from an invasion, favored using the CIA to get rid of Castro. Although it was considered imprudent to discuss assassination openly, the chief of the CIA's Cuba task force testified to a Senate committee in 1975 that McNamara recommended that the SGA "consider the elimination or assassination of Fidel."[13] CIA agents were appalled that such a delicate subject be talked about openly, although they had made several attempts — under the prodding of the Kennedys — to "get rid of Castro" to implement just such a policy.

With Castro entrenched in power despite the CIA's efforts to eliminate him, the military option gained support. In August, McCone won JFK's approval for a CIA plan to seek to provoke a full-scale revolt against Castro that might require U.S. intervention to succeed. Although Bobby was McCone's strongest backer, the Kennedys still hoped to avoid the domestic and international repercussions from such an intervention by using the Mongoose operation to get rid of Castro.

Castro became convinced that the Americans, having failed in their assassination attempts, were now preparing to invade. Although administration officials denied this, McNamara later admitted: "If I had been a Cuban leader at that time, I might well have concluded that there was a great risk of U.S. invasion. . . . If I had been a Soviet leader at that time, I might have come to the same conclusion."[14]

This is apparently the conclusion Castro and Khrushchev reached. This led them to make a fateful decision. On October 15, 1962, U.S. spy planes returned from flights over Cuba with photographs revealing that the Soviets were building secret missile bases on the island. Suddenly the "intolerable" Castro problem assumed new meaning. A shaken JFK assembled a small team of advisers to which he assigned the deliberately opaque name of Executive Committee, or ExCom. Bobby became its gadfly and deputy leader.

He was not a calming presence. When he first saw the photos of the missile sites, according to a CIA agent then present, "He walked around the room like a boxer between rounds, thumbing his nose and uttering epithets." His first reaction to the Soviet move was to urge that it be countered with an American invasion of the island. Searching for a pretext to justify such an action against an independent country, he suggested that the United States fake a Cuban attack on the Guantánamo base or "sink the *Maine* again or something."[15] Even as the confrontation over Cuba threatened to ignite a direct conflict between the U.S. and the Soviet Union, he remained obsessed with Castro. While the ExCom was arguing over what to do about the Soviet missiles, he met with the Cuba task force to complain about the lack of progress with Mongoose and the fact that for more than a year there had been "no acts of sabotage."

The ExCom quickly split between those who wanted direct military action — an attack on the bases and an invasion of the island — and those hoping to get the missiles out by diplomacy. Nobody argued for ignoring them, even though McNamara pointed out that they made little dent in America's nuclear superiority over the USSR, and that the U.S. had similar missiles in Turkey right on the Soviet border. Although RFK at first sided with the hard-liners, he calmed down as it became apparent that the critical issue was not Castro's defiance or Khrushchev's duplicity, but the danger that the U.S. and the Soviet Union might, under circumstances that neither could fully control, be drawn into a nuclear confrontation.

Unlike some other members of the ExCom, Bobby knew what the CIA had been doing in Cuba and why the Russians might have felt that their Caribbean protectorate was in danger. He even understood why Castro — under death threat from the U.S. — might seek Moscow's protection. This eventually tempered his normal emotionalism. With his brother's full backing, his immunity from losing his job, his reputation for toughness, and his realization that his own zeal to get Castro may have helped provoke the crisis, he had the freedom to consider conciliatory positions without fearing accusations of weakness.

Early in the crisis he had been among those who wanted to bomb the bases to take out the missiles. But he was persuaded by McNamara and others that such an attack could quickly escalate out of control and provoke a Soviet retaliation in Cuba or elsewhere — perhaps Berlin. By the evening of the third day of deliberations he had turned against an air strike as the first resort. Instead, he pressed for a graduated approach: a naval blockade of the island combined with negotiations to persuade the Soviets to remove the missiles. Although he encountered strong opposition, he was able gradually — with the clear authority of the president behind him — to swing the majority over to that position.

Khrushchev, alarmed at the rapid deterioration of events that had brought the Americans to the verge of nuclear war with his country, sent JFK an emotional letter offering to withdraw the missiles in return for an American pledge not to invade Cuba. Before the president could reply Khrushchev — probably pushed by hard-liners in the Kremlin — upped the ante with a second message: the Soviets would pull out only if the Americans would withdraw their own missiles from Turkey.

Although this would solve the problem, it would also deprive JFK of the clear victory he wanted. At this point, Bobby reportedly suggested that the president ignore the harsh second letter and reply positively to the more conciliatory first letter.* Operating as JFK's private negotiator, and without the knowledge of the ExCom, he met secretly with Soviet ambassador Anatoly Dobrynin. The emissary cabled the Kremlin that he found the president's brother "very upset; in any case

* *According to Michael Beschloss, the ploy was first proposed by McGeorge Bundy, but Bobby took credit for it in 1968 to augment his presidential qualifications.*[16]

I've never seen him like this before. He didn't even try to get into fights on various subjects, as he usually does, and only persistently returned to one topic: time is of the essence and we shouldn't miss the chance."[17]

What Bobby knew and Dobrynin didn't was that JFK was having trouble controlling the ExCom. Several members, along with the Joint Chiefs, were demanding an air strike against the bases before the missiles became operational. How the Soviets would respond to such an attack, with the loss of Russian lives and the blow to Soviet prestige, no one knew. Furthermore, the air attacks were to be followed by a U.S. invasion to dismantle the missile sites and depose the Castro regime.

What the Kennedys did not know — and was revealed only years later — was that Soviet troops in Cuba were equipped with battlefield nuclear weapons they were authorized to use if the Americans invaded. In the end the missile crisis was a far closer call than anyone realized at the time. Former secretary of state Dean Acheson, who argued from the start for air strikes, was probably right when he later said that it was "a very near miss," and probably "just blind luck" that the superpowers did not stumble into nuclear war.

Finally, after tense negotiations, the Russians agreed to pull out their missiles and aircraft in return for an American pledge not to invade Cuba. JFK came out of the crisis a hero, acclaimed by journalists orchestrated to interpret the resolution as his triumph, for having won through a judicious application of American power and diplomacy: the mailed fist within the gloved hand.

That was the official story. Only years after the publication of Robert Kennedy's memoir of the crisis, *Thirteen Days*, was it revealed that, under Soviet pressure he had negotiated on the basis of the harsher second letter from the Kremlin for the removal of the U.S. missiles from Turkey. The Kennedys insisted that this withdrawal not be made public, and that it not take place until several months after the Soviets closed down their Cuban bases. Above all, they were determined that the deal not be presented as a quid pro quo.

In other words, what the Kennedys sought, and took grave risks to get, was not only a withdrawal of the Soviet missiles, but the appearance of a political victory. The Russians, who feared even more than the Kennedys that the situation was spiraling out of control, seemed to be getting nothing in return other than a promise from Kennedy, later disavowed, not to invade Cuba.* The price they paid for this, however, was not insignificant. The relatively moderate though bumbling Khrushchev was kicked out of office in 1964 by Politburo hard-liners who sped up a crash building program to erase the nuclear inferiority that had humiliated them.

It was a mark of John Kennedy's political skill that he was able to escape blame for his own part in precipitating the crisis. Khrushchev had indeed engaged in "clandestine, reckless and provocative" action. But what the public did not know, and was never told, was that Operation Mongoose, with its scenarios for overturning the Cuban government and killing Castro, may have led the Soviet leader to take his enormous gamble.

* *What Robert Kennedy never divulged, and what was revealed only recently, was that he and JFK were willing to go even further if necessary. If the Soviets turned down the deal, Robert was prepared to offer an immediate quid pro quo, to pull the missiles from Turkey. As a face-saving device the administration would instruct UN Secretary General U Thant to make an appeal to Moscow and Washington.*[18]

The near-brush with disaster brought the two brothers closer than ever. Throughout the crisis Bobby had been Jack's negotiator, confidant, and alter ego. To a far greater degree than anyone realized, or than his official position entitled him, he had become the deputy president, confining Vice President Lyndon Johnson and Secretary of State Dean Rusk to minor supporting roles. Bobby had become at last what he always wanted to be: not merely Jack's helper and henchman, but his partner. But he was to learn that for all his devotion he could not in the end be his protector.

9

Retribution

From the missile crisis Bobby had learned that he could make an important contribution to his brother's presidency. All during the following year — from the unsuccessful struggle to push through Congress a comprehensive civil rights bill to the spiraling entanglement in Vietnam — he became the second most powerful man in the government.

This brought him new powers, but also greater responsibility and blame. Lacking his brother's charm, and largely unconcerned by how the public perceived him, he became the lightning rod for the administration's most unpopular actions. At times he appeared to revel in this, as though it were a badge of honor. Yet by the fall of 1963 there were signs that the strain was beginning to wear him down.

November 20 was his thirty-eighth birthday, and to honor the occasion his staff at the Justice Department gave him a small party. Bobby was in one of his black moods. His aide John Douglas found him "glum" and "depressed." Standing on his desk he made a little speech heavy with his cutting brand of irony. His brother's reelection campaign would surely be aided, he told his staff, by all the wildly popular actions he had taken as attorney general. Among those he cited were his actions on civil rights, union corruption, and wiretapping — actions that angered racial integrationists and separatists, organized labor, and civil libertarians.

Bobby had become, he was convinced, the lightning rod that attracted the enmity of virtually every group with a grievance. His aides wondered whether he might be resigning his post for another place in his brother's administration after the 1964 elections. They had reason to think so. Later, referring to that period, Kennedy told an interviewer: "[T]he fact that I was Attorney General caused him [JFK] many more problems than if I hadn't been his brother." He offered to resign "because I thought it was such a burden to carry in the 1964 election."[1] But he was given to passing black moods and this may have been one of them. What no one doubted was that he would, in one capacity or another, stay at his brother's side.

Two days later, November 22, Bobby was having lunch beside the pool at Hickory Hill with a few associates on a warm day. A call came from J. Edgar Hoover. The FBI director, with no sign of emotion, reported that the president had been shot in Dallas while riding in a campaign parade. At that moment no one knew whether he would live (he would die from his wounds shortly after being rushed to the hospital).

Bobby seemed in a state of shock. His first thought was of conspiracy. "There's so much bitterness," he said to his press spokesman, Ed Guthman. "I thought they'd get one of us, but Jack, after all he'd been through, never worried about it." And then he added, as though it was the target, not the action, that surprised him: "I thought it would be me."[2]

He did not spell out who "they" were, or why he thought that such persons would want to kill him or Jack. Yet as everyone there that afternoon understood, there was no shortage of candidates. A great many people had reason to hate the Kennedy brothers. Aside from the fame-seekers and crazies who are a constant threat to all prominent people, there were those who harbored deep grievances: Jimmy Hoffa, the Mafia, Fidel Castro, anti-Castro Cubans, and the violent fringe of political and segregationist groups.

When *Air Force One* brought his brother's body back to Washington, Bobby was waiting at the military airport. Rushing into the plane as soon as it landed, he swept past Lyndon Johnson, who had just been sworn in as president, without a sign of acknowledgment, and went straight to Jacqueline Kennedy's side. She was still wearing the pink suit from the motorcade, spattered with her husband's blood. They returned together to the White House. Bobby, shaken and inconsolable, retired to the Lincoln bedroom, where Jack had liked to sleep. "Why, God, why?" chronicles report that he moaned through the night.

During the funeral procession down Pennsylvania Avenue, Bobby, his head bowed and his shoulders drooped, walked beside this proud woman, too sunk in his own grief to realize fully how his brother's legacy had shifted to him. He was not ready for that. A part of him had died with Jack. Forcing himself to the casket for a final goodbye, he had placed on Jack's chest his treasured *PT-109* tie clip, a silver rosary, and a lock of his own hair. He would be joined to his brother in death as he had been in life.

Grieving people often search for some cause that will make a loved one's death meaningful. But there is no good reason, or at least none that can be accepted. For some the cause is simply an arbitrary and mindless fate; for others it is the mysterious will of God. In both cases it defies explanation. Ultimately one has no choice but to accept and move beyond.

Bobby would not accept, and for a long time could not move beyond. "It was much harder for him than for anybody," LeMoyne Billings recalled. "He didn't know where he was . . . everything was just pulled out from under him." Pierre Salinger, JFK's press aide, described him as "the most shattered man I had ever seen in my life. . . . He was virtually nonfunctioning. He would walk for hours by himself."[3]

Bobby could not bring himself to utter the word "death," let alone "assassination." Instead, he would refer cryptically to "what happened on November 22." He could not even bear to look at Jack's photo. He grew thinner and more gaunt, wandering around the house aimlessly and making mordant jokes about death and funerals. He was inconsolable in his grief. It was as though in losing a brother, the very meaning of his own life had been drained away. Even his strong Catholic faith did not appear to help him.

On and on it went, for weeks and even months. He sank into the darkness that surrounded him, not even seeming to want to emerge. He appeared to be burdened by even more than the death of a beloved brother. During this time he and Jacqueline Kennedy grew close, seemingly dependent on each other for the solace that they could not find elsewhere. Robert was the one member of the Kennedy family with whom she seemed to have any rapport. They were together so much during this time that rumors inevitably spread about the degree of their closeness.

Surprisingly, as a man of action rather than of words, he turned to the classics for support. Jacqueline had given him a copy of Edith Hamilton's literary study *The Greek Way*. We are told that he spent hours in his room pondering what the poets and playwrights of ancient Greece had meant as they sought to come to terms with the tragic forces of life. In his heavily marked copy he underlined phrases like "the antagonism at the heart of the world," and, of the doomed soldiers of a misguided military adventure, "having done what men could, they suffered what men must."

Until this time he showed little regard for the life of the mind. For him reflection was an impediment to action. Now he was not so quick to seek out enemies and to execute revenge. Instead, he plunged deeper into his own melancholy. He sought some reason for why he must "feel the giant agony of the world," in the phrase from Keats that he kept quoting. "The innocent suffer — how can that be possible and God be just?" he scrawled on one of the yellow sheets he carried around. "All things are to be examined and called into question — there are no limits set to thought."

There was something terrible about this bottomless grief, and also something strange. He clung to Jack's old garments as though they would somehow keep him afloat. Carrying Jack's overcoat with him on trips, he would curiously often leave it behind, as though trying to unburden himself, and then send an aide to retrieve it. In his sorrow he was like the Hindu wife who throws herself on the funeral pyre of her husband. It was as though his own life had been deprived of meaning; or that it had taken on a meaning that he could not bear to contemplate. He tottered for months on the edge of a despair that went beyond Jack's life to the very heart of his own.

The one thing Bobby did not want to talk about, or even to reflect upon, was the circumstances of Jack's death. If there was ever a political assassination steeped in mysteries, confusions, and contradictions it was that of John Kennedy. Almost from the first day there were accusations of cover-ups and conspiracies. To assuage these suspicions, a governmental blue-ribbon panel was empowered under the direction of Chief Justice Earl Warren to examine the circumstances surrounding the president's murder. But its conclusion that Lee Harvey Oswald, a drifter who had lived in the Soviet Union and publicly protested U.S. policies toward Cuba, had acted alone and without rational motive satisfied few of the skeptics. This was particularly so because Oswald himself was assassinated by a Mafia-linked gunman while in police custody before he could give testimony.

One did not have to be a conspiracy theorist to find the Warren Report inadequate. Yet Bobby would not aid the commission as it conducted its investigation and delegated authority to his deputy. Nor, when the report came out, did he publicly question the commission's verdict that Oswald had acted alone in killing the president and was not linked to any conspiracy. He appears not even to have read the findings. Despite widespread criticisms of the report, he refused to fault or even examine it.

Yet privately he expressed his doubts. When Jim Garrison, the maverick New Orleans district attorney, charged that Oswald was part of a wider conspiracy involving organized crime and renegade forces in the U.S. government, Kennedy told his aide Walter Sheridan that Garrison may have had some reason to charge that the CIA was involved in the assassination. "At the time I asked [CIA director John] McCone . . . if they had killed my brother," he said to his Senate press aide, Frank Mankiewicz, "and I asked him in a way that he couldn't lie to me, and they hadn't." Kennedy also asked the aide whether he believed any part of Garrison's story about CIA and Mafia involvement. When Mankiewicz started to explain why he did, Kennedy cut him off: "Well, I don't want to know any more about it right now."[4]

It is possible that grief alone explains why Kennedy did not want to delve into the depths of his brother's assassination. What he might have found there would have prolonged the pain of his loss. But there is reason to believe that Bobby also feared that the complete story, if ever revealed, could do terrible damage to the memory of John Kennedy. A deeper inquiry might have revealed not, as columnist Anthony Lewis has written in support of the report, that "in this life there is often tragedy without reason," but to the contrary, that this was a tragedy with reason. The greatest service that Bobby could render his dead brother was to preserve his memory by guarding the secrets they shared.

Harris Wofford, Kennedy's civil rights aide, has suggested in his book, *Of Kennedys and Kings*, a very different scenario from the official one. He argues that many were unwilling to dig beneath the comforting conclusions of the Warren Report for fear of what might come to light. The FBI, which provided most of the evidence for the commission, did not want it known that it had failed to put Oswald on its watch list, despite information it had about his involvement with the Russians, the

Cubans, domestic extremists on the right and the left, and the Mafia. Later the FBI issued a blistering internal analysis of its handling of the case, and Hoover carried out a purge of agents who had been derelict in their duties. "The thing I am most concerned about," J. Edgar Hoover said at the time to Lyndon Johnson's aide Walter Jenkins, "and so is [Kennedy's deputy attorney general, Nicholas] Katzenbach, is having something issued so that we can convince the public that Oswald is the real assassin."[5]

The CIA wanted to conceal the fact that since 1960 it had been engaged in efforts to overthrow the government of Cuba and to assassinate Fidel Castro and other leaders. This alone could have provided a motive for Oswald, who had been actively involved in pro-Castro activities. The CIA, as it later became known, had enlisted the Mafia in its assassination plots. Had any of this been revealed, the agency would have been gravely tarnished, and even been accused of indirectly inspiring the murder of Kennedy. To prevent this, former CIA director Allen Dulles, one of the seven members of the commission, argued strenuously that Oswald was a demented extremist acting alone. His fellow members wanted to believe it.

The Warren Commission failed to probe for an adequate explanation of why Oswald was murdered by small-time hoodlum Jack Ruby while in custody in Dallas. Ruby, a former runner for Al Capone in Chicago, had close ties to Mafia chief Santos Trafficante and New Orleans mobster Carlos Marcello. Marcello (whom Bobby had indicted for racketeering) was linked to Jimmy Hoffa and to the anti-Castro Cubans in New Orleans. In 1978 the House Select Committee on Assassinations, as a result of its own investigation, would conclude that Hoffa, Trafficante, and Marcello "had the motive, opportunity and means" to assassinate President Kennedy, although it could find no conclusive proof that they had.

Yet any serious investigation into possible Mafia responsibility would have revealed some politically explosive connections. Among them was the fact that the CIA, as part of its schemes to assassinate Castro, had actually engaged such mobsters as John Rosselli and the ubiquitous Sam Giancana, with whom John Kennedy shared a mistress. Their incentive for murdering Castro was that he had shut down their billion-dollar gambling and prostitution operations in Cuba.

This CIA-Mafia connection would also have established that the murder of foreign leaders, with or without explicit presidential approval, was an operating policy of the U.S. government. The convenient murders of such troublesome foreign leaders as Patrice Lumumba, Rafael Trujillo, and Ngo Dinh Diem would have fallen under far harsher scrutiny than a complacent media had done.

This would have suggested that John Kennedy, like Eisenhower before him, could hardly have been unaware that such methods were being used by agencies of the U.S. government. It would also have suggested that Kennedy's assassination might not have been the act of a demented loner with an incomprehensible grudge, but rather the return blow from a boomerang.

The very possibility of such a complicity in murder was more than any democratic government could willingly admit. Small wonder that the members of the Warren Commission were eager to conclude that the murdered Oswald had killed the admired president.

Robert Kennedy had even more reasons to accept this verdict than did the commission. Knowledge of the links among his brother, the Mafia, and the CIA's Castro assassination plans would forever stain John Kennedy's reputation. Exactly how directly involved the Kennedys were in these activities remains a matter of contention. But there is a compelling trail of circumstantial evidence.

According to a 1975 report by the Senate Select Committee on Assassinations, a CIA team organized by Richard Bissell tried to kill the Cuban leader as early as July 1960. The following month Bissell enlisted the aid of the Mafia on the grounds that it had both motive and experience. When Bobby was told of these efforts in May 1962, he was furious — not about the assassination plots but the use of the Mafia. "If we were going to get involved with Mafia personnel again he wanted to be informed first," Lawrence Houston, the CIA's general counsel, stated of his briefing of Kennedy. What Bobby knew was that some of the very mafiosi used in the scheme were linked to JFK through Judith Campbell. That ruled out continued Mafia involvement, though not the plot itself.

While the Mafia was apparently severed from the scheme — more from exasperation with its failure than from principle — CIA efforts to assassinate Castro continued. On the day that John Kennedy was killed in Dallas, a CIA official in Paris, claiming to speak with the authority of Robert Kennedy, provided a bribed Cuban official with a poison pen to be used against Castro. Efforts by the CIA to kill the Cuban leader continued until President Lyndon Johnson finally halted the operation.

Did the Kennedys specifically endorse these assassination activities? There is no piece of paper to which they have signed their names. CIA officials deliberately avoid using words like "kill" or "assassinate" when securing the approval of their superiors for illegal activities. As Bissell explained to the Senate assassinations committee, covert operations were conducted "in such a way that they could be reasonably disclaimed by the U.S. government." The purpose of "plausible deniability" was precisely to permit the highest officials, and specifically the president, to claim that they had not approved an illegal activity. Instead of giving such an order they would, like Henry II with regard to Thomas à Becket, pointedly ask their courtiers, "Who will free me from this troublesome priest?"

We do know that Robert Kennedy, through Operation Mongoose, had made the removal of Castro his personal responsibility and highest priority. He had also been deeply and personally involved with the anti-Castro Cubans. He was the one who had arranged for the release from Cuban jails of the prisoners taken in the Bay of Pigs operation, and had organized the paying of their ransoms. Compromising the whole purpose of "plausible deniability," he had phoned the anti-Castro Cuban activists at the Washington hotel where they had been lodged, and even entertained them at his home. Even more carelessly, John Kennedy went so far as to bring some of them into the Oval Office, including Tony Varona, who had been hired by the CIA's mob contact to assassinate Castro.[6]

Robert Kennedy's incessant demands to "get Castro" affected not only the CIA and the Mongoose planners, but the inner cabinet as well. Robert McNamara, who sat in on the secret meetings for the removal of the Cuban leadership, impatiently declared, according to White House aide Richard Goodwin, that "the only thing to do is eliminate Castro."[7] Richard Bissell, the

CIA's coordinator for Mongoose, in 1975 told the Senate assassinations committee that he had discussed the murder of Castro with McGeorge Bundy. When questioned by the committee, Kennedy's national security adviser did not deny this, but merely said he had taken no steps to block the plan because it had not yet become operational.

Richard Helms, who took over the dirty tricks operations from Bissell and later became head of the CIA, testified that he believed "assassination was permissible in view of the continued pressure to overthrow the Castro regime," even though the incriminating word was not used. He also said to historian Michael Beschloss in an interview: "There are two things you have to understand. Kennedy wanted to get rid of Castro, and the Agency was not about to undertake anything like that on its own."

In a 1989 interview Helms told author Richard Reeves, when asked about plans for killing Castro: "Robert Kennedy ran with it, ran those operations, and I dealt with him almost every day." Helms described the CIA, "then and now," as a "service organization for the president of the United States." McNamara also conceded that the CIA was "a highly disciplined organization, fully under the control of senior officials of the government."[8]

While there is no smoking gun proving that Robert Kennedy pressed specifically for Castro's assassination, the circumstantial evidence is powerful: the CIA believed that it had a mandate to kill Castro, it organized an extensive operation to perform this task, it was under constant prodding from the president's brother to "do something" about Castro, and on learning of the CIA's assassination projects RFK had done nothing to stop them. Bobby was not normally known for his passivity. When he wanted results he could be brutal. "He could sack a town and enjoy it," his friend Maxwell Taylor said after observing him berate senior government officials of the Special Group for their failure to dispose of the Cuban leader.

Bobby was a fanatic about Castro, and about using Mongoose to get rid of him once and for all. John Kennedy, when testing the idea of assassinating Castro on the *New York Times* reporter, said that he was under "terrific pressure" to approve the murder of the Cuban leader — although he claimed that he was resisting. Assuming that the president was telling the truth, who, Harris Wofford pointedly asks, could have applied such "terrific pressure" if not someone very close to him?

Arthur Schlesinger, who has defended the Kennedy brothers against such charges, has argued that the assassination operation was entirely confined to the CIA, "undoubtedly misled by the urgency with which the Kennedys, especially Robert, pursued Mongoose." Yet was the agency misled? In 1967 the CIA's former inspector general declared: "We cannot overemphasize the extent to which responsible Agency officers felt themselves subject to the Kennedy administration's severe pressure to do something about Castro and his regime."

Since "do something" here meant removal from power as soon as possible, and the CIA was under relentless goading from Robert Kennedy to produce results, and to achieve its goal it had even hired Mafia hit men, it hardly seems likely that harried CIA agents would have concealed from him their efforts to achieve the goal he so insistently demanded of them. Yet he did not halt the project. His only protest was that he had not been informed of the Mafia connection early enough.

In addition to the wealth of circumstantial evidence indicating Robert Kennedy's direct involvement in the murder plot, information has more recently come to light from an inquiry conducted by historians under a congressional mandate to provide greater public information on assassination activities involving U.S. government officials.

According to the historians' report, in 1975, Henry Kissinger, then secretary of state, met with President Gerald Ford in the Oval Office to discuss problems raised by scheduled Senate hearings on secret government assassination operations. Kissinger informed the president that he had just spoken with Richard Helms, and that the CIA director had informed him that "Robert Kennedy personally managed the operations on the assassination of Castro."[9]

In light of the terrible secrets that might have emerged from an uncompromised examination of the circumstances surrounding John Kennedy's assassination, it is not surprising that Bobby was quick to endorse the reassuring conclusion of the Warren Report that the president was killed by a single gunman.

Any other finding would have revealed things that could have fatally compromised the reputation of the Kennedy administration and shattered the saintly image of the dead president. It would have made public the CIA's efforts to kill Castro and to use the Mafia as hired killers. It would have strongly implicated both the Kennedys in these illegal activities. It would have revealed that the president of the United States shared a mistress with a Mafia capo. It would have suggested that Castro, and those like Oswald who supported him, had a motive in trying to get Kennedy first.*

This alone would explain Robert Kennedy's eagerness to accept the report as conclusive. But his deep withdrawal and depression had further cause. It was he who had provoked the enmity of the Mafia by his vendetta against crooks like Marcello and Giancana; he who had hounded the CIA to get rid of Castro by virtually any means. This tied his hands against the Mafia, and against any serious attempt to find an assassin other than the

* *Indeed, Castro had stated in September 1962, in regard to attempts against his life, "We are prepared to fight and answer in kind. U.S. leaders should think that if they are aiding terrorist plans to eliminate Cuban leaders, they themselves will not be safe."*[10]

convenient Lee Harvey Oswald. Bobby had reason to protect those who might possibly have killed his brother in order to save John Kennedy's reputation.

Any investigation of a possible Mafia link to the CIA assassination schemes against Castro would likely have revealed not only his own role, but the link between John Kennedy and the Mafia through Judith Campbell. Furthermore, and most terrible of all, was the fear that RFK's own vendetta against the Mafia may have triggered a retaliation that killed his brother — that, in mafioso Carlos Marcello's grim words, "The dog will keep biting you if you only cut off its tail. But if you cut off the dog's head it will die."

And if retaliation had not come from the Mafia it could have come from Castro — the direct target of Bobby's efforts to even scores for the Kennedy brothers' embarrassment at the Bay of Pigs. As a target of CIA assassination efforts, Castro had reason to strike at John Kennedy. If Castro became strongly suspect, public pressure for an attack on Cuba might have been irresistible. In a replay of the missile crisis, this could have drawn the U.S. and the Soviet Union into a nuclear war. For this reason, too, it was critical that the entire blame be placed on an isolated and demented single gunman.

The Kennedy administration's war against Castro had unleashed forces that it could not control: not only the targeted Castro, but also the mafiosi who were being hired by the CIA and pursued by the Justice Department; the anti-Castro Cubans who felt that JFK had betrayed them at the Bay of Pigs; the Cuban government that the Kennedys had vowed to overthrow; pro-Castro sympathizers like the unstable Oswald; and perhaps individuals linked to the CIA who feared, after the missile crisis of 1962, that the Kennedys were not pushing hard enough against Castro.

It was Bobby who had hounded the Mafia; who had goaded the CIA to get rid of Castro; who knew of his brother's connection to the very Mafia don the CIA had hired to kill the Cuban leader. The psychic weight of such a burden of knowledge and responsibility must have been enormous — the fear that in his single-minded zeal to destroy those whom he considered to be evil, he had set in motion actions that resulted in the murder of his brother. This is the horrible irony he carried with him and kept secret until the day he died. He had trafficked in the darkest realms of conspiracy and murder, and he had brought this fate upon himself. It was the classic definition of Greek tragedy.

His sense of guilt was overwhelming. "All arrogance will reap a harvest rich in tears," was a phrase from Aeschylus he had underlined. "God calls men to a heavy reckoning for overweening pride." Nonetheless, other words of the ancient Greeks seem to have brought him some solace. "Take heart. Suffering, when it climbs highest, lasts but a little time," he wrote in his notebook, quoting Aeschylus. "The suffering of a soul that can suffer greatly — that and only that is tragedy," he quoted Edith Hamilton. Interestingly, it was not the church's teachings of atonement and forgiveness that drew him, but the demands of a destiny that promised understanding through suffering and courage.

Ultimately he learned stoicism and acceptance. Of all the poets the one he found most meaningful was Aeschylus, whom he often quoted by heart. "He who learns must suffer. And even in our sleep pain that cannot forget, falls drop by drop upon the heart, and in our own despair, against our will, comes wisdom to us by the awful grace of God."

Whereas the Christian church teaches that God works in mysterious ways, the ancient Greeks believed that man brought his fate upon himself by his deeds. Often, like Oedipus, man was unaware of how his actions defied the order of the gods until punishment was inflicted — and with that punishment came recognition of the crime that was committed. Bobby turned to the Greek poets for a reason. It was through them that this pious Catholic found a way of working through his despair.

Only gradually and partially did he emerge from his grief. It left a melancholy that could be seen in his eyes, and it tempered his arrogance and impatience. Grief helped humanize him. It pulled him into the world of human imperfection and suffering. It even made him more tolerant. And it forced him, bit by bit, to begin the effort to reevaluate a life based on power, will, and the drive to conquer.

His own tragedy had left him bereft and confused. So much of his life had been defined by others: by the needs and expectations of the Kennedy family, by service to his brother. That would not change. What had changed was that with John dead and his father felled by a stroke he himself now had to carry the burden. For him that burden was also a trust — to carry forth the legacy of the Kennedy presidency. In this way he would not only assuage his guilt, and honor Jack's memory, but find a worthy meaning in life for himself. He would immortalize Jack and vindicate himself from his culpable grief by becoming what Jack would have been. He became the self-anointed but inevitable inheritor. In good works he would seek release from his self-destructive impulses. And from the public emotion generated by the violent end to his brother's stylish but undistinguished presidency he would seek to build a legend.

It was a legend based in part on a reformulation, indeed even a reimagination, of John Kennedy's presidency. JFK would be remembered and honored not only for the expectations that he raised and did not — either from lack of time or commitment — quite fulfill, but also for what he might have done had he lived. In the months that followed John Kennedy's death Robert would refashion the Kennedy image into one where achievement and expectation intertwined so indistinguishably that it was difficult to determine where reality left off and hope began. What Robert's efforts by themselves could not achieve, the public's longing and the media's encouragement would accomplish. The Kennedy legend, which immortalized John Kennedy as much for what he might have been as for what he was, became the vehicle for Robert's own inheritance of power.

It is from this period following John's murder and Robert's terrible recognition of his own possible, and unintended, complicity that the notion of his ostensible "transformation" is taken. It was during these months that the "new Bobby" is said to have emerged from the chrysalis of the old. This is where the legend of John Kennedy leaves off and the legend of Robert Kennedy begins.

10

The Making of a Legend

The legend of John Kennedy, like any work of art, was carefully crafted. It took form in the work of thousands of chroniclers and image-makers, in an unending stream of articles and books by those who knew him and those who admired from afar. Gradually, under their cumulative weight, and shaped by powerful feelings of loss and regret, a new mythology was created. "Jack's life had more to do with myth, magic, legend, saga, and story than with political theory or political science," his widow rightly observed a week after his death.[1]

As the logical inheritor of that myth, Bobby presided over the transformation of John Kennedy from a politician killed on a political foray into hostile territory into a martyr for all mankind. Only by turning him from a man into a symbol could his brother gain a new and even greater life: honored not merely for what he was, but for everything he might have been. Only in this way could Robert Kennedy, the abandoned survivor, submerge what he had been into what he now sought to be. In Jack's immortalization lay the foundation of Bobby's re-creation.

What is striking about the legend of John Kennedy is how much it is related to style. When one examines his record and pierces the inspiring rhetoric, it is hard to find any great legacy of programs ready to be transferred into law or promises on the verge of fulfillment. His "thousand days" pale beside Franklin Roosevelt's first one hundred. He was a practical man, not a visionary; a stylish one, but not an innovator. As president he did not so much anticipate issues as respond to them as they arose. The key word of his administration was "crisis," and it is as a crisis manager that he is best known. Had he lived to complete a normal term of office, he would be remembered far less reverentially.

But with great success he had conveyed — through his wit, youth, and charm — a sense of purpose and innovation. This gave rise to high expectations that were an ineffable part of his image. The American public, informed by a media that found both profit and pleasure in providing a chronicle of the Kennedy style, enjoyed John Kennedy, his lovely wife, and beautiful children. They shared, to some degree, the administration's image of itself as an energetic source of new ideas ready to be tested and confirmed.

Because this youthful and attractive man died violently under circumstances and for reasons that many do not fully understand or accept even to this day, the nation was swept by an intense sense of loss. This cannot be explained entirely by the bereavement that a tribe feels on the death of a king, for the reaction was not confined to the United States. In response to the dominant position of the United States in the world, prayers were dedicated, flags lowered, church bells tolled, and streets renamed around the globe.

Since his was a politics more of expectation than of achievement, the underlying theme of his death, and of the public mourning, was that of a mission unfulfilled. That is what gave the protracted period of public grief its great poignancy. As *New York Times* columnist James Reston wrote at the time: "What was killed at

Dallas was not only the president but the promise, the death of youth and the hope of youth, of the beauty and grace and the touch of magic. The heart of the Kennedy legend is what he might have been."

Today this rhetoric — the "death of youth," "hope of youth," "touch of magic" — sounds overwrought and melodramatic, more hype than analysis. But it expressed a real enough feeling at the time. The media fell in love with John Kennedy, and the public saw him not only as a symbol of youth and glamour, but also of an energetic America's coronation as the world's leader. Kennedy made Americans feel that they had won the future, and they honored him for this.

Thus his death was treated not only as a human tragedy but as an assault upon America itself. *New York Times* columnist Tom Wicker described a pervasive feeling after Dallas of vulnerability among Americans of all ranks and political beliefs; suddenly the world appeared a "dark and malignant place; the chill of the unknown shivered across the nation." After it became clear that the state itself was not collapsing, and that there was no plot to take over the government, the reaction to his death became intensely personal. Kennedy's ability to use the media to establish a rapport with the public, and the media's fascination with the Kennedy clan, had established an unusual intimacy. Americans felt that someone they knew personally had been taken from them.

Yet for all its pervasiveness and intensity, this sense of loss at the murder of the head of state was not unprecedented. Even the dour President William McKinley, shot by a distraught anarchist in 1901, was mourned effusively. "A universal spasm of grief passed from end to end of the land," the press reported after his assassination, ". . . the sentiment of deep grief, the feeling of intense sadness, filled every soul. . . . The whole nation swung downward into a vale of grief, only slowly to rise again under the force of that dread blow."[2] People then also expressed anxieties of being leaderless and alone.

Yet it was not McKinley, but Lincoln, that the Kennedy family sought to evoke. The man who saved the Union and freed the slaves, our secular saint, was decreed to be Kennedy's historical forebear. On the very night Jacqueline Kennedy returned from Dallas she sent aides to the Library of Congress to research how Lincoln had been honored. At the White House, Kennedy's coffin rested on a replica of Lincoln's catafalque, and in the Capitol rotunda it lay upon the original. The funeral ceremony, with the procession moving slowly down Pennsylvania Avenue from the Capitol to the White House and then across the Potomac bridge to Arlington Cemetery, the flag-draped casket atop a caisson drawn by a blinkered black stallion with boots facing backwards from the stirrups, the eerie silence broken only by the slow, incessant throb of drums were all designed to evoke the death of Lincoln. An estimated quarter-million people filed by Kennedy's coffin, and one million lined the route to Arlington.

Hardly a single American avoided exposure to the protracted mourning period. During the four days following Kennedy's assassination 95 percent of the public absorbed the events on radio or television. The average adult was tuned in for an astonishing eight hours a day. Four out of five Americans polled stated that in Kennedy's death they experienced "the loss of someone very close and dear." Even 62 percent of voters in the anti-Kennedy South expressed such feelings. Although slightly less than half of those participating in the 1960 elections had voted for him, immediately after his death two out of three Americans claimed that they had.

John Kennedy represented the state with all its power to evoke unity and command allegiance. The posthumous homage that has been rendered to him and Robert Kennedy is in part related to the symbol for which they stood. Yet only in part, for other great leaders are buried in far less grandiose surroundings. In the words of a skeptical British journalist: "The graves are there, immense in their sweep, ample in their design, commanding in their situation, like the tombs which in a vanished age were erected only for the proudest dynasts. . . . To an outsider, it seems as if the American people, for the first time in their history, have buried an emperor."[3] It was not the majesty of their office that commanded such an exalted burial site as it was the manner of their deaths. Had they been elderly politicians a place would have been found for them on Cape Cod. It was as though Americans wanted to accord them a high honor for what was viewed as their sacrifice.

There was also, in those solemn funeral proceedings, an underlying sense of anxiety mixed with the sadness. Kennedy's reign is remembered as more triumphant than it was. Major problems festered beneath the placid surface of American optimism. Some of these — the growing tension over civil rights, the awareness of great poverty amidst America's plenty, reverberations from an Asian war into which Kennedy's bold frontiersmen had enthusiastically plunged, and cracks in the consensus over the nation's goals and values — would not be felt fully for another few years. But the shock of Kennedy's death had made them more apparent. Much of John Kennedy's continuing allure rests on the fact that he died before he had to deal seriously with these issues. His successor did — and paid dearly for it.

Kennedy's death, coming when and in the way it did, dramatized that an era was passing. Beyond that it suggested that this was happening in some way because of his death. This intensified the sense of loss and fed an unfocused hope that an earlier optimism could be recaptured. As troubles mounted at home and abroad, the yearning grew greater. It took on the power of myth. Forged out of empathy, regret, loss, and a vague sense of national guilt, this myth later endowed the Kennedy presidency with an aura it did not have at the time. Ultimately it enveloped Bobby and became the vehicle for his quest for power.

He not only benefited from that myth, but also was beholden to it. It defined him for others, and even more importantly for himself. He assumed the identity of the survivor. It was he, as much as Jacqueline, who was the widow; he whose place in life was shattered by an assassin's gun. Eventually she would break loose from her widow's weeds; he never would. He was a creature of the myth. Even as it imprisoned him, it also transferred to him a power of the surviving heir: the power of hereditary succession.

With the death of his brother Robert Kennedy no longer knew who he was or where he was going. He had lost his compass and even part of his identity. The life of politics was virtually the only one he had known. The demands of the family were the only ones he fully honored. His service to Jack had dominated his career. These three imperatives — politics, the family, Jack — came together in a way that was as logical as it was inevitable. He would overcome tragedy and death, and purge his own sense of guilt, by carrying forward John Kennedy's legacy.

He found support in a public belief,

carefully nourished by the family and the court, that there *was* a Kennedy legacy, that Jack would have achieved heroic deeds had he not been cut down. John Kennedy's death left many Americans with a "vague, uneasy feeling of guilt about it," wrote columnist Max Lerner. "They can no longer make it good to the former president, but they can make it good to his very able brother. It is, if you will, the politics of expiation, of atonement, not for any personal guilt but for the burden assumed by history."[4]

Bobby seized upon this sentiment as an instrument. He made the notion of an unfinished agenda the theme of his public appearances as he gradually emerged from mourning. He began to take on Jack's mannerisms: one hand stuffed in his suit jacket, the other jabbing the air with little thrusts for emphasis. He let his crew-cut hair grow and started smoking little cigars, as Jack had done. By deliberately trying to infuse his own identity with Jack's, he ensured that his dead brother would possess him even more than he had in life.

The mythicization of John Kennedy rested on a public need to believe in an idealized past that the gods had snatched away. Robert learned to harness that need, transfer to himself some of the nostalgic emotions focused on his brother. He built his new identity. And it was by the idealization of John and the supposedly "unfinished legacy" of his thousand days in office that he rationalized his own ambition to sit in the chair once occupied by his brother. He would be the instrument by which John Kennedy's ideals could be achieved.

Robert Kennedy was himself the most fervent believer in the Kennedy myth. He wore it without any sense of guile or artifice. To immortalize his brother and incarnate the myth he had to believe that he was serving a higher purpose than his own grief or ambition. It sustained him in the dark months following Jack's death, and sanctified his ultimate emergence as successor. His assumption of the mantle, like his prolonged grief, was an instrument of his survival.

"The embrace of the dead may, paradoxically enough, serve as the means of maintaining life," psychiatrist Robert Jay Lifton has written. "For in the face of the burden of guilt the survivor carries with him . . . the obeisance before the dead is his best means of justifying and maintaining his own existence. But it remains an existence with a long shadow cast over it, a life which, in a powerful symbolic sense, the survivor does not feel to be his own."

Bobby displayed a morbid obsession with Jack, quoting him constantly, adopting his gestures, returning again and again to his gravesite, and passing out mementos like the ubiquitous *PT-109* tie clips "with the same matter of fact air that one associates with souvenir stands at religious shrines," in the words of one observer. "The regular invocation of the late president's name in his speeches was made with no break in countenance, as if he were a pastor quoting familiar scripture."[5]

By the time that Bobby made his own bid for power four years later, the New Frontier rhetoric was beginning to sound inappropriately Homeric. JFK's vocabulary, like his politics, was inadequate to deal with the problems he bequeathed his successor. His 1961 inaugural address with its stirring appeal to Americans to "pay any price, bear any burden" in the contest with communism had too much of a heroic ring at a time when Cold War certainties were under assault and the consensus on the domestic society had begun to evaporate. However, Bobby's own future rested on persuading the public of the vitality and relevance of Jack's legacy. The best strategy lay not in extolling the glories of the unretrievable past but of a vague though inspiring conditional future. The Kennedy legend would have to be revitalized by linking it to what JFK *would have done* had he lived.

This meant that Bobby had to transmute his brother, brush away his failures and omissions, and create a legend based on expectation. Bobby then could become the inheritor of the future. The key to JFK's resurrection lay in the notion of "growth." He was portrayed as having grown in office, learning from the bad experiences at the Bay of Pigs and the disastrous encounter with Khrushchev at Vienna, and coming into his triumphant own during the Cuban missile crisis. Even Vietnam, it would be said, was not Kennedy's doing: he was merely testing the waters and would have withdrawn gracefully (with honor intact) once it became clear that the task was hopeless. When Vietnam turned sour it was transformed into Johnson's poisoned creation, not Kennedy's legacy.

And Bobby himself was also said to have grown, to have shed his ill-tempered and dogmatic ways, to have embraced the scorned and deprived, to have taken on the world's sorrows as his own. He became a creature of the prevailing *Zeitgeist*: as John had been celebrated for his detached "cool," Bobby was honored for his intensity. Theodore Sorensen, who served both brothers, phrased it thus: the pain of others was something with which John Kennedy could "rationally empathize," whereas Bobby could "feel it in his bones."

Sorensen did not, of course, intend this as a criticism of JFK. Rather it was meant to convey that although the two brothers shared a common concern for the grief of the world, because of their temperaments they expressed it differently. Since the mood of the late sixties was to value feeling over thought, passion over "cool," what had earlier been Bobby's handicap became his virtue. The political and cultural period we call the sixties began not with JFK's election in 1960 but with his death in November 1963. Thus Bobby's mystique rested in part in nourishing the belief that he was what Jack *would have become.*

For the Kennedy myth to have continued validity it had to be updated. By the time that Robert Kennedy began slowly to emerge from his grief in 1964 (he continued to wear a black tie of mourning until 1965), the liberal consensus that JFK embodied had developed serious cracks.

John Kennedy was celebrated in part because he so perfectly incarnated American success. "The United States was in an imperial mood, and Kennedy was an imperial president," a British commentator has observed. ". . . He was the embodiment of the aspirations of the whole of the new, expanded upper-middle class."[6] That is in part why he was so adored.

But for those not blinded by his luster there were signs that not everyone basked in this success. As early as 1955, Allen Ginsberg, speaking for dissenters of the Beat Generation, wrote "Howl," in which he described "the best minds of my generation destroyed by madness, starving hysterical naked." Over the next ten years it sold 100,000 copies, making it probably the most popular serious poem of the century. Also in 1955 Rosa Parks refused to move to the back of a Montgomery, Alabama, bus. In 1960 four students in Greensboro, North Carolina, launched the "sit-ins" by seeking to be served at a segregated lunch counter. In 1961 the Freedom Riders began nonviolent direct action to integrate bus stations across the Deep South. In 1963, Senator J. W. Fulbright declared that, for all its essential decency, "Our national life, both past and present, has also been marked by a baleful and incongruous strand of intolerance and violence." In 1964, Congress gave Lyndon Johnson a blank check to fight communism in Vietnam by any means he saw fit, and Malcolm X, announcing his program of "black nationalism," declared that "there can be no revolution without bloodshed." The following year deadly riots erupted in the Los Angeles ghetto known as Watts, and later in scores of cities across the nation.

Something was happening in America that did not fit into John Kennedy's celebrations of national greatness or his concerns about creeping communism. Bobby, if he was to be relevant, and if the Kennedy presidency was to endure as more than a historical footnote, had to address these issues. With this in mind he decided, beginning with his entry into the Senate in 1965, to focus on race relations and civil rights, and on the persistence of poverty in an affluent nation.

In doing so he made a particular appeal to the idealism of youth. Perhaps the most popular innovation of the Kennedy administration had been the Peace Corps, run with dedication by Eunice Kennedy's husband, Sargent Shriver. Building on this success, and on JFK's relative youth, as well as his own, Bobby made it the central theme of the legend he was creating. Only two months after JFK's death he went to Japan, where he told a huge gathering of university students that "John Kennedy was not only president of one nation; he was president of young people around the world."

A few months later in Berlin, where JFK held a special place of honor because of his 1963 "Ich bin ein Berliner" speech, he reassured a large public gathering that while "there were many who felt . . . that the torchbearer for a whole generation was gone; that an era was over before its time," they should not despair, for "the torch still burns, and because it does, there remains for all of us a chance to light up the tomorrows and brighten the future." Then he added, in words that hinted at his own future: "For me, this is the challenge that makes life worthwhile."[7]

On this base of youth and change Bobby would create a living memory to his brother, assuage his feelings of guilt and loss, and build his own political future. To redeem his brother he would first immortalize and then replace him.

11

The Usurper

Robert Kennedy and Lyndon Johnson were natural antagonists. Their mutual dislike fed on every slight and insult, real or imagined. It was a consuming passion, even more for Kennedy than for Johnson. In the end it damaged both men greatly, and bound them indissolubly to one another by chains of deep emotion.

Hatred was not foreign to Kennedy. For him the line between disdain and disgust was very narrow. With his proclivity to villainize those he disapproved of, he often perceived evil where others saw only opposition. And because he was so convinced of the justice of whatever cause he believed in, he neither forgave nor forgot easily. As his father once said of him approvingly: "When Bobby hates you, you stay hated."

The Kennedy-Johnson mutual hatred society was one of the great political dramas of the sixties. Part of it was based on the simple fact that Johnson was in the

Oval Office and John Kennedy was in the grave. Although this was hardly Johnson's fault, Bobby treated it as though it somehow was. For him, as for much of the Kennedy court, JFK's presidency had been something akin to the musical comedy fairyland of Camelot that Jacqueline had conjured up for the star-struck Theodore White. In this fantasized Arthurian court there was one Modred, from which all evil and misfortune flowed. This was Lyndon Johnson's role — as it would have been that of any man who succeeded Jack. Perhaps one who was more like the beloved brother in physical grace and charm would have been even more threatening.

Johnson, to be sure, had some severe handicaps. He was in many ways the antithesis of John Kennedy: ungainly rather than handsome, provincial rather than cosmopolitan, shrewd rather than sophisticated, emotional rather than detached, and surprisingly insecure outside the political arena he maneuvered with such mastery. But he had a formidable intellect and a remarkable ability to induce others to do his bidding. As president he managed, for example, to persuade the vain Arthur Goldberg to resign a lifetime seat on the Supreme Court in order to serve as his delegate to the United Nations. He could, it was said, persuade almost anyone to do almost anything.

But he could not persuade the Kennedys to respect, let alone like, him. Bobby, along with the rest of the family and its entourage, could not bear that LBJ was in the place they had come to believe was rightfully their own. They made no attempt to hide their feelings. For them Johnson was simply unqualified to replace Jack, as indeed anyone outside the immediate family would have been. Drafting the speech Johnson would make to Congress several days after Kennedy's death, the faithful Theodore Sorensen seriously proposed that the new president say: "I who cannot fill Kennedy's shoes must occupy his desk."[1]

Resentment was intensified by contempt for Johnson's personal style. The members of the inner circle, who prided themselves on their sophistication, took pleasure in denigrating Johnson for his lack of courtly grace and worldliness. During his time as vice president they had either ignored or surreptitiously ridiculed him. Their shock and unhappiness when he became president were justified; their contempt was not. Viewing the White House as their rightful seat of power, they could not accept that someone they considered so crude should be taking the place of the king with whom they identified. For the Kennedys the White House had become an ancestral home. Before leaving the nation's presidential residence Jacqueline affixed a plaque outside the Lincoln bedroom. It read: "In this room lived John Fitzgerald Kennedy, with his wife Jacqueline during the two years, ten months, and two days he was President of the United States." Lyndon Johnson generously chose to leave the plaque in place.

The fiercest Kennedy loyalists formed a veritable government in exile, with Robert as the heir presumptive, Jacqueline as the dowager queen, and a palace guard of Cambridge academics and Boston politicos. They consoled themselves that Johnson's tenure, though an affront, was merely an interlude between Kennedy dynasties.

Jacqueline publicly displayed the best manners toward Johnson, while he, for his part, indulged her every whim, including having the space center at Cape Canaveral renamed Cape Kennedy. But from the moment of her husband's death she became a ferocious guardian of the legend. Despite Johnson's numerous invitations to social and ceremonial occasions, she did not set foot again in the White House until Nixon was president.

The inner circle of Kennedyites treated Johnson even worse, if possible, than Bobby did. They had made an enormous emotional investment in their dead leader. They could never accept this flamboyant Texan. Yet Johnson depended on them to lend legitimacy and effectiveness to the transfer of power. "I needed that White House staff," he later told his biographer. "Without them I would have lost my link to John Kennedy, and without that I would have had absolutely no chance of gaining the support of the media or the Easterners or the intellectuals. And without that support I would have had absolutely no chance of governing the country."[2]

The most important officials of the old regime did stay on to serve the new president: McGeorge Bundy as national security adviser, Robert McNamara as secretary of defense, Dean Rusk as secretary of state. Although they had admired Kennedy, their highest loyalty was to the institution of the presidency rather than to a single man. But some of the others, such as Schlesinger, O'Donnell, Salinger, and the Irish Mafia, were bereft and resentful.

They had come to Washington to serve John Kennedy, and the very thought of anyone else in his seat — particularly Johnson — was abhorrent. They soon left, but intended to return with Bobby as their champion and standard-bearer.

Bobby could not reconcile himself to the willingness of any of Jack's appointees to work for the man who had taken his place. "I thought that they felt: 'The king was dead, and long live the king,' " he complained to an interviewer. The fact that this is the way public officials are supposed to behave in a democracy eluded him. Only in a dictatorship does the staff flee when a ruler dies. "He honestly believed," McGeorge Bundy recalled, "that if you were fully in the Kennedy administration you had a continuing allegiance that should, in certain circumstances, be more important to you than your allegiance to the existing president. And I didn't see it that way."[3] But in Bobby's mind Bundy was disloyal.

Although he decided to stay on for a time as attorney general, Robert Kennedy did not bother to conceal his disdain for the new president. He knew that Johnson needed him to establish the line of continuity with JFK. But he also knew that it cut both ways: for him to resign precipitously would be seen as trying to undermine Johnson from personal pique or ambition. Considerations for his own political future required at least a public display of loyalty to the institution.

Bobby may have considered Johnson unqualified, but the new president showed himself to be superbly capable. With the formidable skills that he had honed as Senate majority leader, he coaxed, flattered, and cajoled a stunned Congress into passing a sweeping legislative reform program, including an expanded version of Kennedy's civil rights bill that had been blocked in Congress for months. In part it was the efforts of congressmen to honor Kennedy's memory, but even more it was a product of their fear and awe of Lyndon Johnson.

Johnson was a brilliant politician with a formidable grasp of the issues. But he had one debilitating weakness: a deep personal insecurity toward those with more polished social credentials. The Kennedys and their coterie of "Harvards," as he called their Ivy League camp followers, intimidated him. The rural Texan with the outsize manners believed that these people, because of their arrogance and polish, actually were somehow superior. Unable to surmount this, he sought their esteem and feared their condescension. That some of the Kennedyites considered him crude drove him mad.

Yet there was little Johnson could do about it other than fume. He knew that he was the brunt of jokes by Bobby and his entourage. LBJ knew that they referred to him and Lady Bird, in Jacqueline's wittily cruel phrase, as Colonel Cornpone and Little Porkchop. This condescension had begun from the moment of his nomination as vice president, and for three years he had swallowed *his* gall. Even as president he had to endure real and imagined insults from Bobby, to whom he privately referred as "that little runt."

What they were engaged in was, of course, a war of succession. Under the Constitution, Johnson was the legal heir to the throne. But Bobby was, in his own mind and the ardent conviction of the Kennedy court, the hereditary heir. Although they would not have phrased it that way, that is what they meant, and what they began planning to achieve. To Bobby, Johnson's very presence in the Oval Office meant that John Kennedy's legacy was being thwarted and his image defiled.

When he spoke of "the president" he always meant Jack. "[O]ur president," he told an interviewer in May 1964, "was a gentleman and a human being . . . this man is not. . . . He's mean, bitter, vicious — an animal in many ways."

At Hickory Hill, Kennedy gathered regularly with the loyal irredentists to denounce the usurper and plot their return to power. They called themselves a "band of brothers," in emulation of the stylish English aristocrats John Buchan had written about in the novels JFK had so admired. "Our power will last for just eleven months," he told them shortly after Jack's death. "It will disappear the day after the election. . . . We must use that power in these months to the best possible advantage. . . . There are a hundred men scattered through the government who are devoted to the purposes for which we came to Washington. We must all stay in touch and not let them pick us off one by one."[4] So spoke the new president's chief law enforcement officer.

Johnson felt no less threatened. "I'd given three years of loyal service to Jack Kennedy," he told Doris Kearns. "During all that time I'd willingly stayed in the background. . . . Then Kennedy was killed and I became the custodian of his will. . . . But none of this seemed to register with Bobby Kennedy, who acted like *he* was the custodian of the Kennedy dream, some kind of rightful heir to the throne."[5]

If Johnson felt abused and threatened by Bobby, he also knew how to wound. Aware that the White House was a sieve for gossip, he periodically made critical remarks that would get back to Bobby. Pierre Salinger, JFK's adoring press secretary, reported to Bobby that Johnson, referring to the assassinations of Trujillo and Diem during the Kennedy administration, along with the plots against Castro, stated that what happened to JFK might have been "divine retribution." A journalist also reported to Bobby that Johnson had said that the Kennedys "had been operating a damned Murder, Inc. in the Caribbean. Kennedy was trying to get Castro, but Castro got to him first."[6]

While Bobby's disapproval could annoy Johnson, it could not greatly hurt him — so long as Johnson had public support. And it would seem like simple malice and envy on the part of someone known for his "ruthlessness." Johnson, as JFK before him, enjoyed all the prerogatives and respect accorded to the presidency.

Because of his liberal program, his dedication to Kennedy's goals, and his impressive political skills, he retained the support of the liberal establishment and the respect of conservatives. Washington is not a sentimental place. Respect resides with power, and Johnson exercised it brilliantly.

Bobby realized that he was in danger of becoming marginalized. Under his brother he had been the deputy president, and Johnson little more than a ribbon cutter at official ceremonies. As LBJ's attorney general he was now just a glorified sheriff. J. Edgar Hoover, who had held RFK in thinly veiled contempt, no longer bothered speaking to him, but reported directly to the president. The reservoir of affection for JFK was enormous, and growing with the passage of time and the charitable proclivity to speak only well of the dead. But there was no public yearning for a Restoration.

Yet the "band of brothers" had supporters everywhere: people who were nostalgic for what had been, or hopeful for what perhaps could be. They had nowhere else to turn but to Bobby, and he was making ready to receive them. He was the inheritor of a dynasty with enormous unfulfilled ambitions. He enjoyed the loyal services of a battalion of acolytes: the journalists, professors, lawyers, politicos, and ambitious wannabees whom Victor Navasky has termed the "honorary Kennedys." They swarmed around him, offered their fealty, and goaded him to drive out the usurper and fulfill their own dreams. He was their new hero and their hope.

By the summer of 1964, as the Johnson steamroller moved through Congress, flattening opposition to his sweeping reform legislation, Bobby was confined to the sidelines. His anger had not weakened the president, and his sullen opposition had not harmed him. He was being driven to the political periphery. This was intolerable not only to him, but also to those who followed in his wake. They persuaded him that the best hope for advancing what they called the Kennedy legacy lay in his becoming Lyndon Johnson's vice president.

It was, to say the least, a bizarre notion. It also took considerable chutzpah for him even to suggest that Johnson give him the post that he had tried to deny LBJ four years earlier. Only in desperation could Johnson even have considered such an astonishing proposal. Only if he needed the votes of the liberals still yoked to memories of the Kennedy promise could he make such an adversary his own deputy. Putting Bobby on the ticket in 1964 would have meant that JFK was reaching back to reclaim the presidency. If Johnson won the election it would be read as Bobby's victory. He would be weakening the legitimacy of his own government.

"I don't want to go down in history as the guy to have the dog wagged by the tail, and have the vice-president elect me," he recalled. "I'd waited for my turn. Bobby should've waited for his. But he and the Kennedy people wanted it now. . . . I simply couldn't let it happen," he later explained. "With Bobby on the ticket, I'd never know if I could be elected on my own."[7]

While Johnson was prone to using self-pity and self-justification to get his way, there was considerable truth in what he said. Bobby would have been the Trojan horse, and there would be no effort at concealment. Able to call on a considerable number of nostalgia votes because he bore the name of the dead president, Bobby tried to force LBJ's hand by letting his supporters promote him as a write-in candidate for vice president in the New Hampshire primary in March.

A Gallup poll that month showed Kennedy as the leading contender for the post, with five times more supporters than Hubert Humphrey. In an effort to promote a mini-boom, he pushed openly for the nomination. His strategy was to force his candidacy upon Johnson through an open vote at the convention. On a trip to Poland, he made a pitch for the Polish-American vote at home by evoking the memory of his dead brother. "I am not running for president," he told the admiring Poles, "but if I were, I wish you could all come to the United States and vote."

But Robert Kennedy realized that Johnson would do almost anything to avoid letting him restore the clan's claim to the White House. Even while insisting that he was not officially a candidate for the vice presidency, he proposed that Johnson appoint him ambassador to South Vietnam. It is hard to know what he expected to come of such an overture. Even though LBJ would have been pleased to get him out of Washington, he could hardly accept the responsibility of sending a Kennedy to a war zone. Nor did he want to be accused of banishing a rival to the far reaches of the empire. From any angle Kennedy's proposal seemed to him a trap. Johnson declined with effusive gratitude.

Instead, LBJ floated the name of Sargent Shriver as a possible running mate. This was a clever idea. As Arthur Schlesinger had warned Bobby, "LBJ might well prefer Shriver on the ground that Shriver would bring along Bobby's friends without bringing along his enemies."[8] Kennedy was enraged when Shriver refused to dampen the idea. The Kennedyites made it clear, both to the brother-in-law and to LBJ, that if anyone in the Kennedy family was chosen it had to be Bobby.

As the convention neared, Kennedy's chances of forcing LBJ's hand sank. The Republicans, in a fit of fundamentalist zeal on the part of their ideologues, did Johnson a favor by nominating Senator Barry Goldwater instead of the centrist Nelson Rockefeller. The amiable but rhetorically wild Arizonan frightened so many moderate voters that Johnson had no need for any extra votes Kennedy might bring in. LBJ was riding high with approval ratings of 75 percent, a stunning record of legislative accomplishment, and the support of Democratic party officials who distrusted Bobby and did not want him on the ticket. Nor did RFK have support among such key elements of the Democratic coalition as southerners and labor union officials. At this point all he could offer Johnson was trouble.

Kennedy knew this, but he was determined to make Johnson squirm. Called to the White House to be told officially that he would not get the vice presidential nomination, he refused Johnson's request to take his name voluntarily out of the running. He wanted to be publicly fired in order to embarrass Johnson. Nor would he accept a safe ambassadorial appointment, or the post of campaign manager for the 1964 elections.

For both men the situation ended with bad feelings. Each felt mistreated by the other. The divide between them was too wide to be bridged by compromise. Bobby sought a Kennedy Restoration; Johnson was determined to be president in his own right. Their goals were irreconcilable. Only one of them could succeed — or neither. The denouement had been unpleasant, but at least the fantasy was over. There would be no Johnson administration bracketed by two Kennedys. If the Kennedy era was to be revived, Bobby would have to do it himself.

It is remarkable how these two men

brought out the worst, and the most self-defeating, behavior in each other. Johnson's personal insecurities made it impossible for him simply to ignore Kennedy and bask in his high public approval ratings and the accolades for his successful legislative program. Kennedy, for his part, was so driven by his resentment and anger that anybody — particularly Lyndon Johnson — should be sitting in his brother's chair that he hardly seemed to be thinking rationally. After all, he needed Johnson more than Johnson needed him. But instead of conquering his anger he wallowed in it.

One can imagine how John Kennedy, were he in Bobby's place, would have handled the situation. He would have ladled out charm and flattery, rather than radiating hostility and contempt, and would have had the approval-craving Johnson begging him to grace his ticket as vice president and heir apparent. But Bobby, in virtually every way, was not Jack. He had a knack for making even the easy look hard.

Over the next few weeks Kennedy met with his advisers to plot strategy. Staying on in the administration had now become impossible. He needed his own power base. For some time he had toyed with the notion of running for the U.S. Senate. Although he lived in Virginia and all the family ties were with Massachusetts, his best shot lay in New York, where the incumbent Republican was up for reelection. Kennedy had lived in New York for a while as a child, and the family kept an apartment there. More importantly, there was a solid core of Democratic voters who could be roused.

At the end of August he took up residence at the Carlyle Hotel in Manhattan and launched his campaign. From the lawn of Gracie Mansion, the official home of New York's mayor, he announced on August 25 that he was running for the Senate. Two days later he was in Atlantic City, where the Democrats had exuberantly nominated Johnson as their standard-bearer and Humphrey as his running mate.

Kennedy stayed on as attorney general and a member of Johnson's administration until September 3. But he came to the Democratic convention as a brother: to introduce a film about the life of John Kennedy. Johnson, fearing that sentimental delegates, stampeded by emotion, would put Bobby on the ticket with him, had insisted that Kennedy not appear until the final night, after he and Humphrey had been nominated.

Johnson's fears had not been exaggerated. Bobby, appearing frail and wistful rather than ruthless and angry, stood at the podium. A thunderous ovation erupted from the darkened arena as the delegates rose to their feet, some of them screaming and crying, and gave vent to their feelings about the president they had lost. This was not a rejection of Johnson, but rather a mass purgation of emotion, and an outlet for an unfocused loss and longing. It was, like much of politics, more about feelings than about programs. The convention hall took on the semblance of a revival meeting.

It was as though all the sadness and confusion over Jack's death, and all the hopes that had, rightly or wrongly, been buried with him and had been growing over the previous nine months, had suddenly been released. The crowd responded to the appearance of Bobby with an orgy of mass feeling. It was not for him, but it was in some way about him, and about the powerful emotions he triggered.

For some quarter of an hour it went on as the standing delegates wept, shouted, and stamped their feet. With a sad smile,

Bobby made feeble efforts to begin speaking, but then stopped until the crowd had exhausted itself. This emotion had been for Jack; he knew that. But it had embraced him as well, and he knew that too. It meant that the Kennedy legend was not dead; that it would live on even without Jack; and that he was entrusted to be its bearer. He would carry on that burden and fulfill what he deemed to be that destiny.

As the cheers finally subsided he began to recite some lines from Shakespeare that Jacqueline had chosen for him, Juliet's words for Romeo:

When he shall die,
Take him and cut him out in little stars,
And he will make the face of heaven so fine
That all the world will be in love with night,
And pay no worship to the garish sun.

He recited the words flatly and without intonation, for he was no orator. But in that emotion-charged arena, and coming from this man who so visibly and hauntingly evoked the dead monarch, they had the power to summon, to move, and in the case of Lyndon Johnson's "garish sun," to taunt.

12

Lord-in-Waiting

He reached for the Senate in the way that a man in a labyrinth moves toward an open door. It seemed to be the only path open to him. His efforts to be named ambassador to Vietnam or, even more improbably, Lyndon Johnson's vice president, had failed. He could not linger on as attorney general in the administration of a man who distrusted him and whom he despised. He had no interest in running the family businesses: Joseph Kennedy had trained his sons for more exalted tasks. Nor could he imagine working as a lawyer, a profession he had never even practiced. The life of politics was all he knew or really cared about. That is where his future, whatever it was, lay.

He was not, to say the least, a natural politician. Indeed, it would be hard to imagine anyone less skilled at ingratiating himself with voters and special-interest groups, or less naturally inclined to do so. Though he had all the backroom skills from managing his brother's campaigns and running a huge federal bureaucracy, he had few of the front room ones. He knew how to threaten but not how to cajole; he got angry easily and held grudges forever; he seethed with moral certainty over whatever course he pursued, and considered compromise to be vaguely immoral.

A virtual teetotaler, he did not drink with the boys, and had no patience for small talk and bonhomie. He could not stand to be touched, a distinct handicap for a politician. Once at a political dinner he became so annoyed when a rambunctious politician at his side kept grabbing his arm and shoulder for emphasis that he turned to the man, narrowing his cold blue eyes to slits, and said in a low, menacing voice: "Take your hands off me right now."

At the beginning of his campaign he could not even give a talk that would engage his listeners. When he read from a prepared text he would drone on in a dull, nasal monotone, holding on to the pages as though for safety. When he tried to speak extemporaneously or from notes he would repeat himself nervously or lapse into awkward silences. Although, like Jack, he had an ironic sense of humor, little of it came through initially. Only late in the campaign did he relax enough to use humor to deflect criticism.

Robert Kennedy made the decision to run for the Senate more from a sense of resignation than from enthusiasm. It was the best alternative open to him, after Johnson's veto of the vice presidency. Yet it also offered opportunities. As he told an interviewer for the Kennedy Library in the spring of 1964, "I'd not be just a Senator. I'd be the Senator from New York. And I'm head of the Kennedy wing of the Democratic party."[1]

In other words, he made it clear, the Senate would be his platform for challenging Johnson's leadership. It provided a national audience, it would help validate him as a political leader in his own right, and it seemed there for the taking. The Republican incumbent, Kenneth Keating, was an amiable moderate whom no one really disliked, but who lacked a dedicated following. Ironically, this was the same man who for months in 1962 had insisted that the Soviets were secretly putting missiles in Cuba, and who greatly embarrassed the Kennedys when he was proven right.

The New York Democrats, a fractious

and often self-defeating lot, were eager to regain the seat and did not at all mind reaching out to a carpetbagger — so long as he had a good chance of winning. Although Kennedy had hardly lived in the state since he was twelve, when his father became ambassador to England and took the family to London, and he himself had always voted in Hyannis Port, he offered the Democrats their best chance to recapture power. In short order he rounded up such party bosses as Carmine de Sapio and Charles Buckley, and was even able to persuade most of the perpetually squabbling reform Democrats to fall into line. But not all: a number of prominent liberals led by Gore Vidal, Paul Newman, Richard Hofstadter, and James Baldwin — neither trusting Kennedy nor forgiving him for his McCarthy period — formed a committee to support Keating.

At the beginning Kennedy attracted wild crowds: screaming teenagers, weeping housewives, misty-eyed retirees, patriotic farmers and workers, excited immigrants — all of whom came to pay homage to the brother of the fallen hero, or simply to see a celebrity. Broadcaster Eric Sevareid captured the feeling at those huge rallies, where hysteria mingled with tribute, when he reported that the genial but colorless Keating, a mere "palpable, flesh and blood human being," was "fighting witchcraft, a symbol of adulation and sorrow, memory of the deepest mass emotion of recent years, a fabulous ghost returned to earth."[2]

Robert Kennedy knew that the cheering crowds saw him as a stand-in for his brother. It would have been impossible not to have known it. Indeed he played upon it, constantly invoking Jack in his speeches, stoking the powerful if amorphous "Kennedy legend," and reminding the audience by his very voice and appearance that he incarnated, and could perhaps restore, the old political magic. At one rally, as the crowd stomped and whistled its allegiance, he turned to an aide and said mournfully: "They're cheering him." And of course they were, but in the process part of that emotion was being transferred to him.

But the excitement peaked too early. The magic was not sticking to him. By October, Keating had inched ahead in the polls. Kennedy's managers were getting nervous. The campaign needed help. Ironically, the person most capable of providing it was Lyndon Johnson, who was moving toward a landslide victory in the state. In desperation and with obvious distaste, Kennedy began pulling at Johnson's coattails. The campaign posters showing Kennedy in shirtsleeves working for New York were replaced by new ones exhorting voters to "Get on the Johnson, Humphrey, Kennedy Team."

LBJ, for practical reasons rather than sentiment, made a special effort to help Kennedy, accompanying him on two barn-storming trips through the state, the final one culminating in a huge evening rally at Madison Square Garden. The circle had come around all the way: the man whom Bobby had tried to veto as vice president in 1960 had now, four years later, become his political life raft.

Aided by Johnson's public embrace, Kennedy won a resounding 720,000-vote margin over Keating. But LBJ had done far better, swamping Barry Goldwater by 2.7 million votes, the greatest margin in the state's history. Nationwide, in his historic victory, he swept nearly every state, garnering 486 electoral votes out of a total 538, and all but six states. New Yorkers had given him a margin over Goldwater nearly four times greater than that of Kennedy's over Keating.

It is questionable whether Kennedy would even have made it without Johnson's support. And being in any way beholden to LBJ was deeply galling to him. He made little effort to hide this, despite his obligation. Standing before his exultant campaign workers on victory night he warmly thanked his family, his friends, his staff, his volunteers, indeed almost everyone he could think of. The one person he did not thank was Lyndon Johnson. He could forgive his brother's successor nothing, not even his help.*

In addition to Kennedy a triumphant phalanx of Democrats came charging in with Johnson, ensuring the party an easy control of the Congress. Whereas JFK, with a margin of only 120,000 votes in the entire nation, had been fearful of offending conservatives, Johnson ignored them as he pushed through an economic reform program rivaling that of his hero, Franklin Roosevelt. Under his prodding the legislators approved not only JFK's stalled agenda, but also a sweeping range of new federal commitments: Medicare and Medicaid, aid to education, voting rights and

* *On the day of Johnson's inauguration Kennedy went with a pack of photographers to JFK's gravesite early in the morning and again in the afternoon.*

other antidiscrimination measures, and immigration reform.

The Senate was an odd and, in many ways, dissatisfying place for Kennedy. He was used to running things. That made him feel useful and significant. In the Senate he was one among equals in a private, hierarchical club of vain and ambitious people, all with independent power bases and largely indifferent to his threats or pleas. Although he came with a political pedigree, and his colleagues knew that he had higher ambitions, he was in this forum not prince-inheritor but rather another, if highly privileged and well-placed, aspirant to the throne. He had to make himself politically visible to a national audience. And to do so he had to reach far beyond the voters of New York.

In the fall of 1965 he toured Latin America with the usual family and media entourage. There he made it a point to meet with youth groups, workers, journalists, and even political dissidents. His goal was twofold. First, he wanted to breathe life into the Alliance for Progress, the Kennedy administration's economic and social reform program to stave off Cuba-style revolutions. Johnson had largely abandoned the emphasis on reform, instead emphasizing stability and hard-line anti-communism. Secondly, he wanted to establish himself as his brother's successor in an ill-defined but forward-sounding "youth revolution." For this reason he insisted on talking to students no matter how hostile they were.

The following year, in the summer of 1966, he moved to cement his ties with American civil rights groups. Many black Americans had come to believe that JFK, despite his cautious civil rights program, had been a martyr to the cause of racial justice. They became an important part of Bobby's constituency. On a triumphant tour of South Africa that June, he toured the black townships, met with dissidents, and made powerful appeals for racial equality.

At the University of Cape Town, where an anti-apartheid student group had invited him to speak, he told a cheering crowd, in one of his most eloquent addresses, that idealistic youth could "from a million different centers of energy . . . build a current which can sweep down the mightiest walls of oppression and resistance." The reporting of these events in the American media helped form an allegiance to him in the black community that became the heart of the political constituency he was building from his own diverse "centers of energy."

His words were eloquent. He had a brilliant speechwriter in Adam Walinsky, joined occasionally by Richard Goodwin. But inspiring words were not enough. If he was to become a political force in his own right, he needed to develop strong allies and meaningful political initiatives. Johnson, with his Great Society program of New Deal–style reforms, had preempted the center and won the support of most liberals. Kennedy could not best him on that terrain. On the left Kennedy had raised suspicions with his open contempt for liberals, those "sons of bitches . . . in love with death,"[3] as he referred to them. Nor could he move right, even though his own law-and-order, anti-union record was essentially conservative. The Republicans could always outflank him.

Instead he improvised, cobbling together a coalition from around the fringes: young people, blacks, and Hispanics, Vietnam War opponents, non-union workers, the poor. From that base he hoped to move on the Democratic center, relying on Kennedy nostalgia and Johnson's inevitable mistakes. Such a coalition of outsiders was not the way that Kennedys normally won elections. Indeed it was not so much a coalition as a motley collection of disparate and ill-matched factions. This was a danger, for it could leave him with a constituency whose only defining identity was himself. Yet Johnson, wooing conservatives with prosperity and patriotism, and liberals with new social programs, left him little alternative.

However, despite the apparent success of the Great Society, there were already signs by 1965 of potentially dangerous cracks in Johnson's popularity. Although the economy was strong, there was a growing uneasiness over such issues as the Watts riots, black nationalists, student radicals, the "discovery" of widespread poverty, a vague but well-publicized "youth rebellion" against mainstream culture, and disquiet over the mounting costs of a frustrating war in Southeast Asia.

The questioning of traditional values that marked the sixties lay beyond the grasp of any single person or political movement. Kennedy played no part in its development and was mystified by much of it. Dutifully he would meet with some of the New Left spokesmen, listen to their music, and even put love beads around his neck. He had a lively curiosity, and a good many unusual things were happening in the sixties culture to be curious about. But his curiosity did not make him a cultural rebel any more than visiting an Indian reservation made him a Navaho. He was trying to put together a coalition of outsiders because LBJ had co-opted the center.

At times he went to extremes to establish his credentials on the romantic left. "I wish I'd been born an Indian," he said to a Senate colleague married to a Native American. "I'm jealous of the fact that you grew up in a ghetto," he told a credulous Jewish journalist. "I wish I'd had that experience." To an admiring counterculture interviewer he mused: "If I hadn't been born rich I'd probably be a revolutionary."

Like any politician he turned his remarks to the expectations of a sympathetic audience. What he meant was that he would have enjoyed having different experiences, just as he would have enjoyed being, for a while at least, an astronaut, a cowboy, or a professional wrestler. Indeed, when asked what he would do if he could lead a different life, he replied, "I'd be a paratrooper."[4] Growing up with the sense of being an outsider, he sympathized with those mistreated by society or fallen on hard times. Or at least he did when he encountered them personally rather than in the abstract as statistics. When he went into the tarpaper shacks of tenant farmers and rubbed the swollen stomachs of children, or held the withered hands of old people in nursing homes, he revealed the no doubt sincere compassion that lay beneath his often aggressive behavior.

As he tried to broaden his constituency, he picked up allies where he could. Held in suspicion by organized labor from his days as a Senate investigator, he sought an alternative in fringe groups like Cesar Chavez's migrant grape-pickers union in California. These groups marshaled few votes, but they softened his image as an anti-labor zealot. No group was too marginal for his concern. Whether or not he really wished he had been born an Indian, he championed their cause, visited their reservations, conferred with their leaders, and prodded the Senate to set up a committee to investigate the quality of Indian education.

He reached out just about everywhere to build a political constituency. At the urging of his young aides he met with radical organizers Tom Hayden and Staughton Lynd, and with poet Allen Ginsberg. The soft-spoken Ginsberg came to his office to explain the scope of the drug problem in New York and other cities. But Kennedy wanted to talk about the connections between the flower-power people and the black-power leaders. "He wanted to know," Ginsberg related, "whether there was any kind of political relationship or any political muscle behind such a coalition. I said that I had turned on to grass a number of times in Nashville with Stokely Carmichael. But it didn't extend to any formal political alliance." Kennedy listened with curiosity, and then they spoke a bit of the Russian poets they had met. Before leaving, Ginsberg sang him the "Hare Krishna" mantra.[5]

Kennedy was a harshly realistic politician who had no illusions about the political weight of the unorganized assemblage of the politically disaffected known as the New Left. But he did feel more comfortable with it than he did with the feuding factions of the Old Left. Like him the young radicals distrusted liberals more than they did conservatives. They did not nurse grievances and scars from ancient battles between communists and socialists, and like him they wanted to overthrow powerful authority figures.

It was his stance as a rebel against the White House that made him attractive to the New Left — and suspect to its leaders. Abbie Hoffman, founder of the Youth International Party (Yippie!), later wrote of his concern that Bobby's appeal was so great that he had become a "real threat" after he announced his bid for the presidency in March 1968, "a direct challenge to the theatre-in-the-streets, a challenge to the charisma of 'Yippie!' "[6]

The youthful radicals could not provide an effective coalition, but they were potentially useful allies. By keeping his lines out to them he could present himself as an essential intermediary between alienated youth and angry blacks on the one hand and distressed working-class whites — even Wallace followers — on the other. He could claim to be the one politician who could speak to both. That ultimately became an important theme of his presidential campaign.

It was not until 1968 that Kennedy had begun to establish himself as a political leader who might be able to unite disparate and contentious factions into a winning coalition. Before then he was still trying to work out a strategy that would give him an independent voice without isolating him as a fringe politician. His only hope for gaining the center was first to seize the periphery.

This meant finding issues that Johnson had either neglected or, because of the conflicts inherent in his office, could not resolve to the satisfaction of each interest group. Kennedy staked out three themes: youth, civil rights, and poverty. None of these could command a mass following, but each could appeal to an important group he targeted as essential to his coalition. And together they offered him an opportunity to carve out a domain of his own on the far frontiers of Johnson's sweeping Great Society program.

On the theme of civil rights Johnson's record was better than John Kennedy's. The sweeping legislation that LBJ pushed through Congress, culminating in his historic 1965 "We shall overcome" speech, exceeded anything that the Kennedy brothers had even proposed. Adam Walinsky was quite direct about this in telling author Jeff Shesol: "Lyndon was much bolder about civil rights legislation . . . than the Kennedys ever would have been."[7]

Johnson, though an earthy man in private, lacked Bobby's ability to make an emotional connection with crowds. Trying to be statesmanlike, he came across as stiff. He was also handicapped among black Americans by being a southerner who had (like the Kennedys themselves) publicly shown no burning concern for civil rights before entering the White House. The deliberate effort to link John Kennedy to Lincoln, beginning with Jacqueline's careful crafting of his funeral, helped create an image of his dedication to their cause and even, by inference, of his martyrdom to it. Bobby reinforced his inheritance of that "legacy" not only by association but by his own actions: his challenge in South Africa to apartheid, his extensively reported visits to northern black slums and the hovels of the black rural South, his efforts to protect the Freedom Riders, and his use of federal power to integrate Ole Miss and the University of Alabama.

Even more than civil rights, Kennedy stressed the theme of youth. "We rely on our youth for all our hopes of a better future . . . for the very meaning of our lives," he told one audience. He had been doing this ever since Jack's death. On his global travels he singled out college audiences, telling them that Jack had been "president of young people around the world." The clear implication was that he himself as a youngish politician was the inheritor of that honor.

Indeed, in his 1967 book, *To Seek a Newer World*, written mostly by aide John Seigenthaler, he relates, in a clear effort to present himself as his brother's hereditary successor, "the story of Moses, who brought his people within sight of the promised land and then died, leaving to Joshua the leadership in achieving goals that both fully shared." Such dynastic claims impelled even a sympathetic observer like columnist Mary McGrory to complain that "Robert Kennedy thinks that American youth belong to him at the bequest of his brother."[8]

He not only extolled and flattered youth, but made it an essential part of his public image and a basis of his claim to power. Most politicians, particularly when young, try to appear mature, thoughtful, and responsible. Kennedy did just the opposite. Letting his hair grow longer he played on his own youthfulness and athleticism, brandishing it as a weapon instead of muting it as a problem. His daredevil exploits on river rapids, mountain peaks, and in jungles, his ferocious games of touch football, the photos by ever-present cameramen of him walking the beach in a worn leather flight jacket, or cavorting with his children were all meant to celebrate his youthfulness as in itself a qualification for high public office.

But for all its theatrics, politically it was a low-risk strategy, for the young, like the poor, carry no political weight once an election is over, Henry Fairlie has observed. Their allegiance can be bought cheaply — with some noble rhetoric and a few vague promises — and need not be redeemed once the candidate is safely in office.[9]

His exploits — almost always in the company of journalists and photographers — bordered on the reckless. Just two months after taking his seat in the Senate, in March 1965, he scaled an unclimbed 14,000-foot peak in the Yukon that the Canadian government had named after his brother. He had never previously climbed a mountain nor undergone any training. This was, to say the least, a curious adventure for a man nearly forty years old with eight small children and, since his father's debilitating stroke, the head of an extended family for which he felt responsible. *Life* magazine, alerted to dramatize the event for its readers, sent a helicopter team to photograph him planting the Kennedy flag on the peak. This dramatic shot went out to millions of readers on the weekly magazine's cover.

In November of the same year he took a trip up the Amazon with the usual entourage of siblings, children, in-laws, aides, and reporters. At one point he left most of them behind on a riverboat steamer to fly a small plane deep into the jungle to a remote Indian fishing port. There he astonished the fishermen by jumping into a river said to be infested with piranha and daring his aides to join him.

Several months later, while traveling in Africa, he stopped in Kenya for a safari tour to look at wild animals. When the guide spotted a rhinoceros Kennedy ordered the driver to stop, jumped out of the Land Rover, and strode over to within fifteen feet of the beast. The two stared at each other for a few moments. Then the rhino turned and shuffled off. Kennedy had bested him, or so he believed.

These incidents were clearly in part publicity stunts. Extensively, usually admiringly, reported and photographed, they made Kennedy seem youthful and fearless. But they also revealed his incessant need to show his courage and conquer his demons. To a skeptical observer this might suggest a disturbing insecurity in one making a claim to the highest public office.

Although he was in no sense a political radical, by the time he entered the Senate in 1965, the mood on campuses had begun to shift toward an experimental cultural, and even political, radicalism. Kennedy hitched on to this while stopping short of identifying himself with it. Asked on the USC campus in 1965 whether he supported blood donations to the communist Viet Cong, he replied: "I'm in favor of giving [to] anybody who needs blood." When in 1966 the Indonesian government provoked the slaughter of 100,000 ethnic Chinese as alleged communists he denounced the action. When authorities denied an American veteran burial in Arlington National Cemetery because he was a communist, Kennedy protested. Such actions antagonized conservatives, who did not much like him anyway. And they appealed to young people drawn to whatever position the establishment abhors. Radical journalists started writing about him as a "rebel," and even an "existentialist" who, in Jack Newfield's terms, "defined and created himself in action."[10]

This was intended as the highest compliment. Whatever it actually meant, it helped solidify the anti-establishment credentials he was assembling as a central part of his political coalition.

It was in the intellectual grounding of his third theme — poverty — that he diverged most dramatically from the prevailing liberal consensus. In contrast to Lyndon Johnson's New Deal–big government approach to social reform, Kennedy emphasized individual initiative, self-reliance, and business participation. His well-publicized visits to rural and urban slums served a double purpose. They focused public attention on the intractable reality of deep and generational poverty in affluent America. And they drew attention away from the successes of LBJ's War on Poverty to its areas of failure.

RFK's program, insofar as it could be called that, was not so much conservative or radical as designed to pick up support where he could. From the left he adopted two premises: that the underclass must be brought into the political system, and that it must gain a share of government power through control of local institutions. The slogan for this was "community action." What it meant was giving the poor — or more often their militant, self-appointed spokesmen — a share in running local programs. As a gesture to the right and as a way of undermining Johnson's Great Society programs, Kennedy denounced government interference, extolled the virtues of self-reliance, and maintained that private enterprise could rebuild the ghettos.

The major laboratory for this experiment was the Bedford-Stuyvesant ghetto of Brooklyn. There Kennedy persuaded his Wall Street friends and private foundations to finance a development project based on job training, housing rehabilitation, and light manufacturing. IBM agreed to build a small plant, and two organizations were set up to restore the community: one to represent the residents and the other private enterprise.

This notion of healing the slums from within through self-help and private financing appealed to conservatives because it restricted the role of government. It also appealed to radicals because it promised to empower the poor: "power to the people," to use the ghetto battle cry. Thus it combined the principle of "community action," through the direct participation of the residents, or those who claimed to speak for them, with that of relying on private rather than government funding.

This went directly counter to the traditional big government approach of federally funded projects and welfare payments — and specifically to Lyndon Johnson's multi-billion-dollar War on Poverty. That well-intentioned war became victim to the far bigger one in Vietnam, which dried up funding for cities. Unsurprisingly, elements of Kennedy's plan were later picked up by Richard Nixon to cut back the government's role in urban renewal projects, although in general Nixon's economic program, which at one point involved a proposed minimum national income, was considerably to the left of Kennedy's.

The Bedford-Stuyvesant plan was innovative in trying to harness private capital to address socioeconomic problems. Had Kennedy lived he might perhaps have been able to extend this experiment. Whether it could have been a workable model elsewhere is questionable since it was so dependent on his own personal involvement and on his ability to enlist his friends on Wall Street and in the philanthropic foundations. What the Bedford-Stuyvesant plan demonstrated most strongly was his impatience with traditional liberal approaches. While this did not put him on the political right, it does demonstrate the futility of trying to label him as either a liberal or a conservative. If he was not an uncritical apostle of free enterprise, he was nonetheless hostile to the New Deal concept of big government.

In his concern for the human tragedies spawned by poverty and neglect he sounded like a traditional liberal. But when he criticized big government for trampling the individual's rights and dignity, he spoke in the language of conservatism. "Reliance on government is dependence and what the people in our ghettos need is . . . not charity and favor of their fellow citizens but equal claim of right and equal power to enforce those claims," he declared. Conservatives had no trouble applauding his insistence that "no welfare system can take the place of a serious program of employment and economic development in the ghetto."

Kennedy's politics were not an evolved doctrine but a work in progress. He himself was not sure where it would take him. He was the link between two competing visions: the welfare state world of the New

Deal and the "middle way" of latter-day New Democrats like Bill Clinton. In Kennedy's complaints about the "growth of organizations, particularly government, so large and powerful that individual effort and importance seem lost" can be seen the complaint of both right- and left-wing populists and of conservatives that it tramples individual initiative. In his attacks on welfare programs as "a system of handouts . . . which damages and demeans its recipients" he echoed the rhetoric of the political right.[11]

Nowhere so much as in his approach to the issues of poverty, welfare, and the role of government did Kennedy make it clear that he was indeed telling the truth when he said he was not a liberal. The angry editors of *Ramparts* magazine may have exaggerated in 1967 when they compared him to California governor Ronald Reagan, but they were not totally amiss.

Kennedy sought both his opportunity and his agenda in the failures of Lyndon Johnson's enormous ambitions. Johnson, with his gargantuan appetites, had taken on more than even he could achieve: the attainment of FDR's vision at home and Woodrow Wilson's abroad. When he stumbled, as he almost inevitably had to, Kennedy found the opening that he needed to advance his own goal: the routing and replacement of the elected president he continued to view as a usurper.

It is a mark of his intellectual nimbleness, and of his speechwriters' cleverness, that he was able simultaneously to pitch to radical leftists and centrist conservatives. By arguing for a smaller, less intrusive government and, as the Vietnam adventure became increasingly unpopular at home, for a smaller war, he was able to cut across constituencies. In this sense he could, until the time was ripe to make a decisive move toward the throne, be all things to all men: a radical to young leftists, an empathetic friend to alienated blacks, a critic of big government to conservatives, a tough law enforcer to blue-collar workers.

It was a delicate balancing act that could last only as long as he did not have to commit himself to a course of action that would alienate an important part of his potential coalition. Although he is remembered to this day as an idealist who brought emotion to politics, he was also an agile and unsentimental realist in the pursuit and the wielding of political power. These two contrasting, and at times conflicting, aspects of his character became increasingly apparent as he moved to claim what he considered to be his inheritance.

13

Cautious Critic

Kennedy gave every indication of running hard, but he wasn't moving. He had assembled his coalition of the young, the dark-skinned, the neglected, the alienated, and, of course, the nostalgic. But even though he was sure where he wanted to lead them eventually, he could not do so yet. The road to the White House seemed blocked until 1972. That gave him time, he thought, to pull together an army from his band of guerrillas. But he had less time than he had reckoned, and the major issue that he had to deal with — where Johnson was the most vulnerable — was one that he dreaded to confront.

Vietnam was Johnson's poisoned inheritance. It was hung around his neck like a wreath of office: the legacy of his predecessor. Although Robert Kennedy gathered to himself virtually every other promise and initiative of his brother, he left the war to Johnson. And Johnson could no more ignore it than he could ignore — or disavow — the national debt. He was its custodian.

The war was, in a very different way, almost as great a problem for Bobby. He had, like JFK, supported it from the beginning, believing that the communists — whether in Moscow, Peking, or Hanoi — had to be shown that "wars of national liberation" against Western-backed governments could not be allowed to succeed. Communist rebels would be defeated by counterguerrilla forces and the elite guard of Mao-quoting Green Berets. In the Kennedy administration schools were set up to train army and police officers from Third World countries in the techniques of counterguerrilla warfare. These American-trained forces became the main instrument by which friendly regimes, particularly in Latin America, put down leftist challenges to their authority.

Later, as the costs of the U.S. intervention in Vietnam mounted and Kennedy's initiative became tagged as "Johnson's war," some argued that JFK would have wound down the war quickly once reelected. There is no evidence for this. He had upped the American ante from a few hundred troops when he took office to more than 16,000 "advisers" when he was killed. He had made the commitment to South Vietnam a test of American credibility, and had given the green light to a military coup against its elected president that resulted in Ngo Dinh Diem's assassination. No more than Johnson would he have found it easy to accept an American defeat.

Bobby understood this, though it did not make him more sympathetic to Johnson's plight. In the spring of 1964 he reaffirmed the "domino theory" used to justify the American commitment. "If you lost Vietnam," he told an interviewer, ". . . the rest of Asia would fall . . . [and] have profound effects on our position throughout the world." When asked specifically whether JFK had given consideration to withdrawal, he replied: "No . . . the President was convinced that we had to stay in there." And when pressed as to whether his brother would have sent in more troops to avoid defeat, he said: "We'd face that when we came to it." Later Theodore Sorensen confirmed that JFK at the time of his death "was simply going to weather it out, a nasty, untidy mess to which there was no other acceptable solution."[1]

That, of course, was Johnson's dilemma.

Although he realized better than anyone else that the war was causing havoc to his Great Society domestic reform program, he was convinced that he had no alternative but to persevere. He remembered what had happened to Harry Truman and Dean Acheson at the hands of the Republicans for "losing" China. And he feared that if he did repudiate the advice of JFK's advisers whom he had retained in office — Bundy, McNamara, Rusk, and Rostow — he would be abandoned by the establishment, whose approval he needed, or so he believed, to govern.

Johnson's political concerns were reinforced by his personal anxieties. "This time there would be Robert Kennedy out in front leading the fight against me, telling everyone that I had betrayed John Kennedy's commitment to South Vietnam," he later said. "That I had let a democracy fall into the hands of the Communists. That I was a coward. An unmanly man. A man without a spine."[2] The tragedy of Lyndon Johnson was that he played by all the Cold War rules, and then those who wrote the rules decided to play a different game.

If Johnson was potentially vulnerable on the war issue, so was Robert Kennedy. He could hardly attack the president for pursuing an action that his own brother had begun. And to challenge the basic premise of the war — the defeat of communist-led revolutions — would be to question the Cold War consensus. Yet he needed to distance himself from Johnson as an essential step toward his own long-term bid for the presidency. A challenge to Johnson over Vietnam, and the assumption that JFK's policies would have been different, was necessary to give Bobby's own candidacy credibility. His guarded repudiation of the war — which was really an argument over tactics rather than objectives — offered a way to salvage JFK's image and enhance his own.

Yet Bobby was unwilling to accept a U.S. defeat in Vietnam. When he learned in January 1965 from inside sources that Johnson was considering pulling out of Vietnam, he told his aides to draft a speech denouncing any withdrawal as a betrayal of American interests. Instead he urged a recommitment to his favorite strategy: counterinsurgency. "The way to defeat the terrorists is to increase our capability to fight their kind of war," the draft stated.[3] Johnson saved him from delivering the speech by launching bombing raids against North Vietnam in February, and by sending 200,000 more American troops to the south.

If Kennedy could not attack Johnson for being too weak, he would attack him for being too tough. On May 6 he proposed to the Senate an alternative to either withdrawal or enlargement: a course of "honorable negotiation." He did not indicate what kind of settlement might result. But he made it clear that it could not mean communist control over the south. "[W]e must show Hanoi that it cannot win the war, and that we are determined to meet our commitments no matter how difficult," he insisted.[4] When the verbiage was stripped aside, it became clear that his disagreement with the administration was over means, not ends. This was confirmed when he went along with a Senate resolution to approve more money for the war and to reaffirm the Tonkin Gulf resolution that gave the president a blank check to fight the war as he saw fit.

A tireless advocate of unconventional warfare, Kennedy had met weekly during his brother's administration with a high-level group on counterinsurgency. "It was Bobby's major touch with foreign affairs," declared aide Michael Forrestal. He considered it to be particularly useful in Latin

America and as an alternative to the use of U.S. troops against leftist rebels.

In July, Kennedy spoke to the International Police Academy, a training school he had helped set up to train such forces in the Third World. "[O]ur approach to revolutionary war must be political — political first, political last, political always," he told the assembled officers the U.S. had trained to fight communism in their countries. As applied in Vietnam this strategy was popularly known as "winning hearts and minds," and more cynically as, "If you've got them by the balls, their hearts and minds will follow."

Lyndon Johnson had not wanted to send hundreds of thousands of American ground troops into Vietnam. He did it because the counterinsurgency strategy had not worked. The Viet Cong was far superior at political warfare. Johnson's dilemma, like John Kennedy's, was that the only real alternative to an American land war in South Vietnam was the loss of the country to the communists. Eventually, of course, that is what happened. But Bobby, too, was not willing to accept that. In May 1965 he declared that withdrawal would be a "repudiation of commitments undertaken and confirmed by three administrations."[5] Not until nearly a year later, in February 1966, did he begin to move beyond "security against terrorism" to consideration of a "negotiated settlement" with the rebels.

The growing Americanization of the conflict offered Kennedy an opportunity and a danger: the opportunity to distance himself from the political fallout of an increasingly costly war, the danger of getting too far ahead of public opinion. Despite the risks involved, Vietnam was the issue that got him the greatest attention. Every time he criticized administration policy the media, eager to publicize a Johnson-Kennedy feud, played it up as high drama. This reinforced his independence from the White House and helped sustain the variegated coalition he was trying to assemble.

At times Johnson played into his hands. In May 1965, LBJ had sent 22,000 American troops to the nearby Dominican Republic when the authoritarian regime there was overthrown by reformers he believed were infiltrated by communists. In fact they were moderates who simply wanted to, and did, restore to power the previously elected democratic government of Juan Bosch. Johnson's ham-handed gesture, which was roundly denounced throughout Latin America as another example of Yanqui gunboat diplomacy, provided Kennedy with the opportunity to jab the administration. "Our determination to stop Communist revolution in the hemisphere," he declared during a Senate debate on funding the Vietnam War, "must not be construed as opposition to popular uprisings against injustice and oppression just because the targets of such popular uprisings say they are Communist-inspired or Communist-led, or even because known Communists take part in them."[6] Of course that was precisely the kind of uprising that initially occurred in South Vietnam and that John Kennedy sent American troops to suppress.

As a result of mounting American casualties and growing draft calls, opinion about the war, particularly among elites, began to shift. In late 1965 Walter Lippmann, whose political column had been molding public opinion since 1933, broke ranks. Turning bitterly against Johnson, he declared that his policies meant "unending war in Asia." In February 1966, J. W. Fulbright, the scholarly chairman of the Senate Foreign Relations Committee, warned against America's growing "arrogance of power" and held extensive hearings on the war widely reported in the press and covered live on television. Kennedy, who was not a member of the committee, came to watch the hearings several times, conspicuous among the spectators.

Prodded by the younger and considerably more radical aides on his staff, Kennedy at the end of January attacked the administration's open-ended bombing campaign against North Vietnam. On February 19 he released a statement, after vetting it with Taylor and McNamara, urging that the communist forces be given "a share of power and responsibility" in South Vietnam's political future. Once again ruling out either a military victory or withdrawal, he went beyond his earlier vague appeal for an "honorable negotiation" to suggest the possible formation of a "compromise government fully acceptable to neither side."

Although he had carefully avoided the forbidden word "coalition," that was the way that an excited media, on the lookout for Kennedy-Johnson fireworks, reported it. Antiwar critics hailed him for opening the path to an eventual settlement in which what he called the "discontented elements" in South Vietnam would be represented. Administration officials including Bundy, Rusk, and Undersecretary of State George Ball, whom JFK had originally appointed, accused him of naiveté. He immediately started backpedaling and, according to Walinsky, became "gun-shy" as a result of criticisms of his speech.[7]

Robert Kennedy wanted to establish his independence without isolating himself on the antiwar fringe. For this reason he did not call for a Senate debate on the issue, and shied away from open confrontation. Richard Goodwin, who had helped draft the controversial press statement, later wrote that Kennedy regretted having made it, fearing that "he had damaged, perhaps destroyed his political future."[8] Fearful of getting too far ahead of public opinion, he vacillated and qualified his positions. This disheartened his supporters without assuaging his opponents. When Senator Wayne Morse of Oregon two weeks later filed a motion to repeal the Tonkin Gulf resolution, Kennedy voted to table it. Eugene McCarthy was among the handful of senators who supported it.

Kennedy's guarded call for a "compromise government" had angered Johnson without gaining much support from voters. And it raised doubts about his motives even among antiwar critics. They taunted him to act upon his principles and challenge Johnson openly. But he would not do this. He feared, with reason, that this would only isolate him on the left and lock him out of any chance for the vice presidency (which he still clung to as a possibility) in 1968. Yet if he pulled his punches he could lose supporters on the left who would drift off in disillusion or disgust. Frustrated by this dilemma he set off for South Africa to denounce the evils of apartheid.

The irony of his situation was that until this time no one had been more ardent than he about the need to defeat communism in Southeast Asia. "We are going to win in Vietnam," he had declared in Saigon in February 1962. "We will remain here until we do win." Persuading himself that Vietnam was now Johnson's war made it far easier for him to question the convictions he had earlier espoused. It is interesting to speculate on what would have happened had Johnson accepted his offer in 1964 to go to South Vietnam as U.S. ambassador. Then he might have been less enthusiastic about a "compromise government" that would have amounted to a disguised U.S. defeat, or about a counterinsurgency strategy that had failed. He would have had to be a cheerleader for the war.

For the rest of 1966 he uttered hardly a word about Vietnam. The controversy over his February press statement had worsened his relations with the White House and lessened his waning hopes that LBJ would be obliged to offer him the vice presidency. His reputation with the public had been badly bruised by the widely reported controversy with William Manchester over the publication of his book on JFK, *Death of a President.*

The Kennedys had chosen Manchester to write their authorized version of the assassination because they believed he would give it the reverential treatment they took as their due. When the manuscript was completed in 1966 and vetted by her minions, Jacqueline — who had not read the manuscript herself — decided that she had been excessively frank with Manchester. Relying on a loosely worded contract drawn up by Bobby designed to give the family veto power over the book, she demanded that the author delete passages that she believed cast her in an unfavorable light.

Bobby, for his own reasons, was also

unhappy with Manchester's work — not because of his worshipful approach to JFK, about which there could be no disagreement, but because of the author's contemptuous treatment of Lyndon Johnson. Still hoping at this point that Johnson might be forced to add him to the ticket in 1968, he had much to lose from egregious insults to the president.

Spurred on by Jacqueline and commanded by Bobby, who was defending not only the widow's honor but his own political ambitions, the family and its retainers descended upon the hapless Manchester. Bobby even pursued him to a hotel where he was listed under an assumed name and pounded furiously on the door, demanding unsuccessfully that the author open it. Aided by various courtiers and emissaries, the Kennedys demanded substantial changes in the manuscript. When Manchester, who saw himself not as an employee but as an interpreter of the late president's greatness, balked at these demands, they tried to block publication. An affair that should have been settled amicably over an elegant afternoon tea in Jacqueline's drawing room, with the awed and admiring Manchester being flattered into making a few "adjustments," degenerated into a public brawl that filled the headlines for weeks.

Images of the "old Bobby" who had hounded Hoffa, sent the FBI against the steel executives, and threatened a newspaper with an antitrust suit if it published unflattering information about JFK's private life were all revived. RFK's poll ratings plummeted and Johnson — who had been treated in the book as representative of everything crude and villainous in American life — came across as the innocent victim of Bobby's aggressiveness and Jacqueline's imperiousness. "The poisonous fallout from this controversy," Sorensen later wrote, "did more than anything else to affix the image of ruthlessness on Bob Kennedy."[9]

To escape the embarrassment that this revealing but totally unnecessary controversy had caused, Bobby went to Europe in February 1967 in hopes of fortifying his foreign policy credentials. Treated as a possible future president, he was received in Paris by President Charles de Gaulle. The French leader, whose country had been torn apart by its own futile war in Indochina in the early 1950s, told Kennedy that the U.S. should end the bombing, withdraw its forces, and strike a deal

— as it already had in neighboring Laos — to neutralize the country.

Trying to act as honest brokers, the French brought Kennedy into contact with high North Vietnamese officials in Paris. In guarded diplomatic language the communist representative told Kennedy that Hanoi was ready to enter into negotiations if the U.S. stopped the bombing unconditionally. Kennedy later claimed he was unfamiliar with diplomatic nuance and did not fully grasp the significance of the offer. The American diplomat accompanying him did, however, and cabled the State Department that there had been an important breakthrough.

After Kennedy returned to Washington the story found its way to *Newsweek*, which reported that he had been given a peace overture. Johnson was furious, convinced that Kennedy was promoting himself as a peacemaker and trying to force negotiations just when victory was near. At a tense confrontation in the White House, Kennedy denied the accusation. "I think that the leak came from someone in your State Department," he said. "It's not *my* State Department," Johnson exploded. "It's *your* State Department, goddam it!" — meaning it was full of Kennedy holdovers and sympathizers. Losing his temper, he told Kennedy that if he kept harping on negotiations and bombing halts at such a critical moment in the war he would regret it. "I'll destroy you and every one of your dove friends in six months. You'll be dead politically."[10]

This did not seem an idle threat. Johnson, encouraged by his advisers, believed that steady American pressure would bring the communists to their knees. By the end of 1966 there were 350,000 Americans in Vietnam, up from 200,000 in January. U.S. casualties had mounted to 9,300 dead and 62,000 wounded. Nonetheless, according to opinion polls, 70 percent of Americans supported the war, while only 24 percent favored a bombing halt. Only two Senate dissenters voted against a $5 billion special appropriation for the war. Kennedy was not one of them.

Now that it was clear there would be no place for him on Johnson's 1968 ticket, he no longer needed to pretend to be a loyal critic. He had become such a pariah that he had little to gain by courting Johnson and a good deal to lose by equivocating about the war. With the White House off bounds, he had little alternative but to move into open opposition.

On March 2, just a month after his acrimonious encounter with the president at the White House, Kennedy broke his year-long silence on Vietnam. In an address to the Senate he attacked not only the administration's tactics but also the very morality of the enterprise. His language reflected the anguish of the aides who had written it and their conviction that he was the one best able to change American policy. Their ardor was intensified by the fact that Johnson had just resumed air attacks against North Vietnam after a five-day suspension. He had done this even though the Soviet premier had confirmed what Kennedy had heard in Paris: Hanoi was now ready to negotiate.

Kennedy began by admitting his own early involvement in the decision to wage war in Vietnam: "I can testify that if fault is to be found or responsibility assessed there is enough to go around for all including myself." Having thus preempted critics, he called on the administration to halt the bombing of North Vietnam immediately and be willing to open peace negotiations within a week. Both U.S. and North Vietnamese forces would be gradually withdrawn, and international monitors would conduct free elections in which the communists could participate. In effect, though not in name, he was proposing a coalition government.

More striking than his proposals was the emotional language in which they were couched. He called on Americans to accept their own personal responsibility for "this horror"; to realize that "it is our chemicals that scorch the children and our bombs that level the villages." Singling out the bombing campaign as a harsh punishment on civilians incapable of controlling their leaders, he insisted: "We are not in Vietnam to play the part of an avenging angel pouring death and destruction on the roads and factories and homes of a guilty land." This was not the language of power brokers, generals, and diplomats. This was the language of the antiwar protesters, and it was their support that Kennedy was now openly seeking.

Opponents of the war hailed his boldness in calling not only for a supervised U.S. withdrawal, but also for a settlement that would allow the communist rebels to "participate" in a future South Vietnamese government. But the media, which had seen him attack and retreat before, were skeptical of his motives and saw this as another battle in his ongoing war with Johnson. Nor did he make much impact on the general public, which still supported the war. In fact, his approval rating, which had been higher than the president's, dropped eleven points to 37 percent after the speech.

Making one of his periodic tours of colleges to drum up support as the candidate of youth, Kennedy found that for many students the war was distant and abstract. At one campus he asked his young listeners whether they were in favor of continued draft deferments. They all cheered. Then: How many wanted to escalate the war? More cheers. Then the punch line: How many who voted for escalation also voted to exempt students from the draft? There was a long silence as the point struck home that the war was being fought mostly by the poor and the dark-skinned. In a Gallup survey in May 1967 half the students polled described themselves as hawks, while 35 percent said they were doves. Not until higher draft calls cut away at student deferments did most campuses turn solidly against the war.[11]

Although Kennedy had guardedly challenged the administration's policies, he refused to make an open break with the president or to move fully into the antiwar camp. In May, along with fifteen other Senate critics of the war, he refused to support a motion for unilateral U.S. troop withdrawals. In June, only three months after his Senate speech, he gave Johnson an effusive introduction at a political fund-raiser in New York. As hundreds of antiwar protesters shouted outside the hall, Kennedy praised the president for having "poured out all his own strength to renew the great strength of this country," and proclaimed that "in 1964 he won the greatest popular victory in modern times, and with our help he will do so again in 1968."[12] Even in a profession whose wheels are oiled with insincerity, this seemed excessive.

In effect Kennedy was presenting himself as an alternative to Johnson without going so far as to make the open challenge that would alienate the party's brokers and its broad base. He was positioning himself in case LBJ stumbled or was abandoned. By criticizing Johnson's tactics — bombing, massive U.S. troop deployment, escalation — without questioning (as Fulbright and several other senators had done) the fundamental principle of American intervention in Vietnam, he sought to turn his brother's legacy into Johnson's war.

Kennedy courted supporters where he could find them. He met with young antiwar leaders like Staughton Lynd and Tom Hayden, while at the same time nourishing ties with party officials and big-city bosses. To bolster his patriotic credentials he cosponsored a bill in May 1967 raising penalties on those desecrating the American flag — legislation expressly designed to punish antiwar protesters.[13] Nobody fully trusted his motives: Democratic loyalists accused him of splitting the party to further his ambition; antiwar activists thought him cowardly for not challenging Johnson directly.

For the rest of the year he wobbled back and forth, trying to appease the party regulars who feared that by dividing Democrats he would ensure their defeat in the elections. At the same time he tossed out morsels of hope to the dissidents who urged him to run. He commiserated with the antiwar activists, but as long as he saw Johnson as invulnerable, all he would offer the peace dissidents was his sympathy. For a practical politician that may have been enough — but not for those who felt deeply about the war.

The many faces of Bobby Kennedy posed a real problem for radicals. They distrusted his motives yet were aware of his political allure. Robert Scheer, writing in the leftist journal *Ramparts*, described him as "a very charming and alive man for a politician," but dangerous because he offered "the illusion of dissent without its substance." Unlike an old-line Democratic loyalist such as Vice President Hubert Humphrey, Kennedy was a problem because "he could easily co-opt prevailing dissent without delivering to it."

In a series of devastating cartoons Jules Feiffer captured the exasperating contradictions of what he called "the Bobby twins." In one of these the "Good Bobby" declares in anguish: "We're going in there and we're killing South Vietnamese . . . innocent people, because we don't want to have the war fought on American soil. . . . I very seriously question whether we have that right." In the next panel the "Bad Bobby" replies: "I will back the Democratic candidate in 1968. I expect that will be President Johnson." In the last panel the Good Bobby turns to the Bad Bobby twin and says: "I think we're going to have a difficult time explaining this to ourselves."[14]

Feiffer cut deep because he asked in vivid form the perennial question of who was the real Bobby Kennedy; the moralist or the politician. Of course both were, and they came together in his turnabout on Vietnam. He could abandon his earlier commitment to the war because the conflict had now become a losing proposition. Thus he could declare it immoral. A realist like his father, he allowed neither sentiment nor ideology to stand in the way when calculating profit and loss. His hatred for Johnson also made it easier for him to reverse his course on Vietnam once he had persuaded himself and could persuade others that it was now LBJ's war and not his brother's.

In the decades since Robert Kennedy's death the nuances of an ancient debate have become blurred, and it has become common to think of him simply as a crusader against war and injustice. But both the times and his own character were more complicated than that. One should not lose sight of the politician in evaluating the icon.

Self-interest governed his conduct. But he was not always sure which way it lay. If he openly challenged the president on the war issue he might find himself rejected by party leaders, and Johnson would be able to trump him by stopping the bombing and opening peace negotiations. But if he continued to back the president even while criticizing his policies, he would look like a hypocrite and alienate his supporters on the left.

Pressure mounted. In October 1967 antiwar mobilizer Allard Lowenstein, who had organized a nationwide "Dump Johnson" movement, offered Kennedy leadership of the organization. Although he carefully cultivated the approval of activists like Lowenstein, Kennedy was unmoved by the appeal. "People would say that I was splitting the party out of ambition and envy," he explained. "No one would believe that I was doing it because of how I feel about Vietnam and poor people." In this assessment he may have been right. But for those morally offended by the war, the fear that some people might misunderstand Bobby Kennedy's motives was not paramount. They had hoped that ending the war would have a higher rank on his list of priorities. Later Lowenstein described the meeting:

> He said he would not run except under unforeseen circumstances. . . . It made me very sad, but angry, too. I kept

> saying that if things were to be judged by traditional political standards, and by traditional politicians, by traditional judgments of what was possible, then of course nothing could be done. But that was the whole point! Nothing was the way it had been before and if he didn't know that, . . . it was hard to believe he cared as much as millions of people thought he did.
>
> He said . . . "It can't be put together."
>
> Then . . . I just glared at him, and said, "You understand, of course, that there are those of us who think the honor and direction of the country are at stake. I don't give a damn whether you think it can be put together or not. . . . We're going to do it without you, and that's too bad because you could have been President of the United States."[15]

Determined to pursue his cause, Lowenstein looked elsewhere: first to retired General James Gavin, who said he would consider running only as a Republican; then to economist John Kenneth Galbraith, who was interested but ineligible because he was born in Canada; and also to South Dakota senator George

McGovern, who thought the effort hopeless.

Then, more in desperation than in expectation, Lowenstein turned to the ironic, poetry-writing senator from Minnesota, Eugene McCarthy, a thoughtful former professor and Catholic seminarian. McCarthy had long been a critic of the war and was not afraid of taking up a challenge that others considered quixotic. Before making it formal, McCarthy wanted to make sure that Kennedy did not intend to run. Kennedy confirmed, according to McCarthy, that he would not be a candidate. On November 30, McCarthy announced that he would enter half a dozen primaries.

Kennedy still refused to break with the administration. The same week that McCarthy announced his candidacy Kennedy labored to explain his position in a rambling television interview. Asked whether it was time to put the national interest over party loyalty and seek the presidency if he really wanted to end the war, he replied cautiously: "If I ran for president . . . I would not strengthen . . . the dialogue that is taking place in connection with these issues." When pressed as to whether this meant he considered President Johnson the best man, he responded: "I expect that he is going to receive the nomination and I will support him." Then "good Bobby" stepped into express anguish over a war in which "we're killing children; we're killing women; we're killing innocent people because we don't want to have the war fought on American soil, or because they're 12,000 miles away and they might get to be 11,000 miles away."[16]

At this point there were powerful reasons Kennedy should have run. He had a huge constituency behind him: not only those opposed to the war, but also millions who were nostalgic for an imagined age of Camelot that they believed he could restore, blacks who felt that he alone among major politicians cared about them, and liberals who were convinced that the Democratic party could not survive Lyndon Johnson. Furthermore, by not trying to defend what he declared to be a moral cause, he risked forever losing the allegiance of those who believed in him. His careful calculations about running in 1972 might become irrelevant.

Another man might have. Another man did. But another man would not have been driven, as all the Kennedys were, by the belief that winning was everything and defeat ignominious. Joe Kennedy had driven into his children the belief that they were either number one or they were nothing. Coming in second was as bad as coming in last. Bobby Kennedy never escaped from this burden. It haunted him his entire life. As even his admirer Jack Newfield has written: "The fear of defeat paralyzed him."[17]

14

Into the Breach

Although Kennedy thought that he could wait indefinitely in the wings until he was sure of success, war critics now had an alternative in McCarthy. Also at this time media reporting on the war was turning more critical, and the public was growing more impatient to conclude it either by withdrawal or major escalation. The U.S. troop presence in South Vietnam mounted to half a million, with no end of the war in sight, and the generals were asking for even more men. Public approval of Johnson's handling of the war plunged to 28 percent.

Within Johnson's administration the consensus was cracking. Robert McNamara, chief planner of the war, decided that it could not be won. Failing to persuade Johnson to scale back a doomed effort, he shuffled off to the World Bank. On campuses antiwar sentiment had become so intense that Johnson had to avoid speaking there. Kennedy was still welcome, but to berate as much as to cheer. At one college students taunted him with a sign they bobbed in front of his face: "Bobby Kennedy: Hawk, Dove or Chicken?"

It was a good question. In theory he had already made his decision. By not trying to dissuade McCarthy, Kennedy had lost his place as the great white hope of the antiwar movement. But in order to hold together even a part of his constituency he had at least to appear to be keeping his options open. He checked with everybody. In January 1968, Arthur Schlesinger took him to see Walter Lippmann. The columnist, who had been among the first establishment figures to come out against the war, told him that if he really felt, as he said, that Johnson's reelection would be a catastrophe, then "the question you must live with is whether you did everything you could to avert this catastrophe."[1]

But still he wavered. Instead of either jumping in or remaining quiet, he criticized the man who had had the courage to act. To journalists at the National Press Club on January 30 he complained that McCarthy's challenge was actually "helpful to President Johnson." The Kennedys were always sore losers. Then he ended the off-the-record session with one statement for attribution: "I have told friends and supporters who are urging me to run that I would not oppose Lyndon Johnson under any foreseeable circumstances."

It could have been even worse. He had originally intended to say "any conceivable circumstances," but his press aide Frank Mankiewicz had persuaded him to tone it down to "foreseeable." Nonetheless he had slammed the door nearly shut and at the worst possible time. Across the world at almost that very moment communist forces in Vietnam launched their biggest operation of the war. In a stunningly coordinated operation on the Buddhist holiday of Tet, they attacked more than a hundred cities and towns simultaneously and even occupied the American embassy in Saigon for several hours.

Ultimately they were driven back and sustained severe losses. Militarily they had gained little, but the psychological impact of the assault was enormous. The belief that the United States was winning the war and that the "light at the end of the tunnel" was growing brighter had been exposed as a self-deluding fiction. Tet was a turning point in the other war for the allegiance of the American public. The patriotic consensus supporting the administration was fast evaporating.

Now Kennedy realized that it was not only safe to move, but also necessary. The Tet offensive, he told a Chicago audience a few days later, "shattered the mask of official illusion with which we have concealed our true circumstances, even from ourselves." It also shattered his illusion that he could be a credible critic from the safety of the sidelines. Declaring that a "military victory is not within sight . . . it is probably beyond our grasp," he called, in bolder words than he had ever used before, for a negotiated "settlement which will give the Vietcong a chance to participate in the political life of the country."[2] The implication of a coalition government seemed clear.

Tet had transformed McCarthy's campaign from a quixotic gesture into a serious challenge. The first test came in the New Hampshire presidential primary on March 12. Marshaling an army of students to ring doorbells and drive voters to the polls, McCarthy stunned the experts by taking 42 percent of the vote. Although Johnson technically won a majority with 49 percent, this was a crushing psychological defeat for a sitting president. Everyone read the results as a vote on the war, and the verdict was that Americans wanted someone to end it. This was a new political landscape. Johnson was revealed as vulnerable, the laconic McCarthy as a viable candidate, and Kennedy as a waffler who had waited too long.

In effect Kennedy was in danger of becoming politically irrelevant. His strategy of waiting until the coast was clear in 1972 now looked like cowardice. If he continued to dawdle on the sidelines he would surrender the fight to McCarthy, and would be accused of having prolonged the war when he could have shortened it. Who, then, would sympathize with his tiresome indecision and agonized calculations? McCarthy's remarkable showing had boxed him into a corner. He had no realistic alternative but to run.

But first Kennedy moved to cement his ties with the head power broker in the party, Chicago's mayor, Richard Daley. At Daley's urging, he proposed that Johnson appoint a commission of "wise men" — including himself — to reevaluate the U.S. role in Vietnam. Kennedy did not expect the idea to go anywhere, but he believed that it would help persuade Daley and other big-city bosses — whose support he needed for any run — that he had tried to avoid splitting the party. Johnson, who saw this idea as a trap by which Bobby could claim credit for any peace gestures by the administration, dismissed it as a challenge to the powers of the presidency.

There remained the matter of McCarthy. The troublesome Minnesotan had not only shown Johnson's political vulnerability, but had also cut broadly into Kennedy's potential constituency. What earlier had seemed to be sincere indecision on Kennedy's part now appeared to many antiwar voters as calculating opportunism. To deflect this criticism the Kennedyites claimed that Bobby had actually decided before the New Hampshire primary that he would challenge Johnson, but had delayed going public in order to avoid crowding out McCarthy. It was an explanation that satisfied only the true believers.

Revealing his anxiety at the prospect of a direct popularity contest, Bobby sent his brother, Ted, to Wisconsin to seek a deal with McCarthy, who was campaigning in the presidential primary there. What he wanted was for McCarthy to agree to divide the remaining state primaries between them. But McCarthy, who had never been an admirer of the Kennedys, had given Bobby his chance. He was now the antiwar candidate, and would see how far he could go even against Kennedy money and charisma. He told Ted Kennedy that he would take his chances on the primaries. The only deal he suggested was that Bobby wait: he was interested in serving only one term as president.

Kennedy was now forced to do what he had resisted for so long. To push ahead meant the real possibility of defeat, but not the end of the game. To sit on the sidelines meant surrendering to a bolder man the possibility of the nomination. On March 16, in the same Senate hearing room where Jack had made his declaration eight years earlier (and in which he himself had served as minority counsel during the televised Army-McCarthy hearings), Robert Kennedy announced to a waiting crowd of reporters: "I am announcing today my candidacy for the presidency of the United States." Some of the journalists snickered when he claimed that he did "not run for the presidency merely to oppose any man," and professed "no personal animosity or disrespect toward President Johnson." His challenge, he insisted, was about "where we are heading and what we want to accomplish."

But he could not resist some of the verbal overkill that had served JFK so well. "At stake," he maintained, in words crafted by Sorensen, "is not simply the leadership of our party and even our country. It is our right to moral leadership of this planet." Kennedy devotees were thrilled by the notion; skeptics saw it as precisely the kind of self-deceiving grandiosity that had gotten the U.S. into so much trouble in places like Vietnam. But in the eyes of Kennedy and his followers this was more than a campaign. It was a crusade — and even a restoration.

Kennedy had a compelling issue. Every American, whether hawk or dove, had come to detest the war in Vietnam. He had an opponent in Lyndon Johnson nearly as unpopular as the war. For two weeks Kennedy hammered relentlessly against both, flying around the nation in his chartered Boeing jet. To delirious crowds in Kansas, Tennessee, Alabama, New York, and California, he attacked the president and the war now tagged as Johnson's. At the end of his litany he would declare, reaching out to the curious and the dedicated who had come to see a celebrity: "*That's* why I run for president of the United States, and *that's* why I come here and ask for your help."

Not everyone was charmed. Party bosses feared that he would fatally divide the Democrats. Media skeptics saw more ambition than idealism in his motives. And many who had found inspiration in McCarthy's bold challenge were bitter. "We woke up after the New Hampshire primary like it was Christmas Day," one young volunteer in McCarthy's band of crusaders told a reporter after Kennedy jumped into the race. "And when we went down to the tree, we found that Bobby Kennedy had stolen our presents."

But his hope, and his strategy, at this point lay not with the bosses or with the idealists he had lost to McCarthy, but with the crowds in the streets. With the bosses pledged to Johnson and the antiwar activists to McCarthy, he had to rely on nostalgia, celebrity, and emotion. He had to be a Kennedy, his brother's brother, the anointed heir of the now-beloved and idealized JFK. He was the inheritor, and it was to that role that the crowds responded: the teenage girls screaming wildly at this harsher version of the handsome JFK, the matrons with rapturous expressions on their faces, the blacks and Hispanics who were persuaded that he was the one candidate who cared about them.

The reporters who trailed around after him, seeing how the crowds were whipped up and how Kennedy played to their emotions, initially kept their distance. Some accused him of demagoguery, particularly after the March speech in Los Angeles where, in a fit of rhetorical overkill, he blamed Johnson for debasing "integrity, truth, honor," and for "calling upon the darker impulses of the American spirit."[3] Some advisers warned him that such extreme attacks on the president could backfire.

But he was convinced that he did not have the luxury of running a gentlemanly race. He needed the crowds and the excitement. It was the only way he stood a chance, the only way to persuade the party bosses that he rather than Johnson could win the election. "I have to win through the people," he told a reporter. "Otherwise I'm not going to win." By "the people" he meant the crowds, whose energy and excitement would force the politicians to abandon their loyalties and gamble on their instincts. "Kennedy's main objective is to stir up such tremendous excitement with an unprecedented springtime nationwide campaign that the shock waves will jar loose Democratic delegates now aligned with the president," Robert Donovan wrote in the *Los Angeles Times.*[4]

Bringing out the crowds, rousing them with fervent rhetoric, capturing it on the TV evening news, said Richard Harwood of the *Washington Post,* was part of a "strategy of revolution, of a popular uprising of such intensity and scale" that the convention would have to choose him. It was all calculated. "Our strategy is to change the rules of nominating a President," explained chief speechwriter Adam Walinsky. "We're going to do it a new way. In the streets."[5] They had to do it through the streets because that was the only way that this angry, emotional politician, lacking Jack's debonair cool, could reignite the Kennedy legend.

Wherever he went it seemed to work: on college campuses and in ghetto streets, in the camps of migrant workers and in suburban shopping centers. The crowds were enthusiastic to the point of frenzy. Senator Barry Goldwater had commented on this emotionalism in 1966 when he noted that "there is a religious fervor building up about this guy that is even stronger than they built up around Jack."[6] The crowds seemed as interested in seeing, and even touching, him as in listening to what he had to say. Hands everywhere reached out as though people wanted to take home some holy relic. They pulled away his cuff links, ripped his shirt, even grabbed his shoes. Above all they wanted, for some reason, to touch his hair. After a day's campaigning his hands were raw and his clothes disheveled.

Who knew what these crowds wanted, or whether this raw emotion could be transferred into votes for a Kennedy presidency? All that could be said was that it made for powerful, and to many people disturbing, images on television. The reaction of the crowds seemed more personal than political, in the view of a British reporting team that covered the campaign. "It had some of the yearning that was once poured out before the great queens of Hollywood, and, before that, was paid as tribute to royalty itself. It was real, that yearning for the young prince of the House of Kennedy; but it was also close to hysteria. It seemed to have more to do with psychopathology than with politics."[7]

The relationship of Robert Kennedy with his followers, like that of their relationship with his brother John, cannot be understood fully in terms of reason. The emotional element was, and remains, so powerful in both cases that it overwhelms any attempt at purely rational analysis. John Kennedy, in part because of his skillful manipulation of the media and deliberate use of heroic rhetoric during his term of office — and later by the incorporation of his assassination into the Lincoln myth — became a symbolic figure of sacrifice and redemption. Robert seized upon the role of inheritor to that myth, virtually by right of succession.

In some ways he was an unlikely vessel to receive the transference of such authority and veneration. He had a squeaky voice, wore ill-fitting clothes that always seemed to be coming undone, and appeared even shorter than his average height because of a pronounced stoop. Often inarticulate, except when stumbling through a prepared speech, he lacked skills of delivery and had none of the orator's ability to move crowds. Yet he had an electrifying presence on crowds. This was less because of what he said than because of his very presence and what he seemed to represent.

Robert Kennedy was not, in the eyes of his followers, an ordinary candidate or even an ordinary man. He was the family heir and the living reincarnation of a beloved king who had been murdered in service to his people. To this JFK legend he had added his own mystique. He walked among the humblest Americans even as he supped with the fashionable and the mighty, and he was beholden to no person or faction but only to all of his people.

Or so he seemed to his followers. And they were followers, not simply admirers. Millions of them believed that he possessed special qualities by which he could lead them from their time of troubles. Those who worked for him did not think of themselves in any way as mere employees. Each felt connected to him personally by iron bonds of belief and commitment. On the Kennedy staff there was no rigid staff hierarchy, but only an interlinked nexus of real and assumed personal ties with the leader. This, too, had been the hallmark of JFK's presidency, where the normal flow of information and procedure through the bureaucracy was supplanted by personal ties emanating directly from the leader.

Those who served Robert, like those who had served JFK, would at his call abandon whatever they were doing to follow his command. When he announced for the presidency people from all parts of the country left their jobs and families to work for him. "I'm a Kennedy man," said aide Edwin Guthman. "I'll go where he asks me." Once they became part of the inner circle, blessed by proximity to their chief, those within the "band of brothers" would remain loyal to their leader even after death had taken him from them. As his Senate and campaign press spokesman later said, looking back on it all: "If they say in my obituary only that I was Robert Kennedy's aide, that's OK with me."[8]

This extraordinary identification with a politician goes far beyond mere empathy, admiration, or party — or even personal — loyalty. It is a form of adulation, and like other forms of worship it rests on deeply rooted emotional feelings. It also assumes that the leader is endowed with certain special qualities. The German sociologist Max Weber described this phenomenon as charisma. By this he did not mean mere glamour or appeal, as the term has popularly come to be used. Rather it refers to the gift of grace by virtue of which the leader "is set apart from other men and treated as endowed with supernatural, superhuman, or at least specifically exceptional powers or qualities."[9]

Among those Weber cites as possessed of this charisma are founders of religions, prophets, warrior heroes, and demagogues. Whether they use their power for good or for evil, they inspire followers among whom their superior authority is freely accepted. Charisma in this sense is a form of authority. But it is unlike other forms: traditional, which relies on custom, such as the line of succession within a monarchy; and rational-legal, such as a set of rules and procedures in a bureaucracy. Charisma, by contrast, emanates from the extraordinary qualities, real or assumed, of a hero or prophet. Such figures emerge in times of great distress or need, and are believed to possess solutions to the ills that beset society. The disciples of a charismatic leader do not follow from fear or favor, but from devotion and enthusiasm. Cult leaders and gurus possess such qualities for their followers.

Charisma of this nature is not eternal; it must continually be reaffirmed. Although not necessarily destroyed by death, it cannot easily survive defeat. This could be interpreted as meaning that the God-given grace had been lost. Part of the mystique of the Kennedys was that they had never lost an election. Although Jesus died, he retained his charisma by virtue of the Resurrection.

Charismatic leaders most often arise during times of crisis. They offer their followers the hope of deliverance from distress: their leadership is salvationist or messianic. Robert Kennedy is often quoted as having said: "I appeal best to people who have problems." That is precisely the prerequisite of a charismatic leader. Those who are content with their lives or the course of society do not need him.

Kennedy's most fervent audiences were the dispossessed, the ignored, the despairing, and above all the blacks. They responded to him with intensity rooted in their belief that he somehow could save them. Such a leader embodies promises of salvation for his followers as Robert C. Tucker has written: "Since he ministers to their most pressing need — the need to believe in the real possibility of escape from an oppressive life-predicament — they not only follow him voluntarily and without thought of material recompense, but tend to revere him and surround him with that spontaneous cult of personality which appears to be one of the symptomatic marks of the charismatic leader-follower relationship."[10] Such charismatic leaders, it should also be noted, inevitably inspire hatred as well as love.

Despite Robert Kennedy's "charisma," Johnson at first had treated him, along with McCarthy, more as a nuisance than a threat. But Tet had had a devastating impact on support for the war. The politicians, ever sensitive to changes in the public mood, were beginning to drift away from the president. The army's request for 200,000 more troops had been leaked to the media, provoking a chorus of alarm. The establishment, which had stood solidly behind the war strategy despite some serious defections, was grumbling audibly about throwing good money after bad.

To reinforce his stance Johnson on March 26 assembled the Wise Men, a group of senior statesmen on whom he relied for support.* They had endorsed his actions in the past. No longer. They now told him it was time to cut the losses. Johnson was stunned. He had done what he thought he was supposed to do, and now

* *Among them were Dean Acheson, Cyrus Vance, Douglas Dillon, Averell Harriman, Henry Cabot Lodge, McGeorge Bundy, and Generals Omar Bradley, Maxwell Taylor, and Matthew Ridgeway.*

he had been abandoned. His beloved dream of a Great Society was a shambles. He had been humiliated in New Hampshire, and his pollsters told him that in a few days he would be humiliated again by McCarthy in the Wisconsin primaries. He was so unpopular that he could scarcely appear in public. He was mortally tired and feared a second heart attack. And now the nightmare that haunted him — that Robert Kennedy, as he told his biographer, would "reclaim the throne in the memory of his brother" and that the American people, "swayed by the magic of the name," would be "dancing in the streets" — was coming true.[11]

Lyndon Johnson had had enough. On March 31, at the end of a television address to the nation in which he had warned Americans to "guard against divisiveness and all its ugly consequences," he astonished his listeners by concluding: "I shall not seek and I will not accept the nomination of my party for another term as your president."

Kennedy heard the news when he arrived in New York late that night from a meeting in Arizona on the plight of the Indians. "I wonder if he'd have done this if I hadn't come in," he mused to an aide.[12] On his return to his East Side apartment his staff greeted him boisterously. He scotched the celebration. Immediately he recognized that Johnson's withdrawal had complicated his situation. His two most powerful issues — the war and LBJ's unpopularity — had been taken away from him.

No longer was he the rightful alternative to a failed president, but merely, along with McCarthy and Vice President Hubert Humphrey, one of three contenders for the vacant throne. During his two-week campaign he had shown that he could rouse vast crowds of the curious and the nostalgic. But now what was it that he stood for? Suddenly, in the words of his political adviser Milton Gwirtzman, "it was a campaign without a theme." And without an opponent — or so Kennedy at first thought.

From the beginning he had underrated McCarthy, whom he considered vain and envious. There was some, though not a great deal, of truth in this. McCarthy, as a former professor and Catholic intellectual, had made it evident that he was not impressed by any of the Kennedys. Indeed he had tried to block JFK's nomination in 1960 by making an eloquent convention speech for Adlai Stevenson that had rocked the halls with waves of doomed nostalgia. A grudge-bearing Bobby had never forgiven him for this. McCarthy was a serious opponent — handsome, urbane, intelligent, and articulate — and in many ways more appealing than Kennedy to the middle-class voter. With his calm self-assurance and sardonic smile he was able to espouse even seemingly heretical views in a way that frightened no one.

Robert Kennedy did not soothe. He was, in Marshall McLuhan's formulation, "hot" to McCarthy's "cool," just as he was hot to Jack's cool. He agitated people, polarized opinion, operated on the emotions of crowds — and often deliberately provoked them. When one reporter described a Kennedy rally as a "happening," to use the jargon of the 1960s, he meant that it was a free-flowing theatrical event without a plot line, but with a great deal of action. One could not be sure where it was going, but there would be plenty of movement along the way. Kennedy invoked emotion, McCarthy applied reason. That is why the little-known Minnesotan had done so well in conservative New Hampshire. The voters could not believe that such a calm, distinguished-looking man would do anything radical. And for the most part they were right.

McCarthy swept the Wisconsin primary and, with Johnson now out of the running, had changed the whole nature of the race. He had become a serious candidate, an effective vote-getter who had stolen the antiwar idealists from the overly cautious Kennedy. No longer could he be dismissed as merely the protesters' candidate. The most serious doubters were among his own staff, who wondered whether their sometimes lackadaisical candidate really wanted to win, or was in it just for the experience.

But for Kennedy everything had changed. Not only had Johnson's withdrawal diffused the war issue, but McCarthy now had to be taken seriously. So did the vice president, who had the near-unanimous support of the party officials who largely controlled the nominating process. Through years of faithful service, the chronically cheerful Hubert Humphrey had won the allegiance of party bosses, union leaders, schoolteachers, farmers, and other core elements of the New Deal–Great Society coalition.

Now, ironically, Kennedy found himself needing Johnson. On the night of March 31 he called every major party leader in the country to seek support, and the next morning asked for a meeting with the president. "I won't bother answering that grandstanding little runt," Johnson snorted. But Kennedy was doing more than simply trying to make up. He wanted something from LBJ: a pledge of neutrality in the primary battles.

To smooth the way he took a leaf from Johnson's own book and tried flattery. In Philadelphia on April 2 he praised Johnson's "act of leadership and sacrifice" in withdrawing, and saluted the president for having shown "his devotion to duty and to the search for peace in Vietnam." The next day Johnson agreed to see him in the Oval Office. After giving Kennedy a briefing on the war, the president mused on the inequities of his life. He had tried to carry out JFK's policies despite the unfair attacks upon him, he told Bobby. But he had done his best, and "as [John] Kennedy looked down at him every day from then until now, he would agree that he kept the faith." This time Bobby was looking for a blessing, not a fight. "You are a brave and dedicated man, Mr. President," he mumbled, but so softly that Johnson made him repeat it.[13]

There was no way that he could be

ingratiating enough. Johnson could hardly be neutral between him and Humphrey. The vice president was his stand-in — a man who could not run against Johnson's record without, in view of his role as cheerleader over the preceding four years, implicitly running against himself. Humphrey was a sanitized LBJ and, since few took him seriously enough to be offended, was in many ways a more serious opponent than Johnson himself.

So, too, Kennedy was now becoming aware, was Eugene McCarthy. Having done better than he himself thought possible, the dark horse was beginning to enjoy the race. He had put Kennedy on the defensive, and even stood a chance of blocking him from the nomination. "It's narrowed down to Bobby and me," McCarthy told his chief speechwriter, Jeremy Larner, the day after his big victory in Wisconsin. "So far he's run with the ghost of his brother. Now we're going to make him run against it. It's purely Greek: he either has to kill him or be killed by him. We'll make him run against Jack. And I'm Jack."[14]

By this he meant that Bobby could no longer blame the war on Johnson, but would have to confront the fact that his own brother had started it. If he did not repudiate JFK's legacy, which McCarthy knew for Bobby would amount to a form of fratricide, he would be burned by it. And McCarthy was going to hold his feet to the fire. He would "be Jack" in the sense that he would not allow Bobby to escape this legacy.

But Bobby was determined not to be sunk by JFK's, and his own, early enthusiasm for a war that everyone now wished would go away. It was not enough for him to disavow a disastrous war: John Kennedy had to be purged of it as well. In this way Johnson's responsibility would be complete. For this reason JFK was "discovered" to secretly have changed his mind about Vietnam. Aides stepped forward to claim that he had told them he was secretly planning to withdraw in 1965, just as soon as he was safely reelected. He would never, they insisted, have made the mistake of sending in a huge American army to save Vietnam, even though this is what Kennedy's own advisers had urged Johnson to do.

But Johnson's withdrawal from the race had defused the war as a major election year issue. Bobby no longer had LBJ and the war to run against. This forced him to focus almost entirely on domestic concerns: poverty, inequality, injustice. This theme worked with urban liberals and blacks. But to win over suburbanites and blue-collar workers he also had to mask his image as the candidate of war protesters and race rioters. He started lacing his speeches, particularly in the suburbs and in working-class districts, with references to his role as attorney general and law enforcer.

There was Bobby the tough and Bobby the tender, depending on the audience. While the old Kennedy magic of glamour and nostalgia brought out wild crowds on the streets and the campuses, TV images of shrieking mobs raised anxieties in the suburbs. His popularity with black and Hispanic voters rested on their assumption that he understood and sympathized with their problems — indeed he was a fellow sufferer of their sadness. Yet in politically conservative areas where some of the primary battles would be fought, this image as the tribune of the unruly worked against him.

He had to woo several different and, in some cases, conflicting constituencies in order to be a viable candidate. It was not enough for him to be the inheritor of a fabulous legend and the reincarnation of a now-sanctified king. At the same time he also had to be a patriot, a cop, a peacemaker, and an exemplar of middle-class virtues, as well as a paladin of the poor, a closet revolutionary, and an honorary soul brother. Of these the most improbable, but ultimately most successful, was the last.

15

Soul Man

The legend tells us that during the last years of his life Robert Kennedy was a healer; that he felt the pain of the impoverished and the excluded like no other politician of his time; that he would have bridged the racial and economic divisions among Americans. He was not, of course, considered to be a figure of reconciliation during most of his career: as an investigator and prosecutor, as his brother's campaign manager, and as attorney general. His concern for blacks, Indians, Hispanics, and the poor was not noted until after he entered the Senate. The shock of his brother's death is said to have triggered a "transformation" in him tantamount to a religious conversion. No longer was he the angry, vindictive protector of the Kennedy name and power celebrated for his "ruthlessness." Rather, it is believed, he had become a caring, sensitive pastor to life's victims; a "tribune of the underclass" was the phrase sometimes used to describe him.

Black Americans were particularly drawn to him during the last three years of his life. He reached out to them with the message that he, too, rich and privileged though he was, had suffered; that he understood their sorrow and anger; and that he would remedy their misfortunes. For those beyond despair, he offered not only empathy but hope. This is, of course, precisely the definition of a leader believed to be the bearer of charismatic powers: he would bring salvation and redemption.

Robert Kennedy was an unlikely person to become a hero to black Americans. "I did not lie awake at night worrying about the problems of Negroes," he admitted in 1964. The same was true of his brother John. Both brothers came late to the cause of civil rights and participated reluctantly. They were driven, at least initially, less by conscience than by the inescapable pressure of political events. They made the most of necessity, and in so doing became the beneficiaries of a legend for which they themselves were only partly responsible.

Ultimately their political needs fused with the unfulfilled yearnings of black people to enshrine the two Kennedys as martyrs to the cause of equality and justice. Together with Martin Luther King they form a powerful triumvirate of martyrs. Their faces, joined in a single assembled portrait, grace hundreds of thousands of black homes and innumerable T-shirts.

There are reasons for this. JFK's celebrated phone call to Coretta King when Martin was in jail, the calculated linkage to Lincoln the liberator in JFK's funeral ceremony, Robert's walks in the ghettos and appeals for racial understanding all left a deep reservoir of empathy among black Americans. This empathy, translated into votes, played a critical role in election races for the two Kennedys.

But JFK's paper-thin majority in 1960 rested not only on the votes of urban northern blacks but also on those of white southerners. He had won some of that support when he criticized Eisenhower's use of federal troops to enforce school desegregation at Little Rock in 1957. His strategy as president was to appease rather than confront the powerful southern legislators who controlled key congressional committees. His natural caution was reinforced by the belief among most northern whites that conditions for blacks were steadily improving and that no exceptional measures were necessary.

Rather than alienate southern legislators

with controversial civil rights legislation that might get in the way of the foreign policy issues that he really cared about, John Kennedy tried to bypass Capitol Hill through executive actions not subject to congressional control. In this way, without disturbing the prerogatives of southern committee chairmen, the White House was able to appoint some three dozen blacks to major government positions; named five black federal judges, including Thurgood Marshall, who later went to the Supreme Court as the first black justice*; set up a commission to promote opportunities for blacks to gain government contracts; and named civil rights advocate Harris Wofford as a special White House adviser.

Kennedy's objective was to funnel black

* *Robert Kennedy preferred Judge William Hastie for the court seat, but backed down when Chief Justice Earl Warren (an Eisenhower appointee) complained that the black jurist was too conservative. Marshall, who was close to LBJ, never did warm to Robert Kennedy. In a taped interview for Columbia University in 1977, not released until after his death in 1993, he said that although John Kennedy was "a very sweet man," his brother "Bobby was like his father. He was a cold, calculating character. 'What's in it for me?' I mean not like his brother. He had no warm feelings at all."*[1]

aspirations through the Justice Department. In this way the emphasis could be placed on enforcing existing legislation rather than on seeking new remedies that could run into congressional roadblocks. Kennedy's enthusiastic staff of young lawyers enforced existing civil rights laws, pressured school boards to enforce desegregation orders, and brought more than fifty voting rights suits in the South.

But for Robert Kennedy, as for most white Americans, civil rights was a problem, not a crusade. Instead of naming Wofford, a dedicated rights advocate, to head the department's Civil Rights Division, he chose a Yale professor of antitrust law, Burke Marshall. The problem with Wofford, Kennedy later explained, was that he "was very emotionally involved in all of these matters and was rather in some areas a slight madman."[2] Kennedy's goal was to hold off the "madmen" on both sides: the die-hard southern segregationists and the increasingly militant young activists who had lost patience with slow reform.

Wofford was suspect not only for his zeal but also for his close association with black leaders like Martin Luther King. It was Wofford who had urged John Kennedy during the 1960 campaign to call Coretta

King to express his sympathy when her husband was imprisoned by a Georgia judge. When Robert learned of this he berated Wofford. But after cooling down he made the most of the situation by calling the judge himself to urge King's release. The Kennedys' gestures made a huge impact on black voters. From 40 percent of the black vote in 1956, the Democrats took 60 percent in 1960 — enough to give John Kennedy the winning margin in critical northern states.

For men like Wofford and Kennedy brother-in-law Sargent Shriver, civil rights was a moral cause of the highest priority. For the Kennedy brothers it was one political problem among many. It had to be weighed against other issues and against the political clout of entrenched southern committee chairmen in the Congress. John Kennedy, like Robert, meant well, King told Wofford, but "the moral passion is missing."* So was

* *This seemed to be confirmed when Kennedy appointed five segregationist federal judges who impeded efforts to ensure black voting rights. William Cox, the most notorious, once from the bench derided petitioners as "a bunch of niggers . . . acting like . . . chimpanzees." The Kennedys claimed that this was the price of getting Senate approval for Thurgood Marshall's seat on the federal judiciary.*[3]

Kennedy's attention. Not until the fall of 1961 was the nation's civil rights leader allowed to see the president.

As attorney general Robert was the nation's chief law enforcement officer, but he was also his brother's political protector. He weighed civil rights initiatives in terms of their political impact on the wider Kennedy agenda. For this reason he preferred to emphasize voting rights, which could be funneled through the courts, over desegregation initiatives that would provoke white resistance in the South. He justified this by arguing that the federal government had a stronger position in enforcing voter registration than in desegregating public facilities.

But young activists, white as well as black, were not so patient. They took to heart JFK's own call for a "new generation of leaders." They formed bands of Freedom Riders who traveled on buses through the South to integrate terminals. The deeper they went into the Old Confederacy the more anger they provoked. Confrontations erupted where local police refused to protect them from white mobs. Many were attacked, beaten, and thrown into jails.

The administration was forced to step

into the breach caused by the passivity, and often hostility, of local officials — and by J. Edgar Hoover's refusal to allow FBI agents monitoring the events to protect those he considered agitators. Aware of the political trouble such confrontations would cause his brother, the attorney general had little alternative but to send federal marshals to protect the Freedom Riders when they were assaulted in Montgomery, Alabama, and later in Birmingham. And in 1963 he had to use the National Guard to ensure the safety of black students seeking admission to the state universities in Alabama and Mississippi.

But he did so with reluctance and sometimes with anger. This was not from sympathy for the white segregationists. Rather it was from a concern over the impact that the use of federal power against state officials would have on his brother's political fortunes in the South. "If you cut out this Freedom Rider and sitting-in stuff and concentrate on voter registration, I'll get you a tax exemption," he promised representatives of the student organizations. The Kennedys' reaction to the sit-ins was mostly one of alarm. "Tell them to call it off," JFK told Harris Wofford, declaring that the desegregation riots would weaken his hand in upcoming meetings with De Gaulle and Khrushchev. "This is too much," Robert complained to Wofford after King turned down his appeal to withdraw the demonstrators. "I wonder whether they have the best interests of the country at heart. Do you know that one of them is against the atom bomb? Yes, he even picketed against it in jail! The president is going abroad and all this is embarrassing him."[4]

Even several years later, after John's death and his own growing sensitivity to racial issues, Bobby still showed resentment against the demonstrators. "Everybody then was trying to get into the act for publicity and attention, and I thought they should stay out of there and stay home," he told an interviewer. The president "was fed up with the Freedom Riders who went down there afterwards when it didn't do any good to go down there."[5]

He was particularly annoyed by the rivalries among the civil rights groups — from the traditionalist National Association for the Advancement of Colored People (NAACP) and King's Southern Christian Leadership Conference (SCLC), to more radical organizations like the Congress of Racial Equality (CORE) and the Student

Nonviolent Coordinating Committee (SNCC). These groups looked with suspicion on one another, and particularly on an administration they wanted to move more decisively. Their impatience was understandable. But their competition with one another made it hard to work out a unified strategy. The Kennedys, despite their sympathy, had more pressing agendas.

Bobby gave vent to this frustration in 1964 when he complained that "there was a lot of feeling that the Negroes didn't know exactly what they wanted and that they were not very well led in certain cases." He singled out King as one of those with whom he often "didn't see eye to eye on these matters." King, for his part, was often frustrated with an administration he viewed as "aggressively driving toward the limited goal of token integration."[6]

King had other reasons to be suspicious of the Kennedys. Not only did he feel they were dragging their feet on integration, but he himself was hounded by the FBI — and with Robert Kennedy's support. Hoover had persuaded Kennedy that King's closest adviser, Stanley Levison, was a secret member of the Communist party. As attorney general Kennedy gave Hoover permission to tap King's phone, even though Hoover never provided any solid evidence for his suspicions. This surveillance proved nothing serious against Levison, but it provided damaging information on King's relations with women that the FBI used to taunt him until his death.

"President Kennedy and I . . . were so reserved about him [King] during this period of time, which I'm sure he felt," Robert later said. ". . . We never wanted to get very close to him just because of these contacts and connections that he had, which we felt were damaging to the civil rights movement. And because we were so intimately involved in the struggle for civil rights, it also damaged us." Of his relations with King when attorney general, Kennedy remarked, "I never really had any conversations with him over the period other than what he should be doing with the Communists."[7] This resentment against King was evident at the time of JFK's funeral. King was not invited to the ceremonies and instead watched from the street with other mourners.

Garry Wills has argued that there later came to be a "compensatory ardor" in Robert Kennedy's work for civil rights because of his acquiescence in Hoover's vendetta against King; that Kennedy was "doing penance" for letting Hoover run wild because he feared the damaging revelations that Hoover could have made about John Kennedy's personal life. It is possible. But Robert Kennedy's later concern for civil rights, after he himself became a politician, also could have been simple political calculation: he needed the votes of black Americans if he was to stand a chance of being elected senator or president.

In Navasky's critical words, "From 1961 to 1963 Robert Kennedy had no civil rights program in the sense that he had an organized crime program. . . . His most visible and most significant civil rights activities were responsive, crisis-managing, violence-avoiding."[8] Not until June 1963, following the confrontation with Governor George Wallace at the University of Alabama, and the violence of city officials against demonstrators at Birmingham, did the administration move beyond executive action to announce a comprehensive civil rights bill. Robert Kennedy shaped the writing of that bill, with its guarantee of equal access to public places and its support of black voting rights and school desegregation. Later he helped gain passage of the Criminal Justice Act of 1964, which provided for paid counsel for indigent defendants in criminal trials and initiated federal bail reform.

However one weighs the reasons, it is striking that the two Kennedy brothers have been enshrined in the pantheon of heroes for black Americans. If John Kennedy, as Taylor Branch writes, "gained credit for much of the purpose that King's movement had forced upon him in life," that credit devolved on to Robert and was augmented by his own later expression of concern for some of King's goals.[9*] By 1968 polls indicated that 94 percent of blacks believed that Robert Kennedy had "many of the same outstanding qualities of his brother." By contrast only 39 percent of the wider public agreed.

[*] *Yet relations between the two men were never cordial. In 1966, King had, in response to Robert Kennedy's criticisms that he had ignored problems in the North, taken his nonviolent protest tactics to Chicago. The results were disastrous as hostile whites clashed in riots with the demonstrators and with Black Power militants. This sealed a bad relationship. Indeed, "after the White House years," King's deputy Andrew Young later wrote of King and Kennedy, "they met very seldom, if at all."*[10]

Kennedy's sensitivity to racial issues became evident after he sought a political career of his own. Yet during his years as attorney general he thought that the Freedom Riders were, for the most part, grandstanding troublemakers, and that some black organizations were infiltrated by communists who goaded them to unnecessary confrontations. The Kennedys tried to block the 1963 March on Washington from fear that it would embarrass their administration. When that effort failed they tried to take it over, and forced one of the key speakers, John Lewis of the radical student organization SNCC, to rewrite his speech because, in RFK's words, it "attacked the president."

In the remarkably frank interviews he gave for the Kennedy Library in late 1964, Robert Kennedy resisted the effort of journalist Anthony Lewis to have him make pious statements about his shared pain with black people. There is something refreshing about his candor in the following exchange:

LEWIS: . . . [W]as there anything during the [1960] campaign that you think brought you or your brother face to face with the actual situation that you saw later, as Attorney General, of the Negro in the South?

KENNEDY: No.

LEWIS: This terrible helplessness?

KENNEDY: No. . . . [T]here was a general feeling that Negroes were in difficulty in the South as well as in many of the northern communities — as well as a lot of white people. A lot needed to be done. But we just didn't sit down and wring our hands and shake our heads, and have meetings about how awful it was about the Negro in Mississippi.

LEWIS: . . . I asked you whether you became aware of the rather special horror of life for the Negro in the South.

KENNEDY: No.[11]

As attorney general Robert Kennedy's task was to do enough for black people to win their support without at the same time losing the votes of white conservatives and southerners JFK needed to govern and to be reelected. This was a tight line to walk, as became apparent in 1963 when, at the attorney general's suggestion, author James Baldwin brought him together with a group of black artists and intellectuals.* They met at the family's Manhattan apartment for what he assumed would be their appreciative response to his progress report on all the good things that the administration was doing for blacks.

But some of them had a different agenda in mind. A young rights organizer who had been jailed in the South cut through the polite chatter by declaring that he had about given up on peaceful change and was "close to the moment where I'm ready to take up a gun." Merely being in the same room with Kennedy, he declared, made him want to vomit. Others, roused to militancy by his boldness, joined in to voice their frustration over what they viewed as the administration's foot-dragging. Kennedy fumed as he was subjected, in the words of psychologist Kenneth Clark, a participant, to "one of the most violent, emotional verbal assaults

* *Among them were Harry Belafonte, Lena Horne, psychologist Kenneth Clark, King's lawyer Clarence Jones, and playwright Lorraine Hansberry.*

assaults . . . that I had ever witnessed before or since."[12]

The problem was not only about facts but about feeling. The people Baldwin had invited to talk with Kennedy were offended that he kept quoting statistics to them. Like Martin Luther King, they put a high value on moral gesture. When they suggested to him that the president ought personally to escort students past schoolhouse blockades put up by segregationists, the attorney general laughed. When he defended the racist judges he had appointed in the South on the grounds that the president needed the votes of their southern sponsors for his social legislation, they laughed at him. The two sides talked past, and were ultimately disgusted with, each other.

Kennedy was still fuming about the incident more than a year later when he told an interviewer that most of the people there had "complexes about the fact that they've been successful . . . that they've done so well and this poor boy had been beaten by the police. . . . They hadn't done what they should have done for the Negro. So the way to show that they hadn't forgotten where they came from was to berate me and berate the United States government that had made this position a condition. They didn't really know, with a few exceptions, any of the facts."[13] In other words, he still had not taken their grievances seriously.

What Kennedy had missed was the feeling behind the argument. Eventually he learned to become sensitive to that as well. This encounter is often cited by chroniclers to demonstrate how far Kennedy later came in understanding the frustration of black people. Certainly his vocabulary changed. He learned the value of gesture and empathy. The speeches he made during the last few years of his life were rich in feeling and were designed to show that he identified with black people. He was rewarded by them for making that identification. They came to admire him in the way that they did few other white people, let alone politicians. They continued to do this even when, in addressing white audiences, he used code words like "law and order" they would have criticized as racist coming from anyone else.

He had learned to talk the talk. "[I]f any man claims the Negro should be content or satisfied, let him say he would willingly change the color of his skin and go to live in the Negro section of a large city," he told students at Berkeley in 1966. "But suppose God is black," he asked South African whites that same year. "What if we go to heaven and we, all our lives, have treated the Negro as an inferior, and God is there and we look up and He is not white? What then is our response?"[14]

Had Kennedy's speeches during his Senate years not been so rich in allusion and in noting the special problems of black Americans, his own proposals for dealing with some of those problems might be viewed more critically. As it was, his rhetoric was eloquent and moving when he spoke of "the violence that afflicts the poor, that poisons the relations between men because their skin has different colors," or that "the violent youth of the ghetto is not simply protesting his condition, but making a destructive and self-defeating attempt to assert his worth and dignity as a human being," or when he asked whites to "suppose God is black."[15]

Yet the remedies he proposed surprised and even distressed many liberals concerned with these issues. In this field as in others, Kennedy made it clear that, as he often said, he was not a liberal. Indeed his curious kinship with white radicals like Tom Hayden and Staughton Lynd rested on the fact that on whatever else they disagreed, they had a common enemy: liberals.

Kennedy's language and proposals frequently had more in common with those of conservatives. Using language familiar to Republicans since the days of the New Deal, Kennedy stressed the need to "bring people back to . . . the warmth of community, to the worth of individual effort and responsibility"; opposed trade sanctions against the South African regime (saying this would harm blacks); declared, with regard to school busing, that "compulsory transportation of children over long distances, away from schools in their neighborhood, doesn't make much sense and I am against it"; decried "the brutality of the welfare system itself [which] has done much to divide our people, to alienate us from one another"; criticized a proposed guaranteed national income as resting on "a myth that all the problems of poverty can be solved by ultimate extension of the welfare system"; attacked federal anti-poverty efforts by urging the need "to halt and reverse the growing accumulation of power and authority in the central government in Washington and return that power of decision to the American people in their own local community"; and demanded "that the government begin to accommodate itself to the requirements of its citizens, instead of the other way around." When California governor Ronald Reagan observed during the 1968 primary campaign that "Kennedy was talking more and more like me," he was not the only person who thought so.[16]

These anti-government statements served a double purpose. They were designed to discredit Lyndon Johnson's federally funded War on Poverty, the proud centerpiece of his domestic program; and to broaden the senator's base of support by enlisting those hostile to virtually any major government activity — whether radicals on the right or radicals on the left.

Kennedy's Bedford-Stuyvesant plan for rebuilding the ghetto with private funds is a classic example. This approach, combined with his attacks on welfare, his emphasis on "community" initiative, responsibility, and self-reliance, later emerged as key elements of urban renewal proposals in the Nixon and Bush administrations. His embrace of the goals of "community action" and its handmaiden slogan "maximum feasible participation" of ghetto residents in development programs made him attractive to black radicals who had their own agenda for gaining political and economic power in the ghettos. Kennedy tried to use them as they did him. Latching on to the rhetoric of Black Power by declaring that "blackness must be made a badge of pride and honor," he formed strategic alliances with some of the militants.[17]

It is striking to note the low priority that Kennedy put on racial integration. His main theme was the rebuilding of the ghetto rather than its dispersal or elimination, at least in the foreseeable future. "We must devote our attention to improving living conditions and rebuilding the present Negro areas," he declared in January 1966. Racial integration lay somewhere down the road, after economic self-sufficiency had been won. "Those who speak of ending the colonialism of the ghetto must therefore recognize that the economic and social development of that community is at the heart of any policy of creating full mobility," he declared during his presidential campaign.[18]

This suited Black Power advocates, who favored racial separation both on theoretical grounds and because it gave them a cut of the economic pie. It also, for different reasons, appealed to many white working-class voters who felt threatened by integration programs foisted on them by affluent white liberals. Thus, by undercutting the central role of government, and by stressing local control and the rebuilding of the ghettos, Kennedy appealed to two otherwise hostile constituencies that had little in common with each other, but that both had something to gain from his proposals. A go-slow approach to integration and a hands-off policy by the federal government seemed to serve both his interests and theirs.

Furthermore, keeping the federal government out of urban renewal undercut Lyndon Johnson's War on Poverty all the more effectively for seeming to advance the best interests of the beneficiaries.* Black

* *Kennedy was ingenious in his efforts to discredit or embarrass Johnson. In 1968 he suggested to NAACP lawyer Marian Wright that she tell Martin Luther King that the way to force the administration to do something about poverty was to "bring the people to Washington." From that suggestion came the Poor People's March that brought a sea of tents to the shadow of the White House. It was a brilliant maneuver. "By encouraging thousands of poor people to Washington," as Brian Dooley observed, "Kennedy could ensure that the president was embarrassed on the issue of poverty, and could claim extra credibility for himself with radical leaders by adopting the mantle of direct (if non-violent) confrontation."*[19]

Power, White Power, Big Business were strange bedfellows in Bobby Kennedy's strategic alliance, but each had something real to gain from it. In a speech to the Senate in March 1967, Kennedy claimed that his ultimate goal was integration through black strength. But Eugene McCarthy had a point in arguing that Kennedy was really preaching a kind of "segregated residential apartheid."[20]

Nonetheless, Kennedy emerged during the last years of his life as the blue-eyed soul brother of the black civil rights movement. This rested as much on symbolism and sentiment as it did on programs and performance. His proposals for black self-help through privately funded programs like Bedford-Stuyvesant were innovative, but sputtered out within a few years and did not become an effective model for such programs elsewhere. His arguments for the importance of training and job creation as the key to transforming the ghettos and improving the condition of black Americans appealed, for different reasons, both to many blacks and to whites both liberal and conservative.

Unlike many politicians he did not merely deplore conditions in the ghettos but proposed specific programs of training, education, employment, and community-building for those trapped in them. For these he deserves credit. Whether, had he lived and been elected president, he would have been able to translate these proposals into effective courses of action we will never know. Certainly many believe that he would have, although others since that time have tried and failed.

But in the end it was not Robert Kennedy's embrace of black pride, or his plans for rebuilding the ghettos, or his visits to slums and backwater shacks that made him an admired, even a beloved, figure for millions of black Americans. Nor was it his trip to South Africa or his speculations on the color of God's skin. None of these would have been enough by themselves.

There was something more to this emotional attachment between an aggressive Irish politician who spent his early years as attorney general running away from the civil rights movement and the black masses who came to believe that in some way he spoke for them. Martin Luther King addressed both blacks and whites with higher moral authority. Angry activists like Malcolm X shouted more fervently and apocalyptically. But no white politician or spokesman was able to capture the confidence of black people and win their honor and respect as did Robert Kennedy.

There is no single answer as to why this was so. It rested in part on the fact that he was his brother's inheritor and on the manner of JFK's death. Although John Kennedy had come late and reluctantly to embrace the cause of civil rights, he ultimately did so with some conviction shortly before his assassination. For this reason, and because of his Lincoln-like funeral ceremonies, many black people came to believe that in some way he had, like the Great Emancipator, died for them and because of them.

Whites, too, after all, have mythicized John Kennedy, and millions believe that had he lived everything would have been better. Robert was the inheritor of the legend of his brother's life and death, and he made it an important part of his public persona. What he inherited he ultimately came to accept and believe in himself. Willingly donning the mantle, he was determined not only to redeem his brother's presumed legacy but even to surpass it.

His hold on the sentiments of black Americans was so powerful that some black activists feared that it cut into their own influence. "I would not want to see your man run for president because he can get the votes of my people without coming to me," former SNCC chairman and black separatist Stokely Carmichael told Ted Sorensen. "With the other candidates I'll have bargaining power."[21]

Kennedy's hold over black voters was an obvious advantage, but also posed a problem in a campaign resting so heavily on image. In the heavily charged racial climate of the late 1960s, when even the most well-meaning white voter was disturbed by the violent speeches of black militants and the riots that had erupted in scores of cities, anyone tagged as the "black candidate" was likely to alienate considerable numbers of whites.

This was particularly true in working-class neighborhoods. Kennedy's task was to rouse his supporters in the inner cities without frightening the politically conservative white voters whose support he needed to win the nomination. The problems this posed were to become dramatically apparent in the crucial Indiana and California primaries.

16

An Inconclusive Victory

The Indiana primary was a test of his ability to turn black empathy for the Kennedy mythology into black votes for the Kennedy candidacy. Even more critically, it was a test of whether he could break out of the ghetto into the hearts, or at least the votes, of the white working class. The legend tells us that he did this triumphantly in Indiana and would have repeated it throughout the nation. The reality is somewhat different.

Among liberals, whose support he was also counting on, his agonizing appraisals and reappraisals had been costly. Kennedy, the vaunted man of decision, had dithered for months while McCarthy, the thoughtful intellectual, had moved with bold decisiveness. As a result Kennedy lost many of the idealists who would have backed him enthusiastically as the candidate best able to end the war. And he lost them out of caution.

At first glance this may seem like a

curious word to apply to such a quick-tempered and emotional person. Much of his reputation, after all, rests on his determination and decisiveness. But in fact Kennedy was remarkably cautious in his politics, continually circling around issues like a cat before finally committing himself. Then, as if in compensation, he would move precipitously.

He dithered for months before deciding to run for the Senate, and then hastily tried to assemble an organization and a program. He did the same in the presidential race, waiting until McCarthy showed Johnson's vulnerability, and then behaving in a way that confirmed everyone's worst concerns about his opportunism and ruthlessness. In this obsessed competitor there was a strong element of self-doubt and even of self-defeat.

His hesitations and doubts raise the question of whether he was of two minds about truly wanting the presidency. He had, after all, reason to feel unworthy of actually trying to fill his brother's shoes; that honoring the legacy was more difficult than claiming it; and that he would have to compete with a legend, as Johnson had been forced to do. And with all the passions aroused by an unpopular war abroad and by racial violence at home, the danger of assassination was all too real. As the father of ten children, with an eleventh on the way, he could not ignore that.

Yet whatever his ambivalence he had no real alternative. He had committed himself too deeply not to run. Had he not jumped into the race, especially after being pushed by McCarthy's challenge and Johnson's surprising vulnerability, his career would have been finished. He would have ceded to a bolder man what millions believed to be his rightful place. He would have lost his charisma, the God-given "special grace" bestowed upon superior beings to lead their peoples out of the darkness. He would have been just another politician, a false claimant to a throne he did not deserve. He was trapped. He had to run even though he did not want to, and the odds seemed stacked against him.

After all his angst of indecision his campaign was a curious and, in the end, inconclusive one. It began with a blitz of heartland campuses in Kansas, Tennessee, and Alabama. There, attacking the administration's conduct of the war in Vietnam, and calling for a moral revival, he was greeted as the celebrity he was. Sometimes he boldly challenged the students directly. At

Idaho State he called for an end to student draft deferments, and at Indiana University he chided medical students for letting "black people carry the burden of fighting in Vietnam."[1]

During the first fifteen days of the campaign he toured sixteen states, visited an Indian tribal gathering in Arizona, and made a whistle-stop tour through California's Central Valley that culminated in street parades and an amphitheater speech in Los Angeles. Indians and Hispanics were two groups he had particularly targeted, and they turned out for him with rapturous support as tens of thousands of people filled the streets, screaming his name and reaching out to touch him. These crowds, generated by the advance men, and roused to near-hysterical excitement by the music and the drama, were powerful and, to many, disturbing in their intensity.

Kennedy had a strong hold on the allegiance of racial minorities and mastered the streets. But he was a long way from the nomination. Students were suspicious, party chiefs were unresponsive, the white South was hostile, and the vast middle class could not yet be gauged. Then there was also Vice President Hubert Humphrey, with all the party apparatus behind him, and Eugene McCarthy, who on April 2 had run away with the Wisconsin primary.

In 1968 primaries were not nearly as important as they became after the Democratic party reforms of 1972. Of the fourteen primaries held between March and early June, the ones of importance were in New Hampshire, Wisconsin, Indiana, Nebraska, Oregon, South Dakota, and California. Each of these had its own rules. In New Hampshire a candidate's name can be placed on the ballot by petition even without his consent. In Wisconsin, Nebraska, and Oregon state officials can nominate any person they think ought to be a candidate.

Kennedy decided to enter the Indiana primary at virtually the last minute. This was one that he could not afford to duck. Racially mixed in the industrial north, the state is solidly middle America in the center, with traces of old Dixie in the south. Tensions between blacks and whites in the industrial cities had helped George Wallace gain more than a third of the votes in the 1964 primary.

Kennedy had to do more than merely win Indiana if he was to stand a chance.

He also had to go beyond his core constituency of black voters to reach deep into the white middle class. Only that would persuade party regulars that he had broad appeal. This was no sure thing. Organized labor, controlled by the conservative leadership of the AFL-CIO, was against him. So, of course, were the Teamsters, although they had relatively little clout in the state because of internal quarrels. White backlash against black militancy and racial rioting was strong. Among traditionally patriotic Hoosiers there was relatively little opposition to the Vietnam War. A popular governor, Roger Branigan, was on the ballot as a stand-in for Humphrey, siphoning off traditionally Democratic voters from both Kennedy and McCarthy.

There was no question of Kennedy's appeal to black voters. Wherever he went among them he was greeted as a hero. This was dramatized by his April 4 appearance in the Indianapolis ghetto. Shortly before his plane landed he learned that Martin Luther King had been assassinated in Memphis. Scrapping the speech prepared for him, he made a few notes before landing. When he arrived in the ghetto it was already dark. An enthusiastic crowd was waiting for him. They had not yet heard the news.

Mounting a flatbed truck in a parking lot, he looked out at the eager people and told them the news. There was a horrified gasp. Urging his audience to reject hatred and the desire for revenge, he pointedly identified himself with the loss of their revered leader. "For those of you who are black and are tempted to be filled with hatred and distrust at the injustice of such an act, against all white people," he told them, "I can only say that I feel in my own heart the same kind of feeling. I had a member of my family killed, but he was killed by a white man."

This sense of common suffering was a major reason for the strong link between Kennedy and black people, and of their allegiance to him. Imploring his listeners to express their sorrow not in violence but in a rededication to King's principles of compassion, he drew on the Greek poets who had brought him comfort in his own anguish, particularly on Aeschylus, who counseled the need to "tame the savageness of man and to make gentle the life of this world."[2]

His words clearly affected and also calmed his audience. In the days that followed the nation was swept by riots in 110 cities, 39 people were killed, more than 2,500 injured, and some 75,000 troops sent to patrol the streets. But Indianapolis was untouched by violence. On his return to Washington, Kennedy walked through ghetto streets littered with glass and charred by fire. The troops stood back and the people walked with him as they would have done with almost no other white politician. Then he went to Atlanta to march in King's funeral procession.

But if Robert Kennedy was one of the few white politicians whom black voters felt they could trust, this did not help him among blue-collar whites. He could not afford to be viewed as the black candidate. "So far in Indiana they seem to want to see me as a member of the black race — I don't think I can win if that happens," he told journalist David Halberstam. He cut back appearances in the ghetto to avoid television images of ecstatic crowds reaching for him. But he also had to be careful not to appear to be walking away from blacks. He was dependent on their support — which could run to 25 percent of the turnout. It was a dilemma. "The only way we're going to win this thing is to get 90 percent of the black vote," aide

Richard Wade told campaign manager Stephen Smith.[3]

Yet that dependency threatened to cut into the support he needed from white working-class voters to impress party bosses. To be a viable candidate nationally he had to address the concerns of blue-collar workers. They were dubious about his antiwar stance and believed that their values — work, patriotism, family — were being violated in a climate of disrespect, disloyalty, and urban violence. Some of them had voted for George Wallace in 1964, and in the 1980s would become Reagan Democrats. To win them over, the "new Bobby" had to call on the "old Bobby." His campaign began to take a different tone. "I was the chief law enforcement officer of this country for three and a half years," he kept reminding his audiences. Translation: "I will crack down on rioters."

Although he brought out the crowds, his support was confined largely to blacks, blue-collar ethnics, people under thirty, and those with no more than a grade school education. Among voters aged thirty to forty-nine, McCarthy bested him in opinion polls with 35 percent of the vote to Kennedy's 27 percent. Among the college educated McCarthy scored 44 percent to Kennedy's 18 percent, thus confirming McCarthy's impolitic boast that "the better-educated people vote for us." However, among Catholics, particularly Irish and Polish, he ran ahead of McCarthy, whose nonethnic, intellectual brand of Catholicism invoked no tribal loyalty.

When Indiana voters were polled on their attitude toward the war, it was clear how deeply McCarthy had cut into Kennedy's base. Among those who opposed the war McCarthy polled 41 percent, while among those who supported it only 26 percent. But curiously, Kennedy scored 28 percent among those who favored Johnson's conduct of the war and also 28 percent among those who opposed it. In other words, his stance on the war, which had caused him so much public agonizing, had made no discernable difference.[4]

Among white voters Kennedy stressed not only his law enforcement credentials to show he would be tough on rioters, but also his fiscal conservatism. To blue-collar whites suspicious of Great Society programs they viewed as benefiting only blacks, he promised both to punish rioters and lawbreakers and also to get private industry to take over the costs of ghetto rebuilding.

Outside the state he continued to mix themes of racial injustice into his law-and-order pitch. In Denver he told a white audience that it must "recognize the fundamental injustice of minority life in the United States," and students at Michigan State University that "the violent youth of the ghetto is not simply protesting his condition, but making a destructive and self-defeating attempt to assert his worth and dignity as a human being."[5] But to white audiences in Indiana he criticized Great Society programs they considered to be giveaways to blacks, and he promised to punish "lawbreakers" — a code word for black rioters. With one message for white listeners and another one for blacks, he hoped that neither was paying too close attention to the message meant for the other.

With the black vote firmly in his pocket he could tell blue-collar whites what they wanted to hear: that he had been a tough attorney general who would keep lawbreakers in their place, that school busing to achieve integration should be ended, that local control was better than federal interference, and that welfare was evil.

Nonetheless, he did not make many real inroads among blue-collar whites beyond his core constituency of Irish attracted to his heritage and Slavs to his fervent brand of Catholicism.

For all his efforts to put together a black-white coalition with street parades and rallies, polls showed that he picked up hardly any new votes during the last three weeks of the campaign. His audience responded to him as much for who he was as for what he said. His appeal was more personal than political: the appeal of a celebrity and an inheritor.

When the votes were counted on May 7, Kennedy's 42.3 percent of the 776,000 votes cast, against 30.7 percent for Branigan and 27 percent for McCarthy, gave him a strong plurality, but not the majority he sought in order to impress party chiefs. He took virtually all of the black vote and did relatively well among the heavily Catholic white working-class voters in industrial cities like Gary. Some whites told pollsters that despite his words of compassion for blacks, he was a tough guy who would keep them in check. Black voters, by contrast, believed that despite his "old Bobby" law-and-order pitch to blue-collar whites, he would protect their interests. Through carefully crafted rhetoric he was able to persuade each camp to believe the message it wanted to hear.

What was important to Kennedy were not the electoral votes of Indiana, which were few, but that he be viewed by party leaders as one who could put together a winning national coalition. This is why Kennedy's staff stressed to reporters his popularity in white working-class districts. Many picked this up and made it a major theme of their stories. From this came the belief, which became a central part of the Kennedy legend, that he was the one politician in America capable of uniting blacks and blue-collar whites, "the last liberal politician," in the words of Paul Cowan in *The Village Voice*, "who could communicate with white working class America."[6]

Every year on the anniversary of his death commentators write with melancholy longing about reforging the black-white coalition that Kennedy presumably put together. They cite Kennedy's nine-hour motorcade through industrial northwestern Indiana where he rode in an open convertible through crowded streets, flanked by Richard Hatcher, the black mayor of Gary, and Tony Zale, the Slavic former middleweight world champion from Gary. "Here," reporter Jules Witcover later wrote, "was the black and blue-collar coalition that was at the core of Kennedy's political base." Or in the description of his biographer Jack Newfield: "Together, the three men, in a pose symbolizing the Kennedy alliance that might have been, clung to each other's waists, standing on the back seat of the convertible, waving to the cheering citizens of the city that so recently seemed at the edge of a race war."[7]

The spin applied by Kennedy's aides had the desired effect on the media. On election day the *New York Times* reported that "In the areas surrounding Gary, Mr. Kennedy has found substantial support in the white working class wards that went heavily to George Wallace in 1964. Some of those voters indicated to reporters that although Mr. Kennedy had the Negro vote they looked upon him as a tough Irishman with whom they could identify."[8] These voters may have been influenced by the half-hour TV commercials Kennedy ran the night before the election stressing his law enforcement credentials and his support for local control over federal programs. Other commentators picked up on this interpretation of the election results, and over time it has become a critical part of the Kennedy legend: the dream coalition that might have been.

But on analysis it has turned out to be a combination of wishful thinking, misperception, and spin control. The notion that Kennedy was the candidate of the white working class, as well as of the blacks, seems to have originated with a post–election day column by Rowland Evans and Robert Novak in which they credited him with "running two-to-one ahead in some Polish districts" in Gary. It was reinforced by statements such as those of Newfield, who wrote that Kennedy "carried the seven backlash counties that George Wallace had won in 1964," and by Jules Witcover's claim that he got "more than the usual number of blue collar whites for a Democrat in the backlash neighborhoods."[9]

But in fact Kennedy ran two-to-one ahead of his opponents in only two Gary precincts and took only eleven of seventy white precincts. Although he carried industrial Lake County, which went for Wallace in 1964, his 15,500-vote margin over McCarthy came almost entirely from the black voters of Gary. Of the fifteen other Lake County cities and townships that Wallace carried four years earlier, McCarthy took thirteen and Kennedy only one. Of Kennedy's total vote in Gary, 80 percent came from blacks. In the seventy Gary precincts where the white voters live, Kennedy got only 34 percent, compared to McCarthy's 49 percent and Branigan's 17 percent.

As William vanden Heuvel, Kennedy aide and self-described "close friend and political associate," and Milton Gwirtzman, Kennedy's issue man for the 1968 campaign, write in their book on Kennedy's Senate years: "The lesson of Lake County, then, was that the more personally involved the white voters were with the racial struggle, the more they identified Kennedy with the black side of it, and turned to his opponents as an outlet for their protest." It was, they admit, a misconception to claim that he had won over the white working class, but "the Kennedy organization believed the misconception and encouraged it."[10]

Kennedy himself spoke as though he believed it. When asked by Newfield what he thought the Indiana vote meant, he replied: "That I really have a chance now, just a chance, to organize a new coalition of Negroes and working-class white people, against the union and party Establishments."[11] To blacks he had spoken with such compassion and empathy that few seemed to mind that he wanted to curtail severely the big federal welfare and housing programs designed to benefit them. They rewarded him with a remarkable 86 percent of their votes.

According to the Harris-*Newsweek* analysis, his entire margin of victory was won in the cities, where he bested McCarthy 54 to 28 percent, and among Catholics, whom he swept by 50 to 28 percent. However, he finished in last place among professionals, with 24 percent of the vote, against 36 percent for McCarthy and 35 percent for Branigan — although he took 48 percent of the industrial-worker vote. His sharp criticism of welfare, advocacy of stern law-and-order policies, and opposition to federal programs alienated the most affluent, who gave him only 27 percent of their vote. Among the best educated he finished in last place.[12]

While his strenuous campaign had brought out black voters in great numbers, and those whites responsive to a Kennedy legend, it had not attracted enough blue-collar Democrats to impress party leaders. All in all it was, as the *New York*

Times concluded editorially, "An Inconclusive Victory."

Equally importantly, it was not a victory that knocked McCarthy out of the race. Only a more decisive Kennedy margin, cutting deeper into the white middle-class vote, could have done that. McCarthy was, in fact, encouraged by the results. He was, he told Witcover, the only Democrat who could pull in enough independents and suburbanites to win, whereas almost any Democrat could rally blacks and blue-collar voters against Nixon.[13]

The real prize lay in California, with its early June primary just a month away, preceded by primaries in Nebraska and in Oregon. McCarthy, who thought he had a chance of actually taking Oregon, devoted only one day to Nebraska. Kennedy, by contrast, blitzed the state, determined to show that he could appeal even to farmers. He succeeded, taking 52 percent of the vote, with overwhelming support from blacks in Omaha. McCarthy, who had hardly campaigned, took 31 percent, performing well in the suburbs and small towns.

Kennedy went on to Oregon for the primary of May 28 with serious problems. A prosperous and tranquil state with relatively few blacks or blue-collar ethnics, Oregon lacked the urban tensions and seething sense of injustices on which Kennedy thrived. His staff denigrated it as "one vast suburb." By this they (mostly suburbanites themselves) meant that Oregonians were predominantly, like most Americans, middle-class whites. For a candidate who boasted that "I do best among people who have problems," this was not ideal Kennedy country. To speak disparagingly of it for its lack of problems, as vanden Heuvel and Gwirtzman observe, not only ignored the liberal sympathies of Oregon voters, but also "assumes the candidate of 'reconciliation' needed votes from the poor and black to cancel out opposition from the middle class."[14]

Oregonians seemed to have few problems that a presidential candidate could convincingly promise to resolve, other than the war that had become deeply unpopular, and had been denounced for years by their independent-minded senator, Wayne Morse. For this reason McCarthy's willingness to take on Johnson when no one else dared had won him particular credit in the face of Kennedy's calculating indecision. In other ways as well McCarthy seemed attuned to Oregon voters: his wry sense of humor, his professorial demeanor, his quirky independence, and his irreverence toward the usual platitudes. For many young people in the Aquarian age of peace and love, the fact that he lacked Kennedy's aggressive toughness worked in his favor.

On the issue of Vietnam, McCarthy was by far the more radical candidate. Although Kennedy had criticized the way the war was being fought and had spoken vaguely of a compromise settlement, McCarthy attacked both the war itself and the mentality of those — including the Kennedys — who had conceived it. "Involvement in Vietnam was no accident," he charged to a huge and enthusiastic rally in Portland, but was inspired by "the idea that somehow we had a great moral mission to control the entire world." This was clearly a direct jab at Kennedy's declaration, in announcing his run for the presidency, of "our right to moral leadership of this planet." Only the labels had changed since the days of John Foster Dulles in the early 1950s, he insisted. "Instead of containment it is counterinsurgency . . . the same diplomacy assuming for itself the role of the world's judge and the world's policeman." Bobby, of course, had been the Kennedy administration's most ardent promoter of counterinsurgency to combat communism in the Third World.[15]

This kind of attack struck not only at Bobby, but even at the hallowed JFK, who in death had been elevated beyond criticism. It enraged the Kennedy loyalists who were continually proclaiming that their candidate represented a new kind of politics — one that had gone beyond the stale formulas of the New Deal and the Cold War. It raised the disturbing question of whether the "new Bobby" was really much different from the "old Bobby," and in doing so struck at the emotional commitment that the "band of brothers" had made to their chosen leader. For this reason Kennedy's inner circle not only treated McCarthy with more than the usual contempt they reserved for political opponents, but also failed to understand the nature of his appeal.

Nor did they know how to deal with the kind of voters — mostly white, middle-class, and essentially optimistic — that they found in Oregon. Their circuslike mass rallies and parades — with the bands, noise, screaming crowds, and eager arms reaching out to touch the candidate — did not work there. Kennedy also made a bad mistake in turning down McCarthy's invitation to debate him on television, just as he had turned down Keating when he ran for the Senate in 1964. By indicating that he thought McCarthy too lowly to be treated as an equal, he came across as arrogant — and to some even cowardly.

Instead of joining McCarthy at the TV studio, he assembled a crew of press photographers for a walk along a windswept beach. Then he suddenly stripped to his shorts and plunged into the Pacific, still icy at that time of year. This was not a performance that impressed sober Oregonians. But the techniques he had tried in Indiana among the ethnic voters were not working either. The crowds came out, but instead of screaming they applauded politely and smiled inscrutably.

By the final days of the campaign it became clear that he was locked into his core constituency of blacks, Hispanics, some blue-collar ethnics, and Camelot sentimentalists. He ran a dispirited campaign, with frequent disappearances to California, whose big primary was only a week later. At one point he blurted out to a reporter, in a remark he soon regretted: "If I get beaten in any primary, I am not a very viable candidate." To this McCarthy quipped that "Bobby threatened to hold his breath unless the people of Oregon voted for him."[16]

Privately McCarthy was more charitable, but in a way more devastating. "He's in a tough spot . . . I feel kind of sorry for him," he told an associate. "When Jack Kennedy ran for president he figured if he didn't make it, life would go on somehow." As the campaign wound down and defeat loomed, the spirit seemed to go out of Bobby. "When he'd read the writing upon the wall," one reporter noted, "Bobby's public facade betrayed an inner devastation; his grins were wan, often desolate."

He seemed to recognize what his acolytes shrank from facing: that perhaps the Kennedy magic had worn off. For a charismatic leader this is dangerous, since the devotion of his followers depends upon continual success. Failure is fatal: it indicates that the leader is a false prophet, or one who has lost his "divine grace." At that point his career is finished. For this reason the results in Oregon were more disturbing for him than they would have been for another politician. Over twenty-seven consecutive elections no Kennedy had ever been defeated. Bobby was. He got only 39 percent of the vote to McCarthy's 45 percent.

The Kennedyites consoled themselves by maintaining that Oregon was an anomaly because it had so few blacks and blue-collar ethnics. But similarly it could be said that Gary was the anomaly. Kennedy, putting his own twist on it, told reporters that party leaders "will use Oregon as an excuse for not supporting me," as though they needed an excuse. The real beneficiary, he mused, would be the party leaders' favorite, Hubert Humphrey. The vice president had earlier been awarded two-thirds of Pennsylvania's delegates by the state party committee, even though McCarthy beat him eight to one in the state's primary.

The way Kennedy saw it, however, it was McCarthy, not he himself as the latecomer, who was the spoiler. "I think what he wanted most was to knock me off," he said of McCarthy. "I guess he may hate me that much."[17] It was a curious remark from a man who always said that the only important thing in politics was winning. The Kennedys had always personalized politics, which is why they put such a premium on loyalty. His bitter comment also revealed the depths of the insecurities from which his aggressions sprang: the fear of rejection that fed his deeply buried self-doubts and led him to be so hostile and aggressive to those he found threatening. Whereas the "old Bobby" had been content with victory, the new one sought love as well. And he would do whatever he had to do to win both.

17

The End and the Beginning

Oregon had seriously dented Kennedy's image and slowed down the charisma machine. A defeat in California, a state that was America in microcosm, would knock him out of the race. If he could not win there he would be finished as a presidential candidate. The myth itself, which decreed his right to reclaim the throne, would be discredited. His pledged delegates, many of whom were Democratic party regulars, would likely switch over to Humphrey. But if he could pull off at least "an inconclusive victory," as in Indiana, the marathon would then move on to New York. Although he had strength in the state he represented, McCarthy's forces there were dedicated and energized. Each side had an impressive list of donors and celebrity endorsements.

Kennedy's hopes in California hinged on

rousing a huge turnout of black and Hispanic voters. Only in this way could he compensate for McCarthy's appeal to the white middle class. Kennedy was in his element among these people, and he played to their emotions as well as to their obvious affection for him. Flying to Los Angeles the morning after the dispiriting Oregon vote, he set off on an all-day motorcade across the city. In the Chicano barrios east of downtown and in the canyons of the central city, he rode standing in an open convertible, anchored to the back seat by husky aides, hailed like the votive effigy of a saint in some ancient religious procession.

Women stuck their babies in his face, teenage girls grabbed at his clothes and screamed, men tried to pull him from his car. The reception was of the kind given to an emperor or a film star, and the crowds were roused to even higher pitches of emotion by the music and the loudspeakers and the ticker tape provided by the advance men. In the shouting, exultant people who surged around him and tore at his clothes in hopes of gaining the holy relic of a button or cuff link, one could imagine the crowds that with equal fervor had greeted earlier political messiahs.

Kennedy alone among American politicians at that time could have inspired such feverish displays of emotion. It was an impressive, even a moving, spectacle. Yet it was also disturbing, particularly to white middle-class voters. As Theodore White writes in his study of the 1968 election, "Carried away by his own emotions and their echo among the volatile, cheering young, he could not quite grasp how television outlined his figure on the forty-second and one-minute snatches of evening news where the larger, national, mature audience saw him: hysterical, high-pitched, hair blowing in the wind, almost demoniac, frightening. In short, the ruthless, vindictive Bobby Kennedy again, action without thought, position without plan." When pollsters asked respondents to react to the statement: "Robert Kennedy is the man who can bring peace to the cities," 71 percent disagreed.[1]

Kennedy made a greater effort to connect with Hispanics than with any other group. They seemed as needy as blacks, but were not split into bitterly contentious rival factions. They were at that time not as numerous or as politically influential. But by espousing their cause when no other major white politician did, he won their undying loyalty — and their votes, which were crucial in a close election. Also, by supporting Cesar Chavez's grape-pickers union, he was able to counter the image, strongly held by most union leaders, that he was anti-labor.

California Hispanics were impressed that in early March, on the eve of the critical New Hampshire primary, when trying to decide whether to enter the race, he had flown to California's Central Valley to celebrate the end of Chavez's protest fast against the grape growers. They also recalled that in 1966 he had brought his Senate subcommittee on migratory labor there to hold hearings on the bitter struggle between labor and management. The loyalty of Mexican-Americans to him was evident when he returned to California to fight for its convention delegates. In some precincts he took 100 percent of their vote. This was a critical element of his narrow victory over McCarthy in the state.

If Kennedy had won the hearts of Latinos, Indians, and blacks — all the people who, in his words, "have problems" — he lost the college students who should have been at the heart of his campaign. He alienated the most idealistic among them by failing to put his principles above politics, and he never got them back. These were the students who had left their campuses in March to ring doorbells, stuff envelopes, and drive voters to the polls in New Hampshire. And these were the people who, along with their professors, and often their parents, formed a volunteer army and made up the McCarthy delegate slate in California.

Kennedy could never quite reconcile himself to the fact that he had lost them — and had done so by his own failure to act on his principles. Instead of an army of idealistic amateurs he had an agglomeration of activists and professionals ranging from the iconoclastic SDS radical Tom Hayden to the politically agile Daniel Patrick Moynihan, who later went on to serve in the Nixon administration. His delegate slate, which had been put together by the old California pro Jesse Unruh was derided by the antiwar Peace and Freedom party as being a collection of political hacks who shared none of Kennedy's proclaimed views. In a state where radical sentiment was running high, this cut sharply into his support.

Although Kennedy had not wanted to debate McCarthy on TV in California, he felt that he had no choice after his defeat in Oregon. He could hardly claim that McCarthy was not a serious candidate. He prepared for the June 1 event — just three days before the crucial vote — like a prize-fighter, going over all the issues and responses with his aides. McCarthy, diffident and self-assured as always, was relaxed and casual to a point that disturbed his aides.

McCarthy took the first question. Asked what he would do differently in Vietnam, he stated that a negotiated settlement required a new government in Saigon that would include the communist-dominated National Liberation Front. There was nothing exceptional in this remark. Kennedy had been saying more or less the same thing for two years. In February 1966, for example, regarding the front and other such "discontented elements," Kennedy had said that "to admit them to a share of power and responsibility is at the heart of the hope for a negotiated settlement" and that this might "mean a compromise government fully acceptable to neither side."[2]

But, now sensing that he was in trouble, Kennedy dropped his good manners and pounced on a vulnerable spot in McCarthy's response. Invoking the "old Bobby," he accused his rival of "forcing a coalition" on the Saigon government. It was a cheap shot, and McCarthy denied that he was trying to force anything. In effect the two men were in agreement on a coalition. Kennedy's reaction was the kind for which the "old Bobby" was well known. He apparently had not been put to rest.

This became clear when the focus switched to the urban crisis. A few days earlier in a major policy speech at Davis, McCarthy had challenged Kennedy's proposal to build up the ghettos with private capital and to turn over political control to local groups. McCarthy charged that this plan, by keeping people locked in the ghettos and giving power to black separatists, would simply intensify the "growing isolation of the poor" and perpetuate segregation. Instead he urged a massive federal program to build low-income housing outside as well as inside the ghettos, along with a mass transport network to allow its inhabitants to reach jobs in other parts of their cities.

McCarthy's position was actually more radical than Kennedy's, for it meant breaking up the ghettos rather than making them more habitable. Proposing that the nation build a million houses a year for low-income people, McCarthy declared that blacks and other racial minorities had been kept as a "colonial nation living in our midst."

Stung by this critique of its urban program, Kennedy's staff hurriedly put out a detailed retort, citing the Bedford-Stuyvesant experiment as a star example of how run-down areas could be restored to life. But their emphasis was still on making the ghettos better, whereas McCarthy's proposal was to break them up and integrate their inhabitants into the larger community. In this sense not only was it more radical, but also more threatening to racial separatists, both black and white.

Turning to this subject the moderator reminded Kennedy that he had "been telling campaign audiences that if you become president you're going to do away with riots and violence in this country, that they simply won't be tolerated," and asked specifically how he hoped to accomplish this. In response Kennedy went through the litany he had been repeating to white audiences: "as attorney general I was the chief law enforcement officer . . . violence and rioting and lawlessness cannot be tolerated in the United States." And he recalled how he "kept a mob under control at the University of Alabama" and his "experience in dealing with these kinds of problems."

He then spoke of his walks in the ghettos and barrios and how he told the people there that "we can't solve these problems overnight, they cannot be solved by violence and lawlessness." Instead he stressed the need for "bringing the private sector in in a major way and hiring people, doing away as much as possible with the welfare system, the handout of the dole, and getting people jobs by giving the private sector tax incentives and tax credits." This is what he had been saying for some time, particularly to white audiences.

But McCarthy kept arguing that trying to get private industry to rebuild the ghettos was not going to solve the problems of jobs, housing, and training. "We have to get into the suburbs, too, with this kind of housing, because . . . most of the employment is now in the belt line outside of the cities, and I don't think we ought to perpetuate the ghetto . . . ," McCarthy insisted. "Otherwise we are adopting a kind of apartheid in this country."

Sensing an opening, Kennedy jumped for the jugular. "We have 40 million

Negroes who are in the ghettos at the present time . . . ," he declared. "You say you are going to take ten thousand black people and move them into Orange County* . . . in the suburbs where they can't afford the housing, where their children can't keep up with the schools, and where they don't have the skills for the jobs, it is just going to be catastrophic."

It was a demagogic retort that distorted what McCarthy had said, clearly intended to frighten white suburbanites and turn them against his challenger. And Kennedy made his racist appeal in a way cleverly designed to seem like a concern for the welfare of blacks. Even the admiring Witcover described it as "political thuggery."[3] Only Kennedy could make such a remark and not be accused of racism. And he could get away with it because he had persuaded black people, by his visits to ghettos and by the eloquent words his speechwriters had crafted for him, that his heart was with them.

For the most part he won them by sentiment and gestures rather than, like McCarthy, by espousing the kinds of programs that would have offended middle-

* *A conservative middle-class suburban area.*

class whites. Kennedy's actual proposals, however, as distinct from his rhetoric, were hardly radical, or even liberal. It was not without reason Ronald Reagan observed that Kennedy was talking "more and more like me"[4] or that some black separatists thought that he would cooperate with them. He was, after all, critical of welfare, school busing to achieve integration, a guaranteed income, national health insurance, and job preferences. Unlike McCarthy he did not make a fundamental critique of the men and policies that had taken the nation into the Vietnam War, nor of the structural causes of endemic poverty. But he was a master of the art of the personal gesture. His rhetoric was emotional and heart-moving. This served him well in the black community, which enthusiastically delivered its votes to him.

Whether, if implemented, his program would have been more successful than those of the kind that Johnson had attempted to pursue under his Great Society plan, or than McCarthy's more radical alternative, remains a matter of dispute. Certainly by 1968 the general public had soured on costly federal programs to attack poverty, and has largely remained so to this day. Ronald Reagan and Bill

Clinton responded to that public weariness with great electoral success.

But many liberals believe that Kennedy, had he lived, would have done it differently. He would, they maintain, have married his compassion with a "muscular liberalism" that would have encouraged self-reliance among the poor, and persuaded private enterprise to rebuild the ghetto. But this rests on faith. Bedford-Stuyvesant, the one place Kennedy's plan was tried, attracted private investors largely because of his personal connections and had no effect on the larger problem of poverty in New York, let alone in other cities with large, impoverished ghettos. Indeed when Kennedy's friend Jack Newfield visited Bedford-Stuyvesant at the end of the year he wrote that the project was faltering and that corporate investors had lost interest.[5]

Kennedy no doubt wanted to help black Americans. He was appalled, as anyone would be, by the waste, violence, and despair of the ghetto. Perhaps his program was the only politically feasible one at the time. It certainly was the one that had the most appeal to middle-class white voters fed up with Lyndon Johnson's War on Poverty and on Vietnamese communists. But instead of taking McCarthy's critique seriously and debating it honestly, as such a critical issue deserved, he fobbed it off by a thinly disguised appeal to the very fears and prejudices he was ostensibly trying to alleviate. It was the old Kennedy imperative, imbued in childhood: winning was all that mattered. This was not his finest moment.

The debate marked for all purposes the end of the campaign. The general consensus among the reporters was that Kennedy had "won" it because of his aggressiveness, and that McCarthy had been surprisingly mild in responding to what even Kennedy's friend Arthur Schlesinger admitted was a "demagogic" provocation.[6]

Kennedy spent the final night of the campaign with his wife and six of their children at the Malibu beach house of one of their Hollywood friends. As the returns came in on polling day, June 4, it became clear that although McCarthy had taken San Francisco, the northern part of the state, San Diego in the south, and the predominantly white suburban areas, he had not done so by enough votes to offset Kennedy's advantage in Los Angeles County. A huge turnout by African- and Mexican-Americans gave him his 150,000-vote margin, out of nearly 2.8 million votes cast.

As in Indiana he did not — popular mythology notwithstanding — ride the crest of a black-poor white coalition. There was, in fact, no such coalition. It was his cooperation with Chavez and black leaders, and his appearances in the ghettos and the barrios that brought out record numbers of voters. In agricultural areas outside the Central Valley, in the north, and in smaller cities and suburbs, he did not do well at all. If he was going to take the Democratic nomination, somehow he would have to conceal from party chiefs his dependence on ethnic minorities. The "misconception" first spawned in Indiana would require continued spin of the media.

Whether this could have been done was problematical. Kennedy had expected at least 50 percent of the vote in California. Ending up as he did with only 46 percent, to McCarthy's 42 percent, many in the media would have considered that this was, as campaign aide Gwirtzman later said, "not the kind of impressive victory he needed to eliminate McCarthy as a credible candidate, and to hurl the gauntlet of 'I am the people's choice' in front of

Humphrey. And that, plus what was in store for him in New York, would have hurt his candidacy badly, in my judgment."[7]

New York was a strong state for McCarthy and he had a good chance of beating Kennedy there in the June 18 primary. This is why, according to Richard Goodwin, Kennedy said to him as the California votes were coming in: "I think we should tell him [McCarthy] if he withdraws now and supports me, I'll make him secretary of state."[8] Considering how both Bobby and JFK treated Secretary of State Dean Rusk, it is unlikely that McCarthy would have considered the job worth having. Nor, under any circumstances as he said, would he have turned his delegates over to Bobby — although he indicated later that he might have to either Ted Kennedy or to Humphrey.

But if Kennedy's victory was an inconclusive one, it did not feel like that in the ballroom of the Ambassador Hotel where some 1,500 volunteers and party workers had for four hours been listening to the projected returns on TV screens and waiting impatiently for their hero. Finally, a few minutes before midnight, he suddenly appeared at the dais and, like a

Roman emperor, received the adulation of the roaring crowd.

To the enchanted followers gathered there it seemed to be more than just the victory of their candidate. It was the gratification of a longing so intense that even this triumph seemed hardly capable of satisfying it. They wanted not only to honor and adore, but even to possess him. Such was the yearning among many in the nation at that time for a savior.

But crowds seized by such emotions are animals straining at their leashes, threatening at any moment to break loose. "I remember sensing almost a frightening suppressed violence in the way the crowd roared back at him," Milton Gwirtzman recalled. "I remember feeling this sort of mass crowd response which had built up to such a fever pitch, was almost too strong, dangerously strong, the crowd an object for a demagogue. I had never seen such an intensity in one room, in one election night, before or since."[9] What took place in that room was merely a concentrated version of what had been going on in the barrios and ghettos for months whenever Kennedy appeared and pleaded for help. It was impressive, and it was also frightening. If some people could surrender themselves to such paroxysms of adoration, others could just as intensely be consumed with hate.*

Kennedy was as aware as anyone of the risks he was running. The danger of assassination was never far from his mind, but rather than avoiding it by running a less emotional campaign, or surrounding himself with guards, or even taking elementary security precautions, he deliberately fomented hysteria as an electoral device, plunging into the crowds his advance men organized, standing up in open convertibles, presenting his body to the crowds as virtually a sacrificial offering. "If I'm ever elected president, I'm never going to ride in one of those bubble-top cars," he told a reporter in a strange, perhaps only partially conscious, reference to the manner in which his brother had been killed.

"You've just got to give yourself to the people and to trust them, and from then on . . . either [luck is] with you or it isn't," he said to author Romain Gary. "I am pretty sure there'll be an attempt on my

* *Kennedy had long been a target for hatred. A Gallup poll in May 1967 showed his "intensely disliked" rating to be more than 50 percent higher than Johnson's.*[10]

life sooner or later. Not so much for political reasons. . . . Plain nuttiness, that's all." On the night of the death of Martin Luther King he admitted to an aide that "it makes me wonder what they might do to me, too."[11] Yet he never let whatever anxieties he felt prevent him from trying to fulfill what he believed to be an inescapable destiny. He had found a meaning for his life in the creation and now the fulfillment of a Kennedy legend. It was that, rather than any political program or personal glory, that drove him on. What he was seeking lay beyond electoral victory. It could not be satisfied by anything less than immortalization.

To those who had worked for him in the campaign, he spoke only a few words that night, thanking them for their help and assuring them that they were foot soldiers in a crusade by which he would somehow remake America. "I think we can end the divisions in the United States . . . the violence, the disenchantment with our society, the divisions, whether it's between blacks and whites, between the poor and the more affluent, or between age groups, or over the war in Vietnam — that we can start to work together again. We are a great country, an unselfish country, and a compassionate country," he concluded with vague reassurance. ". . . So my thanks to all of you, and it's on to Chicago, and let's win there."[12]

Then suddenly he was gone, spirited by his aides into a pantry that would allow him to bypass the crowd and go directly to the room where the media were waiting for his victory interview. And then he was to take his aides and Ethel to a discotheque for a celebration party.

Had there not been such pandemonium in the ballroom the campaign workers might have heard the eight pistol shots that echoed from the pantry, or the screams that followed. But they learned in a moment. The assassin's bullet had exploded in his brain, just as it had in his brother's less than five years earlier. He lingered on in the hospital for another twenty-five hours. A little before two in the morning of June 6 he passed into history. His life was over. But already the powerful legend he had been working to fulfill was being born.

18

The Bobby Myth

President Johnson arranged for Kennedy's body to be flown to New York in an official jet. There it lay in St. Patrick's Cathedral, where the great and the humble came to pay tribute. Early in the morning of June 7 the people began to arrive, and by the end of the day more than 100,000 of all ages and descriptions, waiting in a line at times a mile long for as much as eight hours in the summer heat, had filed past the bier.

Following the funeral on the morning of the eighth, nearly a thousand people — family, friends, journalists, big shots, publicity hounds, and hangers-on — went to Penn Station to board the special train to Washington for the burial at Arlington Cemetery. The journey was supposed to take four hours; it lasted eight and a half as the train wended its way for 225 miles down tracks lined on both sides by people who had come from their homes to watch and to honor.

The scene resembled the passing of a feudal chief before his assembled subjects. The other America, the people without glamour — housewives in hair curlers, nurses in starched dresses, schoolchildren, factory workers in overalls — came to the tracks for the last journey of Robert Kennedy. "I seen people running all over!" an electrician exclaimed. "They were running toward the train. They tried to touch the train as it went by. . . . A lot of people crying. I seen *nuns* from all around with signs like REST IN PEACE, ROBERT AND I'LL PRAY FOR YOU. A lot of nuns! . . . I seen one fellow there with a gun! He was like he was on guard. . . . He just stood there at attention."

Another train worker reported: "Everyone had a rose or a banner. They were throwing roses at the train. . . . People were praying. The men had their hats off. They were crossing themselves. . . . The signs read, WHO WILL BE THE NEXT ONE? and WE HAVE LOST OUR LAST HOPE. These were signs the colored had. It was mostly whites that had the signs that said, GOOD-BY BOBBY and WE STILL LOVE YOU. Further along a suburban family — a man and a woman in shorts, and two young children — stood next to their station wagon holding up a sign that said simply THE GEBHARTS ARE SAD."[1]

Like an immense coffin on wheels the train rolled on through the long summer day and into the evening, past the sad Gebharts, and the nuns with their sunglasses and rosaries, and the Boy Scouts in uniform, and the saluting Legionnaires, and the people who put coins on the tracks to be flattened into souvenirs, and those who threw roses, and those who softly sang the "Battle Hymn of the Republic."

They were informed, if they had not realized it already, that this was the end of an era. Dick Tuck, the campaign wit, summed it up soberly: "Camelot is ended. It began in violence and ended in violence. It began with John Kennedy's death, not before, and it ended with Bob Kennedy's assassination. It will never exist again, whether Ted gets to be president or not."[2]

Robert Kennedy's death was mourned not like that of a politician seeking his party's nomination for a run at the White House, but like that of a revered leader. Once again television, as it had four and a half years earlier, provided not only a description of the funeral, but a quasi-religious context in which the public — through endless repetition of the details of the event, and pontifical explanations by various shamans and "experts" — could be apprised of its deeper significance, while being reassured that the nation would survive this tragedy by honoring the dead man's memory.

Genuine sorrow was mixed with a media-driven pathos that inevitably descended into portentous morbidity and even banality. As they were to do in later decades with the deaths of other Kennedys, commentators vied in their efforts to sanctify the victim (while embellishing their own personal connection to him) and to deplore the moral condition of a people among whom such terrible things could happen.

Columnist James Reston set the tone for the general morbidity in interpreting the event not as the effort of a deranged young assassin to achieve his immortality, but as demonstration of a "world morality crisis" marked by a "defiance of authority, a contagious irresponsibility, a kind of moral delinquency no longer restrained by religious or ethical faith." Kennedy's admirer, journalist Jack Newfield, declared that "from this time forward, things would get worse" now that his generation had lost its leader, and lamented in a portentous metaphor lifted from Camus, "The stone was at the bottom of the hill and we were alone."[3]

Because much of the mourning was based upon the assumption that Kennedy would have been nominated, there was among many the sense that a future president, a redemptive president, had been lost. Yet there is reason to question such a course of events. His victory in California was another inconclusive one, much narrower than he hoped for, and not nearly big enough to finish off McCarthy. In fact, from McCarthy's point of view the results were ideal. Had McCarthy won the primary, Kennedy would have dropped out of the race and his delegates would have drifted over to Humphrey, thereby assuring the vice president's nomination. McCarthy's only hope was that a three-way deadlock in Chicago would induce party bosses to compromise on him.

One factor in their decision was the upcoming New York primary on June 18. McCarthy had a strong and dedicated following in the state and, unlike Kennedy, few political enemies. He also would have been a stronger candidate nationally among moderates, independents, and mugwump Republicans unable to swallow Nixon than either Kennedy or Humphrey.

Since most of the convention delegates would be chosen not in primaries but by party officials, Kennedy put his own chances at only 50 percent. For a real chance at the nomination he had to sweep the remaining primaries and somehow conceal from party leaders how dependent he was on black voters.

Furthermore, the assumption that George Wallace's supporters were planning to vote for Kennedy but not for any other Democrat is not persuasive. Since Humphrey in the 1968 election easily carried blue-collar areas like Lake County, Indiana (by 47 percent to Nixon's 36 percent and Wallace's 16 percent), "the hard evidence that Kennedy was the first choice of many Wallace voters remains thin," Brian Dooley has written in his informative study of Kennedy's final years.[4]

But even his nomination was hardly a sure thing. He was hated by the powerful southern faction within the party, distrusted by many liberals, opposed by organized labor, and resented by Democratic loyalists for fracturing party unity. His strongest support — among blacks, the poor, and the alienated — lay outside the party's power structure. Thus they would have been relatively ineffective at the convention.

"Couldn't they see," said campaign director Lawrence O'Brien, "he didn't have a chance?" In any case it would have been a tough battle. As journalist Tom Wicker explained: "At one and the same time he wanted to have Mayor Daley's support and the support of the college students. The two are incompatible in the long run . . . it isn't a feasible alliance, and it isn't an alliance that's going to hold political power."[5]

Even if he had been elected, what would he have done as president? What exactly was it that "might have been"? All that we can go by is what he *did* when, as his brother's deputy, he had power — and then by what he *said* when, as Johnson's enemy, he was out of power. As attorney general he was a law enforcer who cracked down on organized crime and came late and grudgingly, though ultimately decisively, to the protection of civil rights. As his brother's unofficial foreign policy adviser he was an ardent and conventional cold warrior. As a U.S. senator he was primarily a candidate for the presidency.

We are informed that he underwent a profound "transformation" following his brother's death that sensitized him to the plight of life's victims. It is difficult to know what to make of assurances of such psychological changes, if indeed they did occur. Certainly he began to speak in moving terms about the problems of the poor, and of racial and ethnic minorities. However, beyond his undoubtedly sincere empathy for such people, and his often-cited declarations that the deplorable conditions in which they lived were "not acceptable," his remedies for dealing with their problems were quite modest.

One should not confuse Kennedy's actions, or his feelings, with the changes in his rhetoric that took place after his entry into the Senate — and even less with the rhetoric of those who wrote for, and about, him. The "transformation" that journalists and admirers discerned in Robert Kennedy once he was on his own might have been real. On the other hand, it might equally have been merely evidence of different speechwriters or new political tactics inspired by the results of opinion polls. Just as JFK's speeches were geared to an Augustan era of great expectations, so Bobby's, with equally sensitive timing, reflected and played upon mid-sixties anxiety. Both men were honored, and are today remembered, more for what they said than for what they actually did.

It is impossible to know what kind of president Robert Kennedy would have been or what policies he would have pursued. Had he been elected, which is far from certain, many admirers would have been disappointed. Although he would probably have worked out some means of extrication from Vietnam earlier than Nixon did, his opposition to unilateral withdrawal and his vague formulas for a negotiated settlement hardly differed from Nixon's "peace with honor" formula.

On domestic policy, his anti-poverty plan was far less radical than McCarthy's, and was essentially designed to get private investors to gild the ghetto so that it would be more tolerable for its inhabitants, not to make it easier for them to live and work elsewhere. The Bedford-Stuyvesant laboratory to which he had devoted much attention helped stabilize the neighborhood, but failed to gain the business investment needed to provide jobs. As a national program to attack the causes of poverty, or as a means of breaking down segregation, it was insignificant.

He likely would also have disillusioned the white radicals who found him a "rebel" because he was youthful, let his hair grow longer, and expressed an interest in their music. He was at heart, and had always been, a Catholic conservative deeply suspicious of the moral license of the radical left, with its celebration of drugs, sexual anarchy, and politics as theater. He was no champion of women's rights, and would likely have been appalled by the very notion of gay liberation, had he ever been confronted with it.

He has become a hero to millions not for what he did, but because he was the ghost of his sanctified brother, and many were persuaded that he would have done things that they desperately wanted. But had he ever gained the high power he sought, he would have had to stop being a challenger and become an administrator, to shed his charisma as redeemer and become a constitutional leader within a bureaucratically confined order. Instead of being the "tribune" of the underclass, he would have had to become what every president ultimately is: a power broker. Signs of this were apparent in his 1968 campaign, for those willing to see them.

A product of troubled times and heir to a thwarted legend, he became a hero to millions who were looking for a hero. But we should be wary of such a yearning. People have a need for heroes, particularly during times of trouble. To escape situations they deem to be intolerable they are willing to suspend disbelief and even surrender their will. The yearning for heroes is deeply embedded in our culture, and perhaps in our consciousness. "Unhappy is the land that breeds no hero," says one of the characters in a play by Bertolt Brecht. "No, Andrea," replies the scientist Galileo, soon to become a martyr to fear and superstition. "Unhappy is the land that needs a hero."

The need to follow, to serve, and to worship is not a healthy thing in a people. Heroes are granted license to do things that men of less exalted reputation, or ambitions, would shrink from. Julius Caesar began, after all, as a hero, and then was deemed a tyrant, only to be transformed back into a hero again by the demagogic interpretation put on his assassination. Napoleon Bonaparte, too, was a hero acclaimed throughout Europe as a liberator until he donned an imperial mantle and began losing battles — thereby losing his vaunted charisma as well. Stalin was for many Russians a hero, as was Hitler to Germans.

Passing time and increasing disillusion with the politicians we have lead us to embellish past events as moments of glory, and to inflate certain figures — particularly dashing, youthful ones cut down in their prime — as tragic heroes. In 1968, Americans were desperately searching for a hero. Robert Kennedy offered himself and millions responded. They saw him as one who would deliver the promise aroused by the rhetoric of his brother, who by this time they had already elevated above the level of mortal men.

This is the Robert Kennedy we honor and whom we have created to fulfill our own needs. In this sense he has become "our Bobby," because of what he was, but more because of what we wanted him to be. He himself seemed not always sure of who he was. A narrow and rigid man, he came near the end of his life to have an awareness of moral complexities that both deepened and troubled him. In the end he seemed no longer the dogmatist he had been. But neither was he the moral redeemer that many saw in him.

He was a man embarked on a journey he did not fully understand. He had been driven to it by forces beyond his control, and had good reason to feel that he would never arrive at an only dimly glimpsed destination. He had done dark deeds, and there was a part of his character, reinforced by his fierce brand of Irish Catholicism, that drove him to seek atonement for them. He had become, as in Robert Frost's melancholy poem that JFK liked to quote, "one acquainted with the night." He was always driving himself to feats of endurance, to gratuitous dangers, to acts of penance toward those less privileged, and ultimately to a political quest whose deepest purpose he only half understood himself.

Ultimately he learned to go through a politician's motions during his last campaign, for he was a tireless worker in whatever task he set for himself. He did everything that had to be done, and even more. But he did not seem to enjoy it much. Watching him those last weeks, both feeding and recoiling from the impassioned crowds that seemed to want to take home a piece of him, he appeared to be carrying out an onerous but inescapable duty.

"To the fervor and adulation of his supporters," the *New York Times* reported just after his narrow victory in the California primary election, "he seemed curiously aloof, exhibiting neither pleasure nor fright. Those close to Mr. Kennedy noticed that his eyes rarely sparkled, but instead were sad and withdrawn, and that his manner, despite a grin, was unemotional."

Some have said, reading backwards from the tragic ending of his life, that disaster was inevitable. "Doom was woven in your nerves," Robert Lowell writes in a posthumous poem to him. "He felt he was doomed, and you knew that he felt that," the poet later explained.[6] Perhaps. But such phrases seem meaningful only after an event. It is enough to say that, even during his campaign for the presidency, it seems likely that the future, whatever it held, would not bring him an easy pleasure.

There was a sense of the obligatory about his last campaign. He had dallied for months before committing himself to making the race for president, continually finding reasons the moment was inopportune, publicly anguishing over the decision. It was as though he were looking for a way to be relieved of the burden. Like a man who finally understood that there was no escape from his fate, he embraced it not with excitement but resignation.

This resignation was reflected in his compulsive risk-taking, his fatalism, his offering of his unprotected body to emotionally aroused crowds, and by his willful indifference to physical security. When asked during the 1968 campaign whether he worried about what would happen to his family if he were shot, he replied: "But they're well taken care of, and there's really nothing else I can do, is there? So I really don't care about anything happening to me. This really isn't such a happy existence, is it?"[7]

This is not to claim that he had a conscious death wish, but rather that in this religious and often pessimistic man there was what educator Michael Novak has called a "quest for martyrdom"[8] rooted in his puritan character. To become a martyr was in the most literal sense to become one with his brother, with whom he was bound by an iron sense of guilt and obligation. It was to compensate for his ruthless drive to win, the other side of his vaunted and often insensitive pragmatism.

Semi-legendary figures like John and Robert Kennedy "represent the hero, handsome, courageous," artist Saul Steinberg noted on the funeral train. "They look for drama; and it attracts the counterpart. Just the way the hero is in search of a dragon, the dragon is always in search of a hero."[9] The mysteriously named Sirhan Sirhan was such a dragon. In that moment in a hotel pantry, very near where, weeks earlier, someone had written enigmatically on a wall, "The Once and Future King," he sought immortalization by slaying the immortal hero.

The mythology that has been generated around Robert Kennedy in the years since his death is simply that: a mythology. Like many legendary figures, the Bobby of legend has been created by us. There is little, beyond hope and need, to lead us to believe that he would have bridged the divisions between blacks and whites, narrowed the chasm between rich and poor, dedicated himself to the values that inspire liberals, quickly ended a divisive war, or brought about the magical restoration of a mythical golden age. Only from his early death have we, as with his brother, created a heroic figure to fill our needs.

Why, then, do so many honor him to this day? Because he generated a set of ideals that resonated deeply among Americans at a time of social crisis, and remain unfulfilled to this day. The very fact that his promise was never fully tested made it possible to believe that he would have been able to achieve the goals he espoused. Like his brother John he had the ability to inspire others, through his words more than his deeds, to hope and to acts of service.

Walter Lippmann, who had been an early supporter of John Kennedy and then had grown critical of his performance, wrote about the Kennedy "legend" at the time that Robert was deciding whether to run for president. He was impressed by the fact that millions had come to believe that the murdered president, despite an undistinguished record in office, was a herald of better things to come. This gave the columnist a new respect for the mythmaking process. "I am glad of that legend, and I think that it contains that part of the truth which is most worth having," he concluded in words that also apply to Robert Kennedy's "legend" today. "This is the conviction, for which he set the example, that a new age has begun and that men can become the masters of their fate."[10]

The best of Robert Kennedy was not in what he did, but in what he has inspired in others. As he told a convocation of university students in South Africa two years to the day before his death, it is crucial to recognize that "idealism, high aspirations, and deep convictions are not incompatible with the most practical and efficient of programs — that there is no basic inconsistency between ideals and realistic possibilities, no separation between the deepest desires of heart and of mind and the rational application of human effort to human problems."[11]

It was not his idealism that made him a more accessible and interesting figure than his brother John. Rather it was his efforts, near the end of his life, to compensate for his failings by identifying himself with the deprived. This gave him a romantic dimension suited to an era of powerful emotions.

More than any other politician of his time Robert Kennedy required, like the improbable scripts and personalities of grand opera, a suspension of disbelief. We have read into him what we have wanted to read. It is his very image as the renegade prince that has given him his allure. For millions he has represented not a rational political alternative, but something more powerful and attractive: an escape from politics. What people found in him was not political but emotional satisfaction. He did not inspire programs; he aroused feelings. The response he stimulated was not polite applause or mild disapproval, but love or hate. He had the compelling, and disturbing, appeal of a demagogue.

Among those who followed him, and later have yearned for him, there is the belief that he could have done miraculous things, that he would not have made the compromises of ordinary politicians, that he would not have disappointed. This belief came not from what he did or said, but from what he represented. It came from the "legend."

There is a danger with legends, and the heroes who embody them. They can paralyze as well as inspire. "The love of the hero," Emerson warned, "corrupts into worship of his statue."[12] Robert Kennedy had no answers that are, like an ancient Egyptian's treasured objects, buried with him. Rather he raised interesting questions, and in so doing, and with the often tormented passions he displayed, influenced many to participate in public affairs. The lesson that they drew from his life, however imperfectly he may have exemplified it, is that politics can be a worthy calling, that even the humblest person can make a difference, and that the greatest satisfaction can lie not in the indulgence of private pleasures but in pursuit of the public good. That is the part of the legend most worth remembering: not what he might have done, but what we can do.

Myths can inspire or they can imp
The important thing is that they lead
thought and action, not to idolatry.
Bobby Myth is our creation, not his.

Notes

1: An American Dream

1. John F. Harris, "Clinton Calls RFK a Personal Inspiration," *Washington Post*, June 5, 1998; Josh Getlin, "The Cult of Bobby," *Los Angeles Times*, Oct. 20, 1992.
2. Jonathan Yardley, "Missing Bobby," *Washington Post*, May 31, 1993; Harrington in Harris Wofford, *Of Kennedys and Kings* (Pittsburgh: University of Pittsburgh Press, 1992), p. 420; Marshall Frady, "The Transformation of Robert Kennedy," *New York Review of Books*, Oct. 12, 1978.
3. "Remembering Bobby," *New York Times*, June 7, 1998; Adam Walinsky, "Why We Search for RFK," ibid., June 5, 1988.
4. Frady; Garry Wills, *The Kennedy Imprisonment* (Boston: Atlantic Monthly Press, 1981), p. 94; Richard N.

Goodwin, *Remembering America* (New York: Harper & Row, 1988), p. 450; Wofford, p. 384; Jack Newfield, *Robert Kennedy: A Memoir* (New York: Bantam, 1970), p. 18; Galbraith in Arthur M. Schlesinger Jr., *Robert Kennedy and His Times* (New York: Ballantine, 1979), p. 869.

5. Todd Gitlin, *The Sixties* (New York: Bantam, 1987), p. 311; William L. O'Neill, *Coming Apart: An Informal History of America in the 1960's* (Chicago: Quadrangle, 1971), p. 374.

2: The Man Nobody Knew

1. Oriana Fallaci, "Robert Kennedy Answers Some Blunt Questions," *Look*, March 9, 1965.
2. "choirboy" in Nancy Gager Clinch, *The Kennedy Neurosis* (New York: Grosset & Dunlap, 1973), p. 260; Hans Morgenthau, "On Robert Kennedy," *New York Review of Books*, Aug. 1, 1968.
3. Arthur M. Schlesinger Jr., *Robert Kennedy and His Times* (New York: Ballantine, 1979), p. 348; Vidal in

Ralph de Toledano, *RFK: The Man Who Would Be President* (New York: Putnam, 1967), p. 12.

4. Harris Wofford, *Of Kennedys and Kings* (Pittsburgh: University of Pittsburgh Press, 1992), pp. 32, 420; Richard Harwood, "Bobby Kennedy and All That Might Have Been," *Washington Post*, June 13, 1988.
5. "time-bomb" in Henry Fairlie, *The Kennedy Promise* (Garden City, NY: Doubleday, 1973), pp. 350–51; "tragedy" in Wofford, p. 6; Fairlie, p. 351.

3: Family Values

1. trips in Nancy Gager Clinch, *The Kennedy Neurosis* (New York: Grosset & Dunlap, 1973), p. 77; "nothing" and Spalding in Peter Collier and David Horowitz, *The Kennedys* (New York: Warner, 1985), pp. 212, 242.
2. Arthur Krock, *Sixty Years on the Firing Line* (New York: Funk & Wagnalls, 1968), p. 348; Edwin O. Guthman and Jeffrey Shulman, eds., *Robert Kennedy: In His Own Words*

(New York: Bantam, 1988), p. 328.

3. Vidal, "Playboy Interview," *Playboy*, June 1969.
4. Doris Kearns Goodwin, *The Fitzgeralds and the Kennedys* (New York: Simon & Schuster, 1987), pp. 367, 786.
5. Collier and Horowitz, p. 217.
6. classmate and Rose in Arthur M. Schlesinger Jr., *Robert Kennedy and His Times* (New York: Ballantine, 1979), pp. 46, 44; RFK in Clinch, p. 263.
7. Collier and Horowitz, p. 431.

4: TRUE BELIEVER

1. O'Brien in Arthur M. Schlesinger Jr., *Robert Kennedy and His Times* (New York: Ballantine, 1979), p. 103; Richard J. Whalen, *The Founding Father: The Story of Joseph P. Kennedy* (New York: New American Library, 1964), pp. 425–26.
2. Garry Wills, *The Kennedy Imprisonment* (Boston: Atlantic Monthly Press, 1981), p. 113.
3. Theodore Sorensen, *The Kennedy Legacy* (New York: Macmillan, 1969),

p. 41; RFK in Schlesinger, pp. 111, 113, 114.

4. JFK in *New York Post*, July 30, 1956; RFK in David Burner and Thomas R. West, *The Kennedy Brothers and American Liberalism* (New York: Atheneum, 1984), p. 197.

5: An Enemy Within

1. Kempton in Jean Stein and George Plimpton, *American Journey: The Times of Robert Kennedy* (New York: Harcourt Brace Jovanovich, 1970), pp. 56–57; "Hiss," "first love," and "giggled" in Arthur M. Schlesinger Jr., *Robert Kennedy and His Times* (New York: Ballantine, 1979), pp. 175, 178.
2. Billings in Peter Collier and David Horowitz, *The Kennedys* (New York: Warner, 1985), p. 279; Alexander M. Bickel, "Robert F. Kennedy: The Case Against Him for Attorney General," *The New Republic*, Jan. 9, 1961.

6: Running Interference

1. Reporter and RFK in Arthur M. Schlesinger Jr., *Robert Kennedy and His Times* (New York: Ballantine, 1979), p. 230; Kempton in Jean Stein and George Plimpton, *American Journey: The Times of Robert Kennedy* (New York: Harcourt Brace Jovanovich, 1970), p. 72.
2. Schlesinger, pp. 211, 216–17.
3. Edwin O. Guthman and Jeffrey Shulman, eds., *Robert Kennedy: In His Own Words* (New York: Bantam, 1988), p. 22.
4. Harris Wofford, *Of Kennedys and Kings* (Pittsburgh: University of Pittsburgh Press, 1992), p. 19.
5. Schlesinger, p. 250.

7: His Brother's Keeper

1. criticisms in Arthur M. Schlesinger Jr., *Robert Kennedy and His Times* (New York: Ballantine, 1979), pp. 250–51; Seigenthaler in Peter Collier and David Horowitz, *The Kennedys* (New York: Warner, 1985), p. 341.
2. "grin" in Schlesinger, p. 261; RFK in

Edwin O. Guthman and Jeffrey Shulman, eds., *Robert Kennedy: In His Own Words* (New York: Bantam, 1988), pp. 333–34.

3. RFK in *Own Words*, pp. 125–26; Victor S. Navasky, *Kennedy Justice* (New York: Atheneum, 1971), p. 73.
4. Collier and Horowitz, p. 385.
5. Seymour M. Hersh, *The Dark Side of Camelot* (Boston: Little, Brown, 1997), pp. 394–95; JFK on RFK in Schlesinger, p. 645.
6. Michael R. Beschloss, *The Crisis Years* (New York: HarperCollins, 1991), p. 614; Bradlee in Garry Wills, *The Kennedy Imprisonment* (Boston: Atlantic Monthly Press, 1981), p. 25.
7. Richard Reeves, *President Kennedy* (New York: Touchstone, 1993), p. 291; Billings in Collier and Horowitz, pp. 213–14; John Hellmann, *The Kennedy Obsession* (New York: Columbia University Press, 1997), p. 30.
8. Nancy Gager Clinch, *The Kennedy Neurosis* (New York: Grosset & Dunlap, 1973), p. 327.

1. Edwin O. Guthman and Jeffrey Shulman, eds., *Robert Kennedy: In His Own Words* (New York: Bantam, 1988), pp. 321, 326, 249.
2. Richard N. Goodwin, *Remembering America* (New York: Harper & Row, 1988), p. 125.
3. Arthur M. Schlesinger Jr., *Robert Kennedy and His Times* (New York: Ballantine, 1979), pp. 529–30.
4. Michael R. Beschloss, *The Crisis Years* (New York: HarperCollins, 1991), p. 139.
5. Aleksandr Fursenko and Timothy Naftali, *One Hell of a Gamble* (New York: Norton, 1997), p. 97.
6. Goodwin, p. 187.
7. Ibid.
8. Beschloss, p. 6.
9. McNamara in Harris Wofford, *Of Kennedys and Kings* (Pittsburgh: University of Pittsburgh Press, 1992), p. 399.
10. RFK in Beschloss, p. 375.
11. RFK in Wofford, p. 410.
12. RFK in Fursenko and Naftali, p. 148.
13. McNamara in ibid., p. 201.
14. McNamara in Beschloss, p. 378.

15. RFK in Fursenko and Naftali, p. 226; also see p. 202.
16. Beschloss, p. 528.
17. Anatoly Dobrynin, cited in Kai Bird, *The Color of Truth* (New York: Simon & Schuster, 1998), p. 239.
18. Beschloss, pp. 536–38.

9: Retribution

1. Edwin O. Guthman and Jeffrey Shulman, eds., *Robert Kennedy: In His Own Words* (New York: Bantam, 1988), p. 75.
2. Harris Wofford, *Of Kennedys and Kings* (Pittsburgh: University of Pittsburgh Press, 1992), pp. 411–12.
3. Arthur M. Schlesinger Jr., *Robert Kennedy and His Times* (New York: Ballantine, 1979), p. 660.
4. Interview with the author.
5. Lewis in Schlesinger, p. 665; Wofford, p. 415.
6. Houston and Bissell in Wofford, pp. 400, 394.
7. Richard N. Goodwin, *Remembering America* (New York: Harper & Row, 1988), p. 189.
8. Helms in Michael R. Beschloss,

The Crisis Years (New York: HarperCollins, 1991), p. 139; Helms in Richard Reeves, *President Kennedy* (New York: Touchstone, 1993), p. 714; McNamara in Beschloss, p. 138.

9. Gerald Ford Presidential Library, NSC Files, Assassination Records, Kissinger-Ford, Jan. 4, 1975.
10. Richard G. Powers, *Secrecy and Power: The Life of J. Edgar Hoover* (New York: Free Press, 1987), p. 385.

10: The Making of a Legend

1. John Hellmann, *The Kennedy Obsession* (New York: Columbia University Press, 1997), p. ix.
2. Reston, Wicker, and McKinley in James S. Wolfe, *The Kennedy Myth: American Civil Religion in the Sixties* (Ann Arbor, MI: University Microfilms, 1991), pp. 434, 298.
3. Lincoln analogy in ibid., pp. 442–45; Henry Fairlie, *The Kennedy Promise* (Garden City, NY: Doubleday, 1973), p. 3.
4. Lerner in Penn Kimball, *Bobby Kennedy and the New Politics* (Englewood

Cliffs, NJ: Prentice-Hall, 1968), p. 127.

5. Lifton in Wolfe, p. 532; "scripture" in Kimball, p. 134.
6. Godfrey Hodgson, *America in Our Time* (New York: Vintage, 1978), p. 165.
7. Jack Newfield, *Robert Kennedy: A Memoir* (New York: Bantam, 1970), p. 20.

11: The Usurper

1. James S. Wolfe, *The Kennedy Myth: American Civil Religion in the Sixties* (Ann Arbor, MI: University Microfilms, 1991), p. 501.
2. Doris Kearns, *Lyndon Johnson & the American Dream* (New York: Harper & Row, 1976), pp. 177–78.
3. RFK in Edwin O. Guthman and Jeffrey Shulman, eds., *Robert Kennedy: In His Own Words* (New York: Bantam, 1988), p. 410; Bundy in Arthur M. Schlesinger Jr., *Robert Kennedy and His Times* (New York: Ballantine, 1979), p. 699.
4. "[O]ur president" in *Own Words*, p. 417; "pick us off" in Schlesinger, pp. 680–81.

5. Kearns, p. 200.
6. Schlesinger, p. 701n.
7. Kearns, pp. 199–200.
8. Schlesinger, p. 702.

12: Lord-in-Waiting

1. Edwin O. Guthman and Jeffrey Shulman, eds., *Robert Kennedy: In His Own Words* (New York: Bantam, 1988), p. 416.
2. C. David Heymann, *RFK* (New York: Dutton, 1998), p. 380.
3. *Own Words*, p. 204.
4. RFK in Peter Collier and David Horowitz, *The Kennedys* (New York: Warner, 1985), p. 420; RFK in Nicholas Lemann, *The Promised Land* (New York: Vintage, 1992), p. 126.
5. Jean Stein and George Plimpton, *American Journey: The Times of Robert Kennedy* (New York: Harcourt Brace Jovanovich, 1970), pp. 186–88.
6. Hoffman in Brian Dooley, *Robert Kennedy: The Final Years* (New York: St. Martin's, 1996), p. 63.
7. Jeff Shesol, *Mutual Contempt* (New York: Norton, 1997), p. 471.
8. James S. Wolfe, *The Kennedy Myth:*

American Civil Religion in the Sixties (Ann Arbor, MI: University Microfilms, 1991), p. 529.

9. Henry Fairlie, *The Kennedy Promise* (Garden City, NY: Doubleday, 1973), p. 356.
10. Jack Newfield, *Robert Kennedy: A Memoir* (New York: Bantam, 1970), p. 4.
11. Robert Kennedy, *To Seek a Newer World* (New York: Bantam, 1968), p. 46.

13: Cautious Critic

1. RFK in Edwin O. Guthman and Jeffrey Shulman, eds., *Robert Kennedy: In His Own Words* (New York: Bantam, 1988), pp. 394–95; Sorensen in Thomas Brown, *JFK: History of an Image* (Bloomington: Indiana University Press, 1988), p. 37.
2. Johnson in Doris Kearns, *Lyndon Johnson & the American Dream* (New York: Harper & Row, 1976), p. 253.
3. RFK in Edwin O. Guthman and C. Richard Allen, eds., *RFK: Collected Speeches* (New York: Viking, 1993), pp. 269–71.
4. Ibid., p. 271.

5. Forrestal and RFK in ibid., pp. 266, 277, 270.
6. Ibid., p. 272.
7. RFK in ibid., p. 283; Walinsky, Oral History, Kennedy Library.
8. Richard N. Goodwin, *Remembering America* (New York: Harper & Row, 1988), pp. 455–56.
9. Garry Wills, *The Kennedy Imprisonment* (Boston: Atlantic Monthly Press, 1981), p. 109.
10. Arthur M. Schlesinger Jr., *Robert Kennedy and His Times* (New York: Ballantine, 1979), p. 827.
11. *Speeches*, p. 297.
12. Jules Witcover, *85 Days: The Last Campaign of Robert Kennedy* (New York: Putnam, 1969), p. 28.
13. Brian Dooley, *Robert Kennedy: The Final Years* (New York: St. Martin's, 1996), p. 99.
14. Scheer in Schlesinger, p. 865; Feiffer in *The New Republic*, Feb. 10, 1968.
15. David Harris, *Dreams Die Hard* (New York: St. Martin's, 1982), pp. 210–211.
16. *Speeches*, p. 301.
17. Jack Newfield, *Robert Kennedy: A Memoir* (New York: Bantam, 1970), p. 223.

14: Into the Breach

1. Arthur M. Schlesinger Jr., *Robert Kennedy and His Times* (New York: Ballantine, 1979), pp. 900–901.
2. Edwin O. Guthman and C. Richard Allen, eds., *RFK: Collected Speeches* (New York: Viking, 1993), p. 308.
3. Ibid., p. 334.
4. Ibid., p. 345.
5. Schlesinger, p. 928.
6. Brian Dooley, *Robert Kennedy: The Final Years* (New York: St. Martin's, 1996), p. 13.
7. Lewis Chester, Godfrey Hodgson, and Bruce Page, *An American Melodrama: The Presidential Campaign of 1968* (New York: Viking, 1969), p. 147.
8. Frank Mankiewicz, interview with the author.
9. Robert C. Tucker, "The Theory of Charismatic Leadership," *Daedalus*, Summer 1968, p. 731.
10. Ibid., p. 747.
11. Schlesinger, p. 931.
12. Doris Kearns, *Lyndon Johnson & the American Dream* (New York: Harper & Row, 1976), p. 343.
13. Schlesinger, p. 933.

14. Jeremy Larner, *Nobody Knows: Reflections on the McCarthy Campaign of 1968* (New York: Macmillan, 1970), pp. 63–64.

15: Soul Man

1. "Marshall's Assessments of the Nation's Notables," *New York Times*, Jan. 31, 1993, p. 13.
2. Harris Wofford, *Of Kennedys and Kings* (Pittsburgh: University of Pittsburgh Press, 1992), p. 129.
3. Ibid., p. 168.
4. "Tax exemption" in David Harris, *Dreams Die Hard* (New York: St. Martin's, 1982), p. 139; "call it off" and "atom bomb" in Wofford, pp. 153, 156.
5. "Everybody" and "fed up" in Edwin O. Guthman and Jeffrey Shulman, eds., *Robert Kennedy: In His Own Words* (New York: Bantam, 1988), pp. 98, 101.
6. Ibid., p. 171; MLK in Henry Fairlie, *The Kennedy Promise* (Garden City, NY: Doubleday, 1973), p. 250.
7. *Own Words*, p. 143; RFK on MLK in Taylor Branch, *Pillar of Fire: America*

in the King Years, 1963–1965 (New York: Simon & Schuster, 1998), p. 537.

8. Garry Wills, *The Kennedy Imprisonment* (Boston: Atlantic Monthly Press, 1981), p. 37; Victor S. Navasky, *Kennedy Justice* (New York: Atheneum, 1971), p. 109.
9. Taylor Branch, *Parting the Waters: America in the King Years, 1954–1963* (New York: Simon & Schuster, 1988), p. 918.
10. Arthur M. Schlesinger Jr., *Robert Kennedy and His Times* (New York: Ballantine, 1979), p. 841.
11. *Own Words*, pp. 71–72.
12. Schlesinger, p. 358.
13. *Own Words*, p. 225.
14. "color" and "suppose" in Edwin O. Guthman and C. Richard Allen, eds., *RFK: Collected Speeches* (New York: Viking, 1993), pp. 141, 250.
15. "poisons" and "assert" in ibid., pp. 356, 365.
16. RFK in ibid., pp. 210, 368, 380–84; Reagan in Brian Dooley, *Robert Kennedy: The Final Years* (New York: St. Martin's, 1996), p. 132.
17. *Congressional Record*, March 18, 1966.

18. *Speeches*, pp. 166, 389.
19. Dooley, p. 43.
20. McCarthy in ibid., p. 38.
21. Fairlie, p. 356.

16: An Inconclusive Victory

1. Edwin O. Guthman and C. Richard Allen, eds., *RFK: Collected Speeches* (New York: Viking, 1993), p. 339.
2. Ibid., pp. 351–53.
3. Halberstam and Wade in Richard D. Kahlenberg, "Finding Common Ground: The Urban Populism of Robert Kennedy," unpublished thesis, pp. 118, 121.
4. Lewis Chester, Godfrey Hodgson, and Bruce Page, *An American Melodrama: The Presidential Campaign of 1968* (New York: Viking, 1969), pp. 182–84.
5. *Speeches*, p. 365.
6. Cowan in Arthur M. Schlesinger Jr., *Robert Kennedy and His Times* (New York: Ballantine, 1979), p. 958.
7. Jules Witcover, *85 Days: The Last Campaign of Robert Kennedy* (New York: Putnam, 1969), p. 199; Jack Newfield, *Robert Kennedy: A Memoir*

(New York: Bantam, 1970), p. 296.

8. Brian Dooley, *Robert Kennedy: The Final Years* (New York: St. Martin's, 1996), p. 124.
9. Witcover in William vanden Heuvel and Milton Gwirtzman, *On His Own: RFK, 1964–1968* (Garden City, NY: Doubleday, 1970), p. 348n.
10. Ibid., pp. 348–49.
11. Newfield, p. 302.
12. Louis Harris, "Part Way with RFK: The Price He Paid," *Newsweek*, May 20, 1968.
13. Witcover, p. 207.
14. vanden Heuvel and Gwirtzman, p. 368.
15. McCarthy in John Phillips, "Bobby," *New York Review of Books*, Aug. 21, 1969.
16. McCarthy in Schlesinger, p. 972.
17. RFK in Witcover, p. 225.

17: The End and the Beginning

1. White in Nancy Gager Clinch, *The Kennedy Neurosis* (New York: Grosset and Dunlap, 1973), p. 312; William vanden Heuvel and Milton Gwirtzman, *On His Own: RFK, 1964–1968*

(Garden City, NY: Doubleday, 1970), p. 373.

2. Edwin O. Guthman and C. Richard Allen, eds., *RFK: Collected Speeches* (New York: Viking, 1993), p. 283.
3. Jules Witcover, *85 Days: The Last Campaign of Robert Kennedy* (New York: Putnam, 1969), p. 243.
4. Lewis Chester, Godfrey Hodgson, and Bruce Page, *An American Melodrama: The Presidential Campaign of 1968* (New York: Viking, 1969), p. 354.
5. Ibid., p. 370.
6. Arthur M. Schlesinger Jr., *Robert Kennedy and His Times* (New York: Ballantine, 1979), p. 979.
7. Milton Gwirtzman, Oral History, Kennedy Library, p. 170.
8. Richard N. Goodwin, *Remembering America* (New York: Harper & Row, 1988), p. 537.
9. Gwirtzman, Oral History, p. 184.
10. Gallup in Jeff Shesol, *Mutual Contempt* (New York: Norton, 1997), p. 467.
11. Gary in Schlesinger, p. 968.
12. *Speeches*, p. 397.

18: The Bobby Myth

1. Jean Stein and George Plimpton, *American Journey: The Times of Robert Kennedy* (New York: Harcourt Brace Jovanovich, 1970), pp. 46–47.
2. Jules Witcover, *85 Days: The Last Campaign of Robert Kennedy* (New York: Putnam, 1969), pp. 320–21.
3. Reston in *New York Times*, June 6, 1968; Jack Newfield, *Robert Kennedy: A Memoir* (New York: Bantam, 1970), pp. 38, 348.
4. Brian Dooley, *Robert Kennedy: The Final Years* (New York: St. Martin's, 1996), p. 135.
5. O'Brien in Garry Wills, *The Kennedy Imprisonment* (Boston: Atlantic Monthly Press, 1981), p. 212; Wicker in *American Journey*, p. 237.
6. *American Journey*, pp. 340–41.
7. Howard E. Wolin, "Grandiosity and Violence in the Kennedy Family," *Psychohistory Review*, vol. 8, n. 3 (Winter 1979).
8. *American Journey*, p. 227.
9. Ibid., p. 339.
10. Ronald Steel, *Walter Lippmann and the American Century* (Boston: Little, Brown, 1980), p. 543.

11. Edwin O. Guthman and C. Richard Allen, eds., *RFK: Collected Speeches* (New York: Viking, 1993), p. 242.
12. Ralph Waldo Emerson, "The American Scholar," quoted in Dooley, p. 153.

Bibliography

There have been hundreds of books about the Kennedys and the times they lived in. These are the ones that I found to be the most instructive and provocative.

Beran, Michael Knox. *The Last Patrician.* New York: St. Martin's, 1998.

Beschloss, Michael R. *The Crisis Years.* New York: HarperCollins, 1991.

Brown, Thomas. *JFK: History of an Image.* Bloomington: Indiana University Press, 1988.

Chester, Lewis, Godfrey Hodgson, and Bruce Page. *An American Melodrama: The Presidential Campaign of 1968.* New York: Viking, 1969.

Clinch, Nancy Gager. *The Kennedy Neurosis.* New York: Grosset & Dunlap, 1973.

Collier, Peter, and David Horowitz. *The Kennedys.* New York: Summit, 1984.

New York: Warner, 1985.
Dooley, Brian. *Robert Kennedy: The Final Years.* New York: St. Martin's, 1996.
Fairlie, Henry. *The Kennedy Promise.* Garden City, NY: Doubleday, 1973.
Fursenko, Aleksandr, and Timothy Naftali. *One Hell of a Gamble.* New York: Norton, 1997.
Goodwin, Richard N. *Remembering America.* New York: Harper & Row, 1988.
Hellmann, John. *The Kennedy Obsession.* New York: Columbia University Press, 1997.
Hersh, Seymour M. *The Dark Side of Camelot.* Boston: Little, Brown, 1997.
Kaiser, Charles. *1968 in America.* New York: Weidenfeld & Nicolson, 1988.
Kimball, Penn. *Bobby Kennedy and the New Politics.* Englewood Cliffs, NJ: Prentice-Hall, 1968.
Matusow, Allen J. *The Unraveling of America.* New York: Harper & Row, 1984.
Navasky, Victor S. *Kennedy Justice.* New York: Atheneum, 1971.
Newfield, Jack. *Robert Kennedy: A Memoir.* New York: Dutton, 1969. New York: Bantam, 1970.
O'Neill, William L. *Coming Apart: An*

Informal History of America in the 1960's. Chicago: Quadrangle, 1971.

Reeves, Richard. *President Kennedy.* New York: Simon & Schuster, 1993. New York: Touchstone, 1993.

Schlesinger, Arthur M., Jr. *Robert Kennedy and His Times.* Boston: Houghton Mifflin, 1978. New York: Ballantine, 1979.

Shannon, William V. *The Heir Apparent: Robert Kennedy and the Struggle for Power.* New York: Macmillan, 1967.

Shesol, Jeff. *Mutual Contempt.* New York: Norton, 1997.

Stein, Jean, and George Plimpton. *American Journey: The Times of Robert Kennedy.* New York: Harcourt Brace Jovanovich, 1970.

vanden Heuvel, William, and Milton Gwirtzman. *On His Own: RFK, 1964–1968.* Garden City, NY: Doubleday, 1970.

Wills, Garry. *The Kennedy Imprisonment.* Boston: Atlantic Monthly Press, 1981.

Witcover, Jules. *85 Days: The Last Campaign of Robert Kennedy.* New York: Putnam, 1969.

Wofford, Harris. *Of Kennedys and Kings.* New York: Farrar, Straus & Giroux, 1980. Pittsburgh: University of Pittsburgh Press, 1992.

Wolfe, James S. *The Kennedy Myth: American Civil Religion in the Sixties.* Ann Arbor, MI: University Microfilms, 1991.

Acknowledgments

While writing a book is a solitary process, this one could not have happened without considerable encouragement, assistance, and advice. I am deeply grateful to Tamar Jacoby, for her immensely helpful comments on the manuscript, as well as to James Chace, Michael Beschloss, and Frances FitzGerald. I also want to thank my agent, Morton Janklow, for his crucial support, and his associate, Anne Sibbald; my editor, Alice Mayhew; Sidney Blumenthal for suggesting the title; my colleagues and staff at the School of International Relations of the University of Southern California, and its director, Jonathan Aronson; Stephen Trachtenberg, president of George Washington University, and Harry Harding, dean of its Elliott School of International Affairs, for inviting me to be a visiting professor; Dorothy Shapiro for her generous endowment of that position; Wolf Lepenies and Joachim Nettelbeck for the opportunity to spend an unforgettable year at the Wissenschaftskolleg zu Berlin; Nathaniel Katz and Andrew Manning of USC for making the manuscript legible; Carlos for his patience; Tony, Dudley, Tammy, James, Peter, and Sue for holding my hand; Max Palevsky for his encouragement; and all those who refrained from asking, with understandable impatience, "Are you still working on that?"

Washington, D.C., September 1999

The employees of Thorndike Press hope you have enjoyed this Large Print book. All our Large Print titles are designed for easy reading, and all our books are made to last. Other Thorndike Press Large Print books are available at your library, through selected bookstores, or directly from the publishers.

For more information about titles, please call:

(800) 223-1244
(800) 223-6121

To share your comments, please write:

Publisher
Thorndike Press
P.O. Box 159
Thorndike, Maine 04986